TABLE TALK

TABLE TALK

Biblical Questions and Answers

Moshe Pinchas Weisblum

JASON ARONSON INC.
Northvale, New Jersey
Jerusalem

This book was set in 11 pt. New Baskerville by A Fine Print LTD, of Elizabeth, NJ, and printed and bound by Book-mart Press of North Bergen, NJ.

Library of Congress Cataloging-in-Publication Data

Weisblum, Moshe Pinchas
    Table Talk : Biblical Questions and Answers / Moshe Pinchas Weisblum.
        p.   cm.
    Includes index.
    ISBN 0-7657-6054-1
    1. Bible, O.T. Pentateuch—Examinations, questions, etc.
    I. Title.
    BS1227.V54   1998
    222.1'0076—dc21   98-30373

Printed in the United States of America on acid-free paper. For information and catalog write to Jason Aronson Inc., 230 Livingston Street, Northvale, NJ 07647-1726, or visit our website: www.aronson.com

This book is dedicated
to the memory of my father-in-law

Rabbi Yitzchak Meir Haeitan (Heitner) זצ"ל

Chief Rabbi of Shomron

renowned rabbi, educator, and
spiritual leader in Israel
who devoted his life to his wife,
ten children and grandchildren
and to the cause of education.

May this book serve as a blessing to his memory.

Contents

Contents

Acknowledgements

Thank You, Almighty God, for all the kindness that You have bestowed upon me and my family.

I wish to take this opportunity to acknowledge with gratitude the following people who assisted me in this project, for without their assistance this project would not have been completed.

To my role models, my father, Rabbi Chaim Naphtali Weisblum, Rabbi of NevaShanan, Haifa, Israel, and my mother Rebbetzin Gittel Tova for their love, encouragement, and support.

To my mother-in-law, Rebbetzin Devorah HaEitan, a beacon of strength, wisdom, and love.

To my wife, Miriam, whose personal devotion to me and our five children, Elimelech, Bracha, Ayala Chana, Yitzhak Meir, and Natan, made it possible for me to undertake this complex project.

To my extended family and teachers who filled me with the wisdom of the Bible.

To Dr. Kenneth and Mrs. Henya Storch for their special encouragement, friendship, and help. No words can adequately describe their devotion and dedication to the production of this book.

To Professor Leonard and Mrs. Ruth Ginsberg for a scholar's eye and a friend's heart, who explored, challenged, and criticized.

To Mrs. Chaviva Aptowitzer-Rosenbluth and Mrs. Hadassah Goldsmith for their invaluable help with proofreading this manuscript.

To Mrs. Debbie Kadosh, who typed and retyped this manuscript many times over. Her help is deeply appreciated.

I am grateful to Mrs. Tamar Sitman and Ms. Etal Trit for their technical support.

I thank Mrs. Judith Sandman, whose editing skills greatly enhanced the quality of this work.

Special thanks to my dear friend Cantor Moshe Bazian and his family.

I thank Mr. Dan Winters, Mr. and Mrs. Horace Bier, Mr. and Mrs. Ari Halpern, and Mr. and Mrs. Sidney Fisch for their advice on various aspects of this work.

Warm thanks to Mrs. Sheila Metz and her children, Eric and Spencer. A special acknowledgement, along with my prayers, to Rabbi Nisim Yagan for his speedy recovery.

My deep appreciation to Noach and Deena Horowitz for their extraodinary efforts in improving this manuscript.

I thank Mrs. Susan Roth for her kind assistance.

Additional thanks are due to my special friends Mr. Marty and Mrs. Sheila Nashofer, Mrs. Sharon Schuster, and Mr. Jacob and Mrs. Jean Zimmer, whose comments, suggestions, and review have greatly enhanced the text.

To Mr. Arthur Kurzweil at Jason Aronson Inc., whose

time and energy guided this project.

A special expression of gratitude to Dana Salzman, Director of Editiorial Production at Jason Aronson, Inc. whose professionalism made working on this project a pleasure.

To my students and congregants, I thank you for the dynamic exchange of ideas and your sincerity in our learning together.

And finally to you, my readers, for joining me on this journey, may God bless you all.

Rabbi Moshe Pinchas Weisblum

Introduction

Every one of us shares the desire to learn and know the secrets of the past, present, and future.

Life is full of questions that disturb, confound, and interest us. Questions that have confronted Man since his presence on this earth. The Bible presents us with solutions, if we would but take the time to study it, and learn from it. Some of these questions are: What is Man's purpose in creation? Does he have control over his own destiny? What are the meanings of our dreams? Why do good people suffer so much? Are there angels, and what is their purpose? Why did the Almighty infuse man with a soul? Do names hold any significance? Does the Bible discuss business dealings? How does the Bible instruct us in interpersonal relationships? Does the Bible discuss nutrition and care of the body? What does the Bible tell us about sickness and healing?

In man's quest for meaning and answers to life's daily problems, one is continually amazed at the scope and relevance of the Bible. One of the most beautiful things about the Bible is that it opens the reader's mind to many possibilities, leaving room for different opinions, questions, and answers. Man often seeks abstract, contemporary philosophy or psychology to resolve issues and shed light on life's mysteries. It is ironic that the Bible as the most perfect reference text, a depository of the world's most profound wisdom and teaching, is often overlooked. Undoubtedly, one of the perks of our Bible lies in its ability to encourage us to think and evaluate, question, and believe. The wisdom and teachings with which it has endowed humanity over the centuries are the bedrock of our civilization.

The reality is, except for religious institutions (schools, synagogues), people are often not exposed to the Bible and its teachings. Families look to these institutions for biblical exploration, when in truth it should be looking inward to foster religious learning. How many members of our very sophisticated, modern society are honestly aware of what is in the Bible?

Entertaining diversions like television, theater, computers, telephone, and other high tech pleasure-oriented lures keep youngsters from studying biblical texts and commentators. Bookstores and libraries are packed with secular reading material, competing for an individual's reading attention. The Bible, in the not too recent past, was one of the most popular choices of the reading public. Unfortunately, its sales have seriously diminished in relation to other entertainment media.

Despite the diversions, it has been my experience over the years as a congregational rabbi that our society craves a comprehensive, straightforward, and digestible synopsis of the Bible. This is borne out of the need to appreciate the Bible's teachings in some meaningful way while cutting through archaic and complex verbiage. *Table Talk: Biblical Questions and Answers* was, therefore, essentially written to be used as a "simple roadmap" for anyone who wants to have an easier grasp of the meaning and messages contained within the Bible. The Bible is a blueprint of creation that is to be studied and understood. A vast world of knowledge is available. The Bible is packed with history, law, psychology, adventure, morality, and ethics.

The table, a place of social gathering, usually at mealtime, is an ideal setting for verbal exchange. By putting a condensed and ready-made script onto the table, a tremendous fullness of conversation and brainstorming has the potential to erupt. The possibilities for fun and learning become endless, and the material acts as glue to unite families and friends through shared conversation about the essence of life.

By accumulating biblical knowledge, one can see one's life, not only from an individual perspective, but from a global and historical one as well. Through this acquisition of knowledge, one gains clarity, balance, and strength through an understanding of the past. The world and creation began way back in time, and yet every day we are told that we are born anew. By learning about the lives and actions of those who came before us, we can begin to understand ourselves and how the world around us came to be. Perhaps our mission or life's purpose would be better understood by seeing patterns from the past and the chain of events that led to our current placement on earth.

I have, therefore, worked vigorously at condensing the biblical stories and encapsulating the words of hundreds of commentators into this book. This selection of questions was done with considerable forethought and with an aim at offering the broadest and deepest understanding of the brilliance of the Bible. This book in no way exhausts the myriad of questions that have been or will be asked. It is my fondest hope that readers of *Table Talk* will become moved, enriched, excited, and so much wiser. Perhaps my book will make you cry or laugh, think, feel, and connect in ways you might not have imagined. It is my dream that, your study of this book will bring the rich rewards that accompany any learning of Torah. If so, I have accomplished my mission.

It is my prayer that *Table Talk: Biblical Questions and Answers* sparks greater love for the Lord and the love of one's fellow man through a deeper appreciation of life's inner meaning. May our studies lead us to live life fully the way God intended. Let us recapture our heritage and our most precious and cherished treasure through our Bible—God's very special gift to the world.

Terminology

Here is a list of commonly used words which the reader will find through-out this volume.

Amidah = The "standing prayer"

Bible = Written part of the Torah
    5 Books of Moses = Bible = Written Torah
    Bereishit = Genesis = first book of the Bible
    Shemot = Exodus = second book of the Bible
    Vayikra = Leviticus = third book of the Bible
    Bamidbar = Numbers = fourth book of the Bible
    Devarim = Deuteronomy = fifth book of the Bible

Gematriah = numerical equivalent for letters

Halachah = Jewish Law

Kabbalah = Jewish Mysticism

Kohen = Priest; Kehuna = Priesthood

Kohen Gadol = High Priest

Korban = sacrifices brought to the Temple

Leviem = served as Musicians in the Temple

Midrash = the moral and philosophical teachings of the Torah

Mishnah = Oral Law, part of the Torah

Mitzvah = Commandment

Moses = Moshe Rabbeinu

Noahite Commandments = the seven commandments given to man after the Flood

Parsha = weekly bible portion read on the Sabbath

Prophets = series of books written and from which the haftorah is taken for each of the weekly parshot

Shabbat = Sabbath = Day of Rest = Friday sundown to Saturday sundown

Talmud = Oral Law, part of the Torah (Mishnah, Gemorah)

Torah = composed of Oral and Written parts

Yom Tov = Jewish Holy Day (Holiday): Passover, Shavuot, Rosh Hashanah, Yom Kippur, Sukkot. Minor Holidays: Chanukah, Purim, and Rosh Chodesh (New Month).

Zohar = Book of Jewish Mysticism

$$\boxed{\text{I}}$$

The Book of Genesis

Bereishit
Chapters: 1 - 6:8

Synopsis:

A day-by-day description of the creation of the universe by the Almighty; Man's creation on day six; life in the Garden of Eden; the temptation by the snake; Man succumbed to the temptation and the punishment for sinning, Cain and Abel offered sacrifice to the Almighty; Cain kills Abel.

Question: According to the written and oral Torah (Bible), which laws did God give to all of mankind?

Answer: The seven *Noahite* laws were given by God to all mankind. They were originally given to Adam after his fall from grace, with the exception of the prohibition of eating the limb of a living animal. Following the restoration of the world after the Flood, they were given to Noah, his wife, and his family, the only humans at the time. Later, the *Noahite* commandments were transmitted as part of the Bible, given by God to Moses. These laws outline the ethical and moral responsibilities of man and are a guide for him that he might realize his value as part of the Almighty's creation. Most of the *Noahite* commandments discussed below are found in the book of Genesis (*Talmud Sanhedrin 57a*).

Question: What are the seven *Noahite* commandments?

Answer: The prohibition against idolatry—the creation of or belief in an idol (*Exodus 20:3-6*).

The prohibition against murder, the intentional taking of a human life (Genesis 9:5-6).

The prohibition against blasphemy—cursing and/or improperly using the name of God (*Leviticus 22:32*).

The prohibition against theft—stealing and/or desiring another's property (Leviticus 19:1; Sefer Hachinuch, commandment 424).

The prohibition against illicit intercourse—incestuous or adulterous relationships (*Exodus 20:13*).

The commandment to appoint honest judges and officers (*Genesis 2:16 and Babylonian Talmud, Sanhedrin 56a*).

The prohibition against eating the limb of a living creature—one must never eat any part of an animal while it is still alive (*Genesis 9:4*).

According to the written and oral Torah (Bible), these seven commandments are obligatory upon all human beings (*Talmud*

Sanhedrin 56-59; Maimonides, Book of Commandments, Mishnah Torah, Laws of Kings 9:1-11; Sefer Hachinuch; Minchat Chinuch Part 11, Pages 93, 103; Nachamanides Critique of Ramban; Genesis 9:5; Rabbi Nissin Gaon, Hakdama; Brachot; Rabbi Sa'adiah Gaon, Azkaroth).

Question: To which creature did God give a special blessing, and why?

Answer: We see from *Genesis 1:22* that the fish were given a special blessing. This blessing was to be fruitful and multiply. This blessing was later renewed after the Flood (*Midrash*). God saw that the fish would be trapped and their numbers depleted. At the time of the Flood, the Almighty saw that they did not take part in the crossbreeding that was occurring among the other forms of life. Because of this they were the only type of creature not brought into the Ark by Noah. They were able to sustain their existence outside the Ark. Because of this special blessing, and because they were seen as wholesome creatures, it is customary in many communities to eat fish on joyous occasions and on the holidays.

Note that the animals, wild beasts, and birds that sinned by crossbreeding were, conversely, not deserving of special consideration or blessing (*Genesis 6:12-13, Rashi*).

Question: "God said 'let us make man ... they shall rule over the fish...and the beast...the animals and creepers. . .'" (*Genesis 1:26-28*). Why does the Bible specifically use the phrase "rule over" in conjunction with this decision?

Answer: Man is created in the image of God. He is the pinnacle of Creation. The Almighty gives man this authority to rule over the rest of creation. This authority does not come without its responsibility. Man does not have the right to abuse this power. Man was given superior intelligence, the ability to analyze situations, and the use of free will in his judgment. God instilled greater physical abilities in animals to compensate them for man's intellectual superiority. If man abuses his power he then lowers himself to the level of the animal, thus making him at risk for domination by the stronger animal (*Kaballah, Zohar-Bereishit*).

This concept is supported in *Genesis 4:1-17,* where it tells the story of Adam's sons, Cain and Abel. Cain gave in to his animal nature by killing his brother Abel. God spared Cain's life but punished him by exiling him to the wilderness, where he was regarded by the rest of creation as an animal. In order for Cain to survive, he was forced to live with a mark on his forehead to avoid being killed by predators *(Targum Yonatan ben Uziel, Genesis 4:15).*

Question: How did the Hebrews, later known as the Jewish people, calculate their day? Why?

Answer: The Bible states, "And there was evening and there was morning, one day" (*Genesis 1:5*). From this source, the sages teach us that the Jewish calendar day begins at sunset and ends with the onset of the following sunset. This concept holds true for every day of the Jewish calendar, including festivals, the New Moon, and fast days.

Question: How many generations separate Adam and Noah? Why?

Answer: Ten generations. Within each generation the Almighty gave man the opportunity to carry out his responsibility to live according to His plan. With the coming of the tenth generation of Noah man still was not living up to his potential as the pinnacle of creation. The Almighty lost patience and the Flood washed the generation away. However, since Noah found favor in the eye of the Almighty (*Genesis 6:8*), Noah and his family were spared that fate.

Question: At the beginning of Creation, what did God allow man, animals, beasts, and birds to eat?

Answer: People ate only herbs and fruits; beasts and birds were permitted to eat green herbs. The food was of exceptionally high quality.

Question: Why is the phrase "it was good" repeated twice on the third day of Creation *(Genesis 1:10,12)*?

Answer: The sage *Rashi* explains *(Genesis 1:7)* sthat the first time the phrase "it was good" was written refers to the fact that God finished the creation of the waters, which began on the second day. The second time comes to indicate the completion of a second creation, the herbs. We learn from this, that God did not create all things in one instance. We come to understand that there is an order in the Almighty's creation. This helps us understand the importance of seeing events in their proper sequence. For example, one cannot eat herbs without first planting the seeds in soil, tilling the field, praying for rain, and harvesting the ripe produce.

Question: What is the meaning of the word *Shamayim (Genesis 1:8)*?

Answer: The Hebrew word *Shamayim*, in its simple form, means heaven. However, the commentators suggest that it may also be a contraction thereby offering other interpretations: to hold water; water is there; carry water, or even the phrase *eish umayim*, fire and water (*Rashi, Genesis 1:8*). The last statement infers that God made fire and water together as part of Heaven (*Rashi and Babylonian Talmud Chagiga, 12a*).

Question: Which is the first commandment, mitzvah, mentioned in the Bible? Is it a positive commandment or a negative one?

Answer: The first commandment mentioned is: "Be fruitful and multiply..." (*Genesis 1:28*). It is seen as a positive commandment. Not only is it a commandment but it is also a blessing. With this blessing, God gave mankind the physical ability to produce future generations to ensure the continuity of mankind (*Book of Commandments, Rabbi Chagiz*).

In addition, the *Sefer Hachinuch* states that if one does not fulfill this commandment, it is considered an act against God's creation. This concept does not include individuals who have physical disabilities and are anatomically incapable of conceiving children.

Question: In *Genesis 2:7* it states: "God blew into man the soul of life." What does this mean?

Answer: The origin of the soul is absolutely spiritual, it cannot be physically touched. The source of the body is made entirely from the earth. God created this perfect combination, forming man's body from dust and energizing his soul with the breath of life. Through this act of blowing, God created the combination of soul and body.

After death, the soul is returned to the heavens and the body reverts back to dust (earth). We encounter many illustrations of this concept within this section of Genesis. We can begin to appreciate that a main source of conflict often lies between our soul, which is completely pure and spiritual, and our body, which is geared completely to the physical world. God entrusts us with freedom of choice to conduct our own lives and to strike a balance between body and soul (*Zohar; Shla'a; Maimonides; Tanya, Chapter 2*).

Question: According to the Bible, the beast and the human are both called living beings. What then makes the human different from other living beings?

Answer: The ability to speak, reason, and remember, along with the freedom of choice (mentioned in the previous answer) were given to Man by God to set him apart from the other living creatures (*Targum Unkelos; Zohar; Tanya, Chapter 2*).

Question: Four rivers flowed in the Garden of Eden (*Genesis 2:10*). What were they called? What do their names imply?

Answer: **Piscine.** An Egyptian river, it was called by this name because its waters flowed upward so that it could irrigate the entire country and water the whole land (*Rashi, Genesis 2:11*).

Gitano. This name infers a very noisy river. The word is compared to the Hebrew *yigach*, meaning that when the tide rolls in, there is a great deal of noise.

Chidekel. Its waters were pure and clear (*Babylonian Talmud Brachot, 59b*).

Prat. Its waters were considered to have the ability to heal the human being (Babylonian Talmud Ketuvot 77b). *Rashi* states that the Prat is the most important of all the rivers because it is a boundary line for the Land of Israel.

These four rivers in Paradise are examples of the four rivers that surround the Holy Land.

Question: In *Genesis 2:18*, the Bible states, "God said, 'It is not good that man should remain alone. I will make a helper against him.'" How do we explain the apparent contradiction of the words "helper" and "against" in the same verse?

Answer: There is much discussion as to how woman was formed. Regardless of one's view, she was created as a helpmate to Adam (*Genesis 2:23*). The sages of the *Babylonian Talmud* (*Yevamot 63a*) explain the above contradiction this way. If a man is worthy and acts according to the Will of the Almighty, the woman (his wife) will help him; if not, she will be against him.

Question: Which commandments did God tell Adam and Eve to observe while in the *Garden of Eden?*

Answer: Adam and Eve were not commanded to observe the 613 commandments. These commandments will be given to Moses later at Mount Sinai. However, the *Midrash* says that the Almighty gave them six of the *Noahite* commandments. God also made them the spiritual and physical guardians of the *Garden of Eden (Ibn Ezra; Yonatan ben Uziel; Sforno, Genesis 2:15)*.

Question: What was the prohibition of against eating from the *Tree of Knowledge?*

Answer: Adam and Eve were pristine and innocent and were not capable of judging between good and evil (*Sforno, Genesis 2:17*). God's intention was to protect this innocence, because He loved them so much and understood their limitations. Eating of this Tree would "open their eyes and they would see…" (*Genesis 3:7*).

Question: According to *Rashi*, what kind of tree was the *Tree of Knowledge?* Why was this information omitted from the Bible? How do we know what kind of tree it was?

Answer: There are varying opinions as to which fruit was growing on the *Tree of Knowledge*. According to *Rashi*, the *Tree of Knowledge* was a fig tree. It was not stated in the Bible so people would not come to speak disdainfully of the fig (*Rashi, Genesis 3:7*). It is written that after they had eaten "their eyes were open, and they saw their nakedness." Adam and Eve then took a fig leaf to cover their nakedness.

Question: As a consequence of their disobedience, God banished Adam and Eve from Paradise. Why, in addition to their being exiled, were they punished individually?

Answer: After they sinned by eating from the *Tree of Knowledge,* they attempted to hide from the Almighty. God "found" them and asked them, "Why did you eat from the tree?" Instead of confessing their sin outright and repenting, and accepting personal responsibility, each tried to justify their actions. Adam sought to place responsibility on Eve by proclaiming "The woman whom You gave to be with me, she gave me of the tree and I ate." Eve responded "The serpent deceived me and I ate."

Question: How did the Almighty punish the snake?

Answer: The snake was punished by having a mating cycle that occurs once in seven years (*Babylonian Talmud, Bechorot 8a*). It was no longer allowed to walk upright; its legs were cut off (*Rashi, Genesis 3:14*); it had to slide on its belly; it had to eat the dust of the earth; it was to carry poison in its mouth; it would have man as a constant enemy (*Rashi, Genesis 3:15; Midrash*).

Question: How were Eve and Adam punished?

Answer: The Torah tells in *Genesis 3:16* that the woman (Eve) will suffer discomfort and pain during pregnancy; suffer labor pains (*Babylonian Talmud, Eruvin 100b*); and encounter difficulties in raising her children.

In *Genesis 3:17* Adam is punished by having to work by the sweat of his brow in order to survive; having thorns grow in place of vegetation when a seed was planted; and with a constant struggle to achieve nourishment.

Question: Were there any additional curses given to future generations as a result of the sin of Adam and Eve?

Answer: Yes. Until this point, death had not entered the world. Now with this sin, man would have a measured existence (*Rambam, Guide to the Perplexed*). Future generations are subjected to the punishments outlined in *Genesis 3:16-17* as well.

Question: Since the snake was at fault, why was Eve punished?

Answer: According to *Rashi* (*Genesis 3:14; Talmud Sanhedrin 29a*), the following conversation took place between the Almighty and Eve. God said to Eve, "When a teacher instructs a student to behave in a certain manner and the student follows the instructions of another, punishment should prevail." God continued, "Therefore, if I prohibited you from eating of the *Tree of Knowledge,* and the snake advised you otherwise, you should not have listened to the snake." Eve allowed herself to be enticed by the snake. She then made her situation worse by enticing Adam to sin as well. Then, when confronted, she did not accept personal responsibility.

Question: Who were Cain and Abel and what transpired between them?

Answer: Cain and Abel were the children of Adam and Eve. Cain chose to be a farmer, to cultivate the land, while Abel was a shepherd. Both gave praise to God and offered sacrifices. Differences existed between the brothers. Abel saw a special relationship between the world and the Almighty and gave to God with all his heart. These offerings were acknowledged by God. Cain did not see the world like this and saw only his domination over the earth. His offerings therefore reflected his relationship to God's creation. Seeing the Almighty's acceptance of his brother's offerings incensed Cain to the point of jealousy that culminated in his murder of his brother.

Question: What do we learn from the connection between the sin of Adam and Eve and the sin of Cain?

Answer: This is a perfect example of how children learn from the deeds of their parents and sometimes take matters one step further. When God found that Adam and Eve had eaten from the *Tree of Knowledge,* Adam and Eve were dishonest with God instead of admitting their sin and repenting. Similarly, with the murder of Abel, God asked Cain, "Where is Abel your brother?" Cain lied when he replied, "I do not know," and then compounded the sin by asking the Almighty, "Am I my brother's keeper?" (*Genesis 4:9*).

Question: This incident between Cain and Abel raises a dilemma. We see from the Torah that Cain kills Abel outright. How is it that the Almighty does not see fit to punish Cain with death?

Answer: We see from this episode a combination of the Almighty's justice, wisdom, and compassion. In truth Cain's crime is punishable by death. However, two factors mitigated against the extreme penalty. First there was no warning given to him that what he was about to do was wrong and the punishment would be his own death. Second there were no witnesses to the crime. In His wisdom the Almighty sentenced him to wander the earth for the remainder of his life. In His compassion the Almighty gave to Cain a mark, which singled him out as a murderer, but also served to protect him from his adversaries.

Question: Cain was forced to live with a God-given mark on his body until the end of his life. This served to protect him as he roamed the earth. What did the mark of Cain look like?

Answer: Here also there is a discussion among the commentators as to what exactly the mark was. The *Ramav* suggests it was a horn on his forehead. Or was it that God took one of the letters of His Holy Name and inscribed it on Cain's forehead (*Targum Yonatan ben Uziel, Genesis 4:15*)? Still others say that he was afflicted with leprosy (*Midrash*).

Question: God cursed the ground two times. When and why?

Answer: The first instance was when Adam sinned. He ate from the *Tree of Knowledge,* whose source was the earth. No longer would the earth give forth nourishment as it once had. Adam was now forced to work the land. The second was after Cain killed his brother, Abel (*Genesis 4:11*). Cain killed his brother and buried him in the ground. The earth had become an unwilling partner and was forced to consume the blood of Abel, thereby being cursed by it.

Question: Who was the first individual to worship idols? Which was the first generation to worship idols?

Answer: The Bible records that Javal, the great grandson of Cain, was the first individual to worship idols (*Rashi, Genesis 4:20*). The generation of Enosh, the son of Seth, grandson of Adam and Eve, was the first generation to worship idols.

Question: It is said of Enoch, the grandson of Adam, that "he disappeared" instead of that he died. Why?

Answer: *Genesis 5:24* says, "Enoch walked with God, and he disappeared for God had taken him." According to *Unkelos* and *Rashi,* Enoch was a God-fearing man during his short life. God was concerned that the wicked environment in which he lived would cause him to stray. Therefore, God took Enoch before his time. A second opinion, offered by the sage *Yonatan Ben Uziel,* indicates that Enoch achieved such a high spiritual level of righteousness that he could no longer exist in this world as a human being. Therefore he was taken back by the Almighty, to be His highest servant, and his name was changed to Metatron (*Zohar, Shla'a*).

Question: What is the meaning of the name Noah?

Answer: Noah means peaceful, resting; *yaniach*, a derivative, means "to leave, let go."

Question: What did Noah invent?

Answer: The *Midrash* says Noah invented agricultural tools to work and improve the soil and also to rid the land of the curse it received by having to absorb the blood of Abel (*Rashi, Genesis 5:29*).

Question: "God reevaluated having put man on earth and He had heartfelt sadness" (*Genesis 6:6*). Does the Almighty have a "heart" that feels sadness?

Answer: Often the Bible speaks in human terms so that we can appreciate its meaning and comprehend its message. With this verse the Torah is trying to convey the Almighty's "sadness" with His Creation and that man up to this point had not lived up to his potential. God "thought" to punish mankind for their negative behavior in order to make their hearts feel sadness (*Rashi; Raem*).

Question: How many years of life did God grant man? From where do we learn this?

Answer: In *Genesis 6:3* the Bible states, "And God said, 'My spirit shall not clash ever more concerning man since he is but flesh; his days shall be a hundred and twenty years.'" The commentators view this verse as a source of blessing. Consequently, when a person wants to bless another person, he or she will often say, "Until a hundred and twenty shall you live" (*Ibn Ezra; Targum; Midrash*).

Question: In *Genesis 6:8* it states, "and Noah found grace in the eyes of God." What can we learn from this?

Answer: In his time, only Noah was considered to be a righteous person. The commentators say that although Noah was righteous, that in and of itself was not enough to save him. It was therefore necessary for the Almighty to bestow His grace to Noah and his family (*Ramban; Ibn Ezra; Yonatan Ben Uziel; and Yerushalmi; Sforno*). No person regardless of one's righteousness is sufficient unto oneself to save one's self. The grace of the Almighty is always necessary.

Question: Every Sabbath, it is customary to read the weekly portion from the Torah (*parsha*) and chapter(s) from the Prophets (*haftorah*). What is the connection between Noah and the corresponding reading from the *Book of Isaiah (Isaiah 42:5-43:10)*?

Answer: Our Sages teach us that there is always a strong connection between the weekly *parsha* and its *haftorah*. In this case, we find that both speak about God's creation of the world.

Noah
Chapters: 6:9 - 11

Synopsis:

Noah's righteousness; God's command to Noah to build the Ark; the Flood; the aftermath of the Flood; Noahite commandments; the rainbow; Tower of Babel.

Question: What are the significant differences between life before and life after the Flood?

Answer:

Before the Flood	After the Flood
Man ate only fruits from the tree. Animals ate food from the ground.	Along with fruits, man now permitted to eat meat to supplement diet.
Climate and environs ideal, clean and comfortable.	The Flood caused destruction to the natural habitat. The soil became hard to manage and food quality suffered.
Food readily available, abundant, and satisfying.	Quality of food deteriorated to where fruit, vegetables, and grains no longer satiated appetites.
Man had been given full control over the other species.	The Almighty took away man's dominance over the animals. God instilled in animals a fear of man. Man was now seen as a predator.

Question: Why did God cause these four changes in His creation?

Answer: God found man's thoughts and behaviors to be offensive and harmful. In His compassion, the Almighty chose to bring about the Flood instead of completely destroying the world. The changes made were not part of God's original plan but came as a direct result of the sins of the wicked, pre-Flood generation. God chose not to renew His creation of the universe as it was before the Flood, but caused the world to undergo major modifications. While man remained the same, God altered the earth, thereby indirectly changing man's way of life. In essence, God chose to give man another chance but made it more difficult for him to survive (*Haktav Vehkabala*).

Question: How can Noah be characterized?

Answer: There are two opposing opinions as how Noah is to be viewed. One group sees Noah as a completely righteous person in his own right, because he followed the way of the Almighty despite having to live in a very difficult and corrupt environment. These sages feel that Noah deserved to be saved from the Flood on his own merit. The other school of thought comments that Noah was a "good man," no more than that. They interpret the Bible's use of the word "righteous" in relative terms. They see Noah living in a corrupt generation and compared to other members of that generation he definitely was more righteous. However, in comparison with Abraham, and righteous people of other generations, Noah is viewed as just another good person. Therefore he needed the Almighty's grace to save him from the Flood's destruction.

Question: Why did God allow the eating of meat after the Flood?

Answer: In Paradise, the *Garden of Eden,* God created an abundance of fruits and vegetables of such high quality that man and animal alike were completely satisfied without needing meat. In fact, neither man nor animal desired meat, even though it was readily available. Once the Flood occurred and destroyed the plants, eating meat became an unavoidable consequence. As the Bible states, when God expelled Adam and Eve from *Eden,* He cursed the ground (*Genesis 3:17*). Thereafter the quality and quantity of grown foods immediately decreased. After the Flood, there was further destruction of the ground. Hence, when Noah and his family finally left the ark, they found nothing growing on the earth and had to resort to eating meat for survival (*Ramban, Abarbanel, Abudraham, Talmud Sanhedrin 59, Tosfot Sanhedrin 56*).

Question: Is there a difference in the relationship of man to animals before and after the Flood *(Genesis 9:2)*?

Answer: Before the Flood there was no desire to eat meat. The Almighty had given man complete authority and domain over animals. After the Flood, the relationship changed. No longer did man have domain over the animals. Man was full of lust. Man in order to survive now needed animals as a food source. Man also became a competitor to the animal. Man now needed the Almighty's assistance in being protected from the stronger animals by having the fear of man instilled in them (*Talmud, Sabbath 51*). If man lost the image of God (likeness), as did Cain, the animals would not fear him, because they would then be perceived as just another animal (*Rabbi Samson R. Hirsch; Ramban; Midrash Rabbah; Tur*).

Question: "Flesh with its soul and blood you shall not eat." Who said this to whom and why?

Answer: This refers to the *Noahite* commandment (*Genesis 9:4*) that forbids man from taking the limb from a living animal and eating it. This commandment was not one of the original commandments given to Adam and Eve. It was given to Noah after he had left the ark and the Almighty told him that all that roamed the earth or flew in the heavens would be to him as food.

Question: What is the meaning of the rainbow that came after the Flood (*Genesis 9:14*)?

Answer: The rainbow comes as a sign to mankind. It usually follows a rainstorm. It is seen as a sign of God's promise of forgiveness to all mankind and His assurance that there will never be another flood that would destroy mankind. It also serves as a symbol of God's everlasting control of the universe (*Rabbi Samson R. Hirsch*). Some also suggest that it is the sign of man's continued existence in the world (*Ba'al Haakeida*). The *Zohar* tells us that the variety of colors of the rainbow remind us of God's attributes of compassion and judgment.

Question: How many nations descended from Noah?

Answer: Seventy *(Talmud, Eruvin 53a; Chulin 89a; Rabbeinu Bechayei; Song of Songs 6:8).*

Question: Who was Nimrod *(Genesis 10:8-10)?*

Answer: Nimrod was a king and a mighty hunter. Before Nimrod there were no kings or rulers, but he took control over the Babylonians and had them crown him as their king *(Radak, Ramban).* He was a calculating and deceitful man. He would wear the robes of a pious man to gain people's trust and then persuade them to rebel against God *(R. Samson R. Hirsch).*

Question: What was the Tower of Babel? What was the purpose in building it *(Genesis: 11:1-9)?*

Answer: In Nimrod's attempt to rebel against God, he decided to build a tower that would reach to the heavens and from there he and his followers could wage war against God. Other opinions suggest that the generation sought to prove the Almighty's non-existence. Still others saw the people as desiring to worship idols and they meant the Tower of Babel to be a giant idol *(Talmud, Sanhedrin 109).* Another opinion sees the erection of the tower as a revolt against Abraham as he attempted to persuade the generation to believe in God. That is why they tried to build a tower against God *(Kuzari, chapters 2 & 68; Kol Yehudah).* A further belief saw the people seeking to elevate their king, Nimrod, to "God's level." They meant to have Nimrod sit at the top of the tower and rule *(Haktav Vehakabala; Sforno).* God had given the people the whole world in which to expand, yet they felt the need to rebel against God and to show Him that He was not in control of them *(Abarbanel).* After the Flood, God sent a storm of water from heaven. People were worried that the next punishment would be fire. Therefore, they tried to build a tower that would absorb the lightning and prevent such a fire *(Rabbeinu Bechayei, Tiferet Yonatan).*

Question: How did God deal with the builders of the Tower of Babel?

Answer: Until the sin of the Tower of Babel, everyone spoke the same holy tongue. After they began building the tower, God punished them by causing them to speak in seventy different languages. No longer could one understand his fellow. Consequently, the builders could not understand each other, and the project became totally chaotic. The construction of the tower could not be completed, and came to a grinding halt. The people were dispersed into seventy nations, each one speaking its own distinct language.

Question: What is the connection between *Parshat Noah* and the corresponding *haftorah?*

Answer: Just as the rainbow symbolizes God's mercy to the generation after the Flood, so, too, in the *haftorah*, the prophet Isaiah expresses a similar message of encouragement to the nation of Israel from God: "For but a brief moment have I forsaken you and with abundant mercy shall I gather you in" *(Isaiah 54:7)*. It is important to note that the Bible and Prophets stress time and again God's attribute of mercy.

Lech Lecha
Chapters: 12 - 17

Synopsis:

God commanded Abram to leave his father's house and go to the strange country of Canaan; Abram's relationship with his nephew Lot; Abram went to Egypt because of famine in the Holy Land; the encounter between Sarai and Pharaoh; Abram and Lot split up; the War of the Four Kings; Abram rescued Lot from captivity; the Almighty appeared to Abram in a vision and reassured him of destiny; the birth of Ishmael; the commandment of circumcision; the Almighty changes the name of Abram to Abraham and the name of Sarai to Sarah.

21

Question: "God said to Abram: Go from your property, from your community, to the land that I will show you" *(Genesis 12:1).* How do our sages explain this act of faith on the part of Abram?

Answer: Abram, the first man to worship God, was being tested by God. Abram had complete faith and trust in the Almighty, even to the point that he would sacrifice his physical well-being to do the will of the Almighty. He was asked to leave everything behind, his property, his home, and his friends. He trustingly followed God's way and traveled to an unknown, faraway land, which God had promised him. This action showed the greatest righteousness of our first forefather, Abram *(Rashi; Ramban; Ohr Hachayim; Kli Yakar).*

Question: How many times did God test Abram and what were the tests?

Answer: God tested Abram ten times. The reader should note that these ten tests span the three parshiot of *Noah, Lech Lecha,* and *Vayeira.*

Abram's father, Terach, told Nimrod that it was Abram who smashed his idols. Because of this Nimrod cast Abram into a fiery pit. Because of his unyielding faith in the Almighty he was saved from this test *(Rashi; Midrash; Genesis 11:28).*

After ten years had passed Abram was once again summoned before Nimrod, and challenged to bow before him, and accept him as a god. Abram refused, and was thrust into the cauldron of Ur Kasdim *(Genesis 15:7; Yalkut Shimoni).*

Abram was commanded to leave his land and go to the land of Canaan, promised him by God *(Genesis 12:1).*

Abram was forced to leave his new land, Canaan, and go down to Egypt due to a famine *(Genesis 12:10).*

Sarai, Abram's wife, was taken by Pharaoh *(Genesis 12:15).*

Lot was captured, and Abram incited a war among the kings to secure his nephew's freedom.

Abram was promised children, even though Sarai was quite old and over childbearing age.

God commanded Abram to circumcise himself. Ishmael, Hagar's son, allowed himself to be circumcised even though he was now thirteen years of age (*Genesis 17:10*).

God told Abram to cast out Hagar and Ishmael (*Genesis 21:10-12*).

God told Abram to sacrifice his son, Isaac, at the *Akaidah* (*Genesis 22:1-2*).

Question: The *Amidah*, the silent prayer, is one of the most important prayers. We recite it three times a day, beginning with the first blessing, "Blessed are You, Lord our God, shield of Abraham." What connection can we draw between this blessing and the *parsha?*

Answer: When we pray we implore the Almighty to protect us as He protected Abraham during these tests (previously mentioned). A spark of Abraham is incorporated into every Jew regardless of how far one may have strayed (*Chiddushei HaRim*).

Question: How was Abram compensated for his strong belief in the Almighty?

Answer: Abram's move from his birthplace to a faraway place caused him to expend much time and energy. He was placed in situations where he had to rely totally upon the Almighty for his and his family's well-being. His status within his new community was lower than when he lived among his father's family. To compensate Abram for these losses, God blessed him in his old age with offspring (*Bereishit Rabba 39:11*).

Question: The Bible states, "I will bless you" *(Genesis 12:2)*. What does this mean?

Answer: This blessing was a unique gift from God to Abram. Abram was ultimately blessed with wealth and success. These gains were not related to any previous loss, nor were they subject to envy or aggravation. The implication of this blessing is that although the Almighty gave to Abram great wealth, he was not at liberty to use it without purpose. The intent was that Abram must use it for responsible purposes (*Rashi; Kli Yakar; Ma'or Vashemesh*).

Question: Immediately following the phrase "I will bless you" *(Genesis 12:2)* it says "And you shall be blessed." What is the need for this apparent duplication of phrases?

Answer: This phrase indicates that the Almighty gave Abraham a special ability: the power to bless whomever he wished (*Rashi*). It does not convey a material blessing.

Note: In the *Amidah*, the silent prayer, the first blessing makes reference to Abraham. It mentions his shield that is a reference to the Almighty. In so doing, we express our gratitude to the Almighty for Abraham's blessing (*Talmud, Pesachim 117b*). For when we bless one another, we do so through the merit of Abraham. We ask God for His forgiveness by saying "remember our forefather Abraham" (*Ramban*).

Question: The Bible states, "Abram took his wife ... and the souls they made in Charan" *(Genesis 12:5)*. What is the meaning of this sentence?

Answer: In this verse the word "souls" refers to the people that Abram and Sarai converted to the belief in God. Abram converted the men, Sarai the women (*Talmud Sanhedrin 99b*). It also referred to all the servants of the house of Abram and Sarai who agreed to follow them to the Holy Land (*Rashi; Radak*).

Question: Who was Lot?

Answer: Lot was Abram's nephew. He was the son of Haran. Haran suffered a horrible death at the hands of Nimrod. Abram took Lot into his household.

Question: What was the argument between Abram's and Lot's shepherds?

Answer: Both Abram and Lot were blessed with wealth after a time in Canaan. Both were land owners and amassed herds of sheep. Abram's shepherds argued with Lot's shepherds for allowing Lot's sheep to graze on other people's property. Lot felt that since the land was promised to Abram, and Abram had no heirs, he was therefore entitled to use the land as he saw fit (*Rashi; Midrash*). Lot was offered a choice by Abram: one of them must leave, but the two could not remain together. Lot chose to leave and head south to Sodom.

Question: How did the relationship between Abram and God change after the departure of Lot *(Genesis 13:13-14)*?

Answer: While Lot lived with Abram, the Almighty did not speak to Abram (*Midrash*). Once Lot left, the Almighty spoke to Abram and told him once again that he would have heirs.

Question: What was the reason behind the war between the kings?

Answer: This is one of the ten trials confronted by Abram. Lot went to live in Sodom after leaving Abram. While there he was captured, and the *Midrash* says he was captured by Nimrod. Lot's captivity was actually the catalyst for the conflict. The more significant reason for the war was the authority and ownership of property that was at stake in the region (*Eruvin 53a*). The Midrash says that the Almighty incited the kings to battle so that their fortunes would fall into Abram's hands.

Question: "The fugitive came" *(Genesis 14:13)*. Who is the fugitive, and why is he referred to like this?

Answer: The fugitive is Og, king of Bashan. He is called the fugitive because he was the only one who survived the Flood, beside Noah and his family. He also escaped from the kings' war (*Rashi*).

Question: The Bible states, "*MalkiTzedek*, King of Salem, brought out bread and wine" *(Genesis 14:18)*. Why did he do this?

Answer: *Rashi* says that this was the custom when officers came back from war.

MalkiTzedek's sons died in the war between the kings, and he wanted to show Abram that he was not angry with him (*Tanchuma 15*).

It was a symbol of the bread and wine that was brought along with the offerings in the time of the Temples in Jerusalem (*Bereishit Rabba*).

Question: What was the special honor that Abram gave *MalkiTzedek (Genesis 14:19)*?

Answer: Abram gave *MalkiTzedek* ten percent of the tithe. The *Midrash* and *Rashi* say that originally the Almighty had planned to have the line of the priesthood come through *MalkiTzedek*, but when *MalkiTzedek* blessed Abram before blessing the Almighty this honor was taken away from him.

Question: Why did Abram not want to take any property from the king of Sodom?

Answer: Abram was faithful to God and trusted God's promise of wealth. Therefore, Abram did not desire any other sources of wealth (*Rashi, Genesis 14:23*).

Question: The Talmud states: "Changing a person's name, changes a persons destiny" *(Yerushalmi Ta'anit 2: 1)*. Where do we find an example of this?

Answer: God changed Abram's name to Abraham *(Genesis 17:5)* and his wife Sarai's to Sarah *(Genesis 17:15)*. With the change of names their luck changed as well. Sarah was able to bear a child and Abraham became the father to the nations of Israel and Edom *(Rashi)*.

It is customary to change a person's name if one is seriously ill. According to Jewish tradition, that new name is used when praying for that person's recovery. A person's name is changed in hopes that it will bring renewed health *(Maharal; Kitvey Haari)*.

Question: God promised Abraham many things. For which promise did Abraham ask God to give him a special sign?

Answer: God promised to give Abraham and his descendants the Holy Land. Abraham asked God for a sign of this promise. Abraham wanted to know how he would inherit the land and how his children would exist in it with so many enemies surrounding them *(Rashi, Genesis 15:6,8)*. God granted Abraham a special vision, which is described in *Genesis 15:1-18*. God told Abraham to look at the heavens and asked him, "Can you count the stars? I promise you that your descendants will be as innumerable as the stars" *(Genesis 15:5)*.

Question: Who in this portion repented and returned to God's ways?

Answer: Two people repented according to the Torah in this parsha. First there is Terach, Abraham's father. We learn this from the verse, "You will return to your father with peace" *(Rashi, Genesis 15:15)*. Second, it is noted that Ishmael, Abraham's son from Hagar, his concubine, as the verse states, "You will be buried with a good reputation" *(Rashi, Genesis 15:15)*. At the end of his life, Ishmael repented and gave his brother Isaac recognition and honor, especially when they buried their father, Abraham.

Question: Who is Hagar, and why was she working as Sarah's servant?

Answer: Hagar was Pharaoh's daughter. According to *Rashi*, when Pharaoh saw the miracles that occurred with Sarah, he thought it better his daughter be a servant to Sarah than a noblewoman in his own kingdom (*Midrash, Genesis 16:1*). Sarah gave Hagar to Abraham as a concubine to bear children since she herself was at that point in time incapable of bearing children.

Question: After Hagar had a baby, why did she stop showing respect for Sarah?

Answer: Hagar boasted to everyone that she immediately became pregnant with Abraham's child while Sarah remained barren. Hagar proclaimed that Sarah must not be as righteous as everyone thought she was (*Rashi*).

Question: The Bible praises Ishmael only once. When and why?

Answer: The Bible says that Ishmael was circumcised when he was thirteen years old and that he did not object to it (*Genesis 16:16*).

Question: Why was Isaac called by this name?

Answer: Isaac stems from the Hebrew word for "happiness" or "laughter." The named reflected the feelings of both when each one received the news of the pregnancy. Abraham was happy and Sarah laughed when God's angel revealed that she would have a child.

Also, the numerical values of the letters in the name Yitzchak (*Isaac*) are 10, 90, 8, and 100. Ten signifies the ten tests with which God tested Abraham; ninety signifies Sarah's age when she gave birth; eight signifies the eighth day after birth when Isaac was circumcised; and 100 signifies the age Abraham was when he had Isaac (*Rashi, Genesis 17:19*).

Question: Which commandment is found in this parsha?

Answer: We find the commandment of *brit milah,* circumcision. This remains for eternity a sign of the covenant between God and the Jewish people (*Genesis 17:11*).

Question: When do we fulfill the commandment of circumcision?

Answer: According to Jewish law, circumcision is performed on the eighth day after a baby boy is born. We count from the first night up to the end of the eighth evening. In the beginning of the *Book of Genesis* it says, "It was night and it was day." In other words, we count the day from sunset the night before, or from the time that we see three stars in the sky, up to sunset on the eighth day.

Question: Why is the concept of the three stars so important?

Answer: It is so important because it is the one determining factor deciding one day from the next. It has legal ramifications of great significance.

If the baby is born toward evening of the seventh day, less than thirteen minutes before the appearance of the first three stars, that day is considered to be the seventh, not the eighth day (*Babylonian Talmud Sabbath 34; Shulchan Aruch, Orah Chaim 261b*).

There is a controversy between the sages about a woman who gives birth on a Thursday evening at sunset. If she gives birth after the sun has set, the circumcision would be on the Sabbath a week later. If she gives birth before sunset, the circumcision would be on Friday of the following week. One group of sages says that we count three stars in one glance, that is, without looking left or right. Others say you can look to the left and then to the right until you see three stars. Because it is a biblical commandment to perform the circumcision exactly on the eighth day, it is very important not to miscount the days. Circumcision is permissible on the Sabbath only if the Sabbath is definitely the eighth day. If the circumcision was performed on the Sabbath in error, because the days have been miscounted, it is considered to be: (a) violating the holy Sabbath (b) not fulfilling the biblical commandment to perform the circumcision on the eighth day. The Bible prohibits performing a circumcision earlier (on the seventh day) or later (on the ninth day). Therefore, the sages concluded that only if there were three stars in a single glance would it be considered a new day. Otherwise, it still counts as the previous day (*Tur*).

Question: The Bible states, "On that very day was Abraham circumcised with his son Ishmael" *(Genesis 17:26)*. Why does the Bible place so much emphasize on the phrase "that very day"?

Answer: On that very day Abraham was ninety-nine years old and Ishmael was thirteen years old. The Bible emphasizes this to show us that once Abraham was commanded to circumcise himself he did not delay. He did not wait for the cover of darkness to perform this deed. He was not fearful that his neighbors would see. Rather, Abraham fulfilled the commandment immediately, during the daytime (*Rashi, Genesis 17:25-26*), to show compliance with God's will.

Question: What is the connection between this *parsha, Lech Lecha,* and the *haftorah* from the *Book of Isaiah*?

Answer: Just as Abraham urged the people of his generation to repent and believe in the Almighty, so too the prophet Isaiah urges the people to repent and return to worship God. Both realized that there is only one path to repentance, the belief in the Almighty combined with the observance of His laws.

Vayeira
Chapters: 18 - 22

Synopsis:

Angels visited Abraham's tent; a son is promised to Sarah; Abraham begged God to save Sodom and Gomorrah; Lot tried to save his guests the angels; the destruction of Sodom and Gomorrah; Lot and his daughters were saved, but his wife was turned into a pillar of salt; interaction between the King Avimelech, Sarah, and Abraham; the birth of Isaac; Hagar was sent away by Abraham; Hagar encounters an angel; Abraham's sacrifice of Isaac at the Akaida.

Question: "And God appeared to Abraham...and he sat in the entrance of the tent in the heat of the day" *(Genesis 18:5)*. What do the sages teach about this sentence?

Answer: According to the *Talmud (Bava Metziah 86b)*, God appeared to Abraham on the third day after Abraham had circumcised himself. Abraham was in great pain. The day was very hot and forced Abraham to stay inside and rest rather than to await visitors, which was his usual routine. The reader must keep in mind that Abraham is ninety-nine years of age at this time. Then God saw that Abraham was suffering more from the lack of visitors than from his physical pain and discomfort. The Almighty, therefore, sent three angels in the form of humans to visit him. Seeing them, Abraham rushed to greet the visitors and offer them his hospitality, although he was in great pain *(Rashi)*.

Question: What *mitzvot* (commandments) do we learn from this story of Abraham and his guests?

Answer: Two very important *mitzvot* are learned from this story. First is the *mitzvah* of visiting the sick. We see from here that even the Almighty visited Abraham during his discomfort after the circumcision *(Talmud, Sotah 14a, Bava Metziah 86b)*. The second *mitzvah* is that of inviting guests, even strangers, into one's home. Our sages see this *mitzvah* as the one most associated with Abraham. We see that even while he was in great distress he did not fail to pay attention to the needs of his guests.

Question: Why did God send the three angels?

Answer: According to *Rashi*, each angel had a specific mission to fulfill. God sent the angels to Abraham to "cheer him up" by their visit. One angel was named Raphael, meaning God-healing. His purpose was to heal Abraham. The second one was sent to destroy the city of Sodom. The third angel's mission was to tell Sarah that she would give birth to a child in exactly one year (*Unkelus; Rashi*).

Question: Angels do not eat, yet the Torah tells us they consumed a feast. How do we explain this apparent contradiction?

Answer: According to the *Talmud* (*Bava Metziah 86b*), the three angels appear to behave in accordance with the accepted behavior at that time and place. Even though they are not in need of food, they ate on this occasion in honor of their host, Abraham.

Question: How does the *parsha* teach us about the importance of a *minyan* (the ten Jewish men required for public prayer)?

Answer: When Abraham begs God to save the cities of Sodom and Gomorrah from destruction, he begins by saying that if there are fifty righteous people in the city, then the Almighty should spare the cities. Not finding the requisite number Abraham proceeds to "negotiate" with God to spare the cities for the sake of fewer and fewer righteous inhabitants, until finally the number is dwindled to ten. God agrees to spare the city for the sake of ten righteous people but no less. That number was not found. Abraham no longer prayed for the city's survival. Because of the importance of this number, the sages require a minimum of ten for public prayer.

Question: Where do we see the level of humility reached by Abraham?

Answer: In *Genesis 18:27* Abraham begged God not to destroy the cities of Sodom and Gomorrah. In addressing God, Abraham said "...although I am nothing but dust and ashes..." Abraham saw himself as only dust and ashes even though he had attained the level where he was capable of speaking directly with the Almighty.

Question: The sages teach us that one is not punished without warning. Where do we learn this?

Answer: In *Genesis 19:15* the angels warned Lot to leave the city immediately before they destroyed the cities. They encouraged him to take his family with him. Otherwise, they would be destroyed along with the rest of the cities' inhabitants.

Question: Where in this *parsha* do we learn the importance of *trup* (cantillation)?

Answer: *Genesis 19:16* uses the word *vayitmahama*, meaning "lingering." The word is cantillized with a long musical repetition called a *shalshelet*. This vocalization expresses the delay that Lot caused, because he refused to leave without his possessions. In the end, the angels had to physically remove Lot from his home, without his possessions, and lead him away from the cities (*Pardes laHaremak Sha'ar 28-29; Zohar Chalak A-15b*).

Question: Where do we find this same trup but with a different meaning?

Answer: Later, in *Genesis 39:8* the Torah uses the word *vayima'an* that means "adamantly refused," and it is here that the same musical cantillization occurs. In this story we see Joseph, one of Jacob's sons, now in Egypt. He is a servant in the home of Potiphar. Potiphar's wife is attempting to seduce Joseph, but Joseph "adamantly refuses" to submit, and runs away (*Pardes laHaremak Sha'ar 28-29; Sha'arai Amunah 170*).

Question: What sin did Lot's wife commit, and how was she punished (*Genesis 19:27*)?

Answer: From Abraham Lot learned the *mitzvah* of welcoming guests into one's home and treating them like members of the family, giving them food and drink. When the angels came, Lot asked his wife to bring bread and salt to the table for the guests. She refused. Lot's wife did not want to participate in Lot's hospitality. As a punishment, when Lot's wife turned back to look upon the city, which she was commanded not to do, she was turned into a pillar of salt. The Almighty's punishment to Lot's wife was "measure for measure" (*Bereishit Rabba 50-51b*).

Question: Why did the angel command Lot and his family not to look back at the cities of Sodom and Gomorrah?

Answer: There is a commandment that forbids a person to receive any enjoyment while other people are being punished (*Talmud*).

Question: According to the biblical commentators what sin did the angels commit?

Answer: The angels of our question are the angels who had previously visited Abraham, and then went on to inform Lot of the fate of his city. In *Genesis 19:13* it says "For we are planning to destroy this place." The use of the word 'we' seemed to imply that it was the angels themselves who were causing this destruction. They seem to be placing themselves above the Almighty. For using this word 'we,' God punished them. *Genesis 28:12* is specific in the roles of angels when it says "Angels of God ascending." The use of the word ascending tells us the angels were sent by God to carry out a specific mission and were to return immediately afterward. As a punishment for their act, they were delayed in their return. The return occurred only after Jacob encountered them in his dream as he saw the ladder with angels ascending and descending (*Midrash*).

Question: What sins did the people of Sodom and Gomorrah commit that warranted such a drastic punishment?

35

Answer: The *Talmud Sanhedrin 109a* says they behaved in an exceedingly antisocial manner. They refused to feed the starving or house the homeless of their own cities (*Rabbeinu Bechayei*). They also committed abominations such as robbery, sodomy, and the like with no accountability; and since these transgressions were committed in the Holy Land they therefore deserved a more extreme punishment (*Ramban*).

Question: Why does the Bible refer to it as the sacrifice of Isaac *(Genesis 22:1-19)*?

Answer: The biblical commentators explain that the sacrifice of Isaac serves as a symbol of those willing to make any and all sacrifices out of respect for God's holiness (*Kiddush Hashem*). This was a test for Abraham to see how far he would go in order to submit to the Will of the Almighty.

The *Ramban* explains that the Almighty gave this last test to Abraham because He was preparing Abraham to become a highly spiritual person capable of being a "vessel for holding blessings." By agreeing to sacrifice Isaac, Abraham showed his complete trust and faith in the Almighty. That regardless, Abraham firmly believed that the Almighty was all good' and just. Abraham thus proved his worthiness to be a recipient of the Almighty's blessings.

Question: What is the connection between this *parsha* and its *haftorah (Kings 2,4:1-37)*?

Answer: In the Bible, an angel promises Sarah that she will give birth to a son in one year's time to the day. The angel promises to return at the time of the birth. In the Haftorah, the prophet Elisha promises Shunamit, wife of Ovadia, that she will give birth to a son within one year's time. He cannot promise to return within a year because he is of flesh and blood and cannot know his future.

Another connection between them is the act of welcoming guests into one's home. Just like Abraham and Sarah had done, so too Shunamit sat and waited for travelers so that she might also convey hospitality. One such traveler was one of the angels who had visited Abraham and Sarah.

Chayei Sarah
Chapters: 23 - 25:18

Synopsis:

Sarah passed away; Abraham bought a burial site; Abraham sent his servant Eliezer to find a wife for his son Isaac; Eliezer met Rebecca; Rebecca's father Betuel and her brother Laban; Rebecca agreed to go with Eliezer to marry Isaac; Abraham passed away.

Question: Why was Hebron called Kiryat Arba *(Genesis 23:2)*?

Answer: *Kiryat Arba* means "Place of Four." One reason that it received this name is that four pairs of our ancestors are buried there: Adam and Eve, Abraham and Sarah, Isaac and Rebecca, and Jacob and Leah *(Bereishit Rabba 58; 2)*. A second reason is that in this city lived four giants: Achiman, Shayshai, Talmai, and their father *(Rashi, Genesis 6:3)*.

Question: Is there any significance of the name *Mearat Hamachpelah*?

Answer: This is the burial site of our patriarchs and matriarchs. The word *machpelah* comes from the Hebrew root *kefel* meaning "multiplied." The architecture of the cave was such that it was built as two caves, one on top of the other. It also refers to the multiple couples of forefathers and their wives who are buried there *(Rashi, Genesis 23:9; Talmud Eruvin 53a)*.

Question: Why does the Bible go into great detail describing the purchase of this burial site by Abraham?

Answer: This stresses the importance of the Holy Land, Israel, not only for the living but for the dead as well. Abraham knew that the Holy Land was so sacred that he spared no expense to purchase this burial ground for himself and Sarah, and also for generations to come *(Ibn Ezra)*.

Abraham was the first Hebrew in the Land of Israel, and he wanted to teach the sacredness of the Holy Land to his generation as well as to all future generations *(Ramav)*.

The Bible gives us, and future generations, documented, accepted, written proof that this land is truly ours. Today, we can appreciate the great importance and significance of this proof of the sale as the dispute over ownership continues *(Yalkut Tehillim 20)*.

Abraham wanted to teach the people of his time and future generations how to carry out land transactions. Efron offered to give *Mearat*

Hamachpelah as a gift to Abraham. Abraham refused, insisting on paying full price for the burial ground. This was to show future generations that the land was owned outright, with no liens, with no one beholding to anyone that the site is the rightful property of the Jewish people (*Talmud Bava Batra 112; Moed Katan 13, Tosafot; Chofetz Chaim*).

Since God promised the Holy Land to Abraham and his descendants, Abraham had full right to obtain the land. Yet he preferred to buy the land outright, making full payment up front. Abraham made a careful and conscious choice not to start a war against Efron in order to obtain the burial land. This was done to ensure that God's name would be sanctified and not disgraced (*Rabbeinu Bechayei*).

In Abraham's time, those owning a burial site were given ownership of the surrounding land as well. It was very important to Abraham to be accredited as having full ownership of his land. By purchasing *Mearat Hamachpelah* Abraham guaranteed himself and his descendants the rights of full citizenship (*Sforno*).

Abraham knew that Adam and Eve were buried there. He wanted the privilege of being buried with them for himself, his wife Sarah, and his descendants.

Note: Jewish law requires a body to be buried underground. Autopsies, cremation, and any other desecration of the dead are prohibited. The *Jerusalem Talmud, Nazir 7:1* states "You have to bury the whole body, not just part of the body, in order to fulfill the entire commandment of burial" (*See Teshuvot, Rabbi Meir Shapiro, Siman 74*).

Question: Why does the Bible state twice "life of Sarah" (*Genesis 23:1*)?

Answer: The commentators tell us that Sarah was equal in her righteousness in old age as she was in younger years. *Rashi* says at age one hundred she was the same as she was at twenty in her virtue.

Question: "And Abraham was an old man...and God blessed Abraham *ba-kol*" (*Genesis 24:11*). What is the meaning of the word *ba-kol*?

Answer: *Ba-kol* means "in every way." The *gematriah,* numerical equivalent, of *ba-kol* is 52, the same as *ben* that means son. After many years of not having children the Almighty blessed Abraham with a *ben,* a son (*Rashi, Genesis 24:1*).

The *Talmud* tells that Abraham and Sarah had a daughter and her name was *Bakol.* At the end of his life Abraham had amassed property and wealth as well as a good name. He had almost everything. The Almighty had blessed him with a son. He wanted a daughter. There is a commandment in the Torah given during the days of creation, and that is to be fruitful and multiply. One fulfills this commandment by having both a son and a daughter. Therefore Abraham was blessed by the Almighty by having both. This is described by the word *ba-kol* (*Rambam, Sefer Hachinuch*).

Question: What insight does the Bible give us about Abraham's behavior toward someone else's property?

Answer: In *Genesis 24:10* it says migmalai adonov, from his master's camels. This refers to the incident involving Eliezer, Abraham's servant, who took Abraham's camels out to walk. Before going out he made sure to put muzzles on the camels so that they would not eat or disturb anyone's property (*Rashi, 24:10*). From this story we learn the lesson that we are obligated to respect other people's property. We are taught this lesson so that we can incorporate it into our own character and lifestyles.

Question: Abraham's servant went to Aram Naharayim *(Genesis 24:10).* Why was it given this name?

Answer: *Rashi* says that it means Aram of two rivers. The city was situated between two rivers, the Perat and the Chidekel (*Rashi, Genesis 24: 10*).

Question: According to *Rashi,* what miracle happened to Eliezer, Abraham's devoted servant, on his way?

Answer: A trip that should have taken a number of days was shortened to just three hours. God caused a shortening of Eliezer's trip (*Talmud Sanhedrin 95a*).

Question: Eliezer was sent by Abraham to find his son Isaac a mate. How did Eliezer identify the appropriate woman for Isaac?

Answer: Eliezer devised a test that would indicate to him the woman who would be appropriate for Isaac. Ultimately Rebecca was chosen. She proved to be Isaac's ideal mate because of her consideration of others. The signs she displayed were: she dressed modestly; she treated Eliezer in a kind and respectful manner even though he was a stranger; she treated Eliezer's animals with great compassion by remembering to give them a drink. Not only did Rebecca care for Eliezer's animals' needs, she did so before considering her own needs. Rebecca graciously offered Eliezer a place to eat and sleep. She was thoughtful enough to provide a separate place for Eliezer's animals to eat and rest.

Question: How does the Bible indicate that Laban was a wicked person who did not honor his father?

Answer: The Bible states, "Then Laban and Bethuel answered [Eliezer]" (*Genesis 24:50*). The sage *Rashi* learns from this verse that Laban showed great disrespect for his father by not allowing his father to speak first. Instead Laban rushed to answer before his father had a chance to speak (*Rashi, Genesis 24:50*).

Question: What other insights are we given into the character of Laban, Rebecca's brother?

Answer: When Eliezer came to Rebecca's home, Laban ran out to greet Eliezer and hug him. This outward behavior appears to show that Laban was truly happy to see Eliezer. However, the sages tell us that Laban was interested only in the riches that Eliezer had brought with him as part of the gifts to the woman chosen. Laban was a greedy person by nature. Laban was also aware of Eliezer's belief in the Almighty. Laban knew Eliezer would not step into his home if Laban possessed idols. Laban disposed of his idols before Eliezer entered the house. He then welcomed Eliezer, blessed him in the name of God, and declared that he kept no idols in his house.

Question: Eliezer asked Rebecca if there was a place to rest for the night. Rebecca replied affirmatively but used different wording. What does the difference in language indicate?

Answer: When Eliezer asked he used the word *lalin*, which means to sleep for one night, implying a limited period. However, when Rebecca answered, she used the word *lalun*, indicating an indefinite period of time, several nights. In doing so, Rebecca offered Eliezer accommodations for as long as he wanted to stay. Again the Torah shows Rebecca's great warmth, sensitivity, and generosity to others (*Rashi, Genesis 24:23*).

Question: What other example does the Bible give highlighting Rebecca's special personality?

Answer: The Bible relates the conversation between Eliezer and Rebecca regarding food and lodging for the night. Rebecca made sure to reply to each question with respect. Her immediate concern was to the well-being of the traveler and his animals. She first said she would feed his animals and him. Then she offered him a place to sleep. She was calm in her exchange with him and did not become excited or nervous upon being approached by a stranger. This showed Eliezer Rebecca's refined mannerisms and intellectual capabilities (*Rashi, Genesis 24:24*).

Question: From where do we learn that one is not allowed to force a girl to marry against her will?

Answer: After Eliezer received the consent of Rebecca's father for the marriage, the Bible states, "Let us call the maiden and ask her decision" (*Genesis 24:57*). This statement is meant to emphasize the principle that a girl should marry only with her full consent (*Rashi*).

Question: The Bible states, "And Isaac brought Rebecca into the tent of Sarah his mother" *(Genesis 24:67)*. What three things do the sages teach us from this verse?

Answer: The *Midrash* tells us that while Sarah was alive, a flame burned constantly in the family's tent, from Sabbath to Sabbath. We also learn that the *challah* (bread) Sarah made was blessed; it was always scrumptious and satisfying. There was always a special heavenly protective cloud above Abraham and Sarah's tent.

Upon Sarah's death these three blessings disappeared. However, when Isaac brought Rebecca into his mother's tent, the three blessings resumed. This was conclusive proof that Rebecca was Isaac's destined partner (*Rashi; Malbim*).

Question: The Bible says, "Abraham gave all that he had to Isaac." What was it that he gave to Isaac?

Answer: *Rashi* on *Genesis 24:4* says Abraham's material wealth had already been handed over to Isaac. So what was left to give Isaac? Abraham transmitted spiritual power to Isaac. Abraham had received from the Almighty the ability to bless others. When Abraham blessed somebody the blessing was fulfilled. This unique power was now given to Isaac.

Question: Where do we learn of Abraham's great love for the Holy Land of Israel?

Answer: When Abraham sent Eliezer to find a wife for Isaac, he told him to go to *Aram Naharayim*. Tradition has it that it lies between the Tigris and Euphrates rivers in Mesopotamia. Eliezer asked what he should do if a suitable girl did not want to come to live in the Holy Land. Abraham replied that the Land of Israel was the one promised to him by God, to be inherited by all generations to come. If the maiden refused to come to this land, then the match would not be the appropriate one.

Question: How do we know that Isaac can be credited with the establishment of our regular afternoon prayers? Who was responsible for establishing our daily morning and evening prayers?

Answer: The Bible states that Isaac was "...in the field toward evening" (*Genesis 24:63*). From this verse, the sages learned that in the late afternoon, Isaac went to pray in the field and instituted the afternoon prayer service, known as *Mincha.* Abraham instituted the morning prayer, *Shacharit* (*Genesis 19:27*), and Jacob established the evening prayer, *Ma'ariv* (*Genesis 28:11*) (*Talmud, Brachot 6b, 26b; Yuma 28a*).

Question: The Bible tells us, "Abraham proceeded and took a wife whose name was *Keturah*" *(Genesis 25:1).* Who is *Keturah?*

Answer: *Keturah* was Hagar, Sarah's maidservant. She was the mother of Ishmael. She was originally banished from the home of Abraham because of the effect that she and her son would have on Isaac. After Sarah's death Abraham remarried Hagar. The Midrash tells us that Hagar repented her previous behaviors. Thus she was named *Keturah* because her deeds were as beautiful as incense, *ketoret.* In Aramaic its meaning is "restrained." This indicates that Hagar remained chaste from the time that she was separated from Abraham to her remarriage to him (*Rashi*).

Question: Why did Abraham not formally bless Isaac before he passed away, as the other patriarchs had done to their children?

Answer: According to *Rashi*, Abraham knew that Esau would come from Isaac. Therefore, Abraham felt that it would be better for Isaac to receive a blessing directly from God (*Genesis 25:11*).

Question: What is the connection between the parsha of *Chayei Sarah* and its corresponding portion from the Prophets?

Answer: In *Parshat Chayei Sarah*, Abraham was looking for someone to fill the role of mother of the nation. Similarly, in the *Book of Kings*, we find that King David had to select a successor to the throne.

Toldot
Chapters: 25:19 - 28:9

Synopsis:

The genealogy of Isaac; the pregnancy of Rebecca; the birth of Esau and Jacob; Esau sold his birthright to Jacob; famine; Isaac went to Garar because of the famine; the dispute over the wells; the blessings given by Isaac to Jacob and Esau; Esau's animosity toward Jacob; Jacob forced to leave to Charan; the marriage of Esau to Ishmael's daughters.

Question: The Bible relates, "And these are the offspring of Isaac, son of Abraham–Abraham had Isaac..." *(Genesis 25:19)*. Why does the Bible repeat that Isaac is the offspring of Abraham?

Answer: Sarah was unable to have a child for many years. She finally gave birth to Isaac. The birth had occurred after King Avimelech had abducted her. To dispel any question of paternity the Almighty made Isaac look physically identical to Abraham so that people were unable to deny Abraham's paternity. This verse reminds us that Isaac was born after Abraham's name change from Abram to Abraham, "Father of Multitudes" *(Rashi, Genesis 25:19)*.

Question: "Isaac was forty years old when he took Rebecca, daughter of Bethuel the Aramean, from Paddan Aram, sister of Laban the Aramean, as wife for himself" *(Genesis 25:20)*. Why does the Bible list the genealogy of Rebecca in such detail?

Answer: The Bible wants to teach us that Rebecca was a pure and righteous person. Despite her father and brother, who were wicked people and lived evil lives, she remained true to the Almighty. The Bible teaches us through this story that a person can follow in the ways of God even though he is in a wicked environment *(Rashi, Genesis 25:20)*. A person's worth is based on their personal behavior, not on the behaviors of his family who went before him. That is how a person is to be judged.

Question: "The children agitated within her womb and she said 'If so, why am I thus?' And she went to inquire of God" *(Genesis 25:22)*. Why did the unborn children within Rebecca fight and argue?

Answer: Rebecca was pregnant with twin sons. When she would pass a place of Torah learning, the fetus Jacob would struggle to get out. When Rebecca would pass a house of idol worship, the fetus Esau would struggle to get out. Additionally, both fetuses struggled within their mother over their portions in this world and the World to Come (*Rashi, Genesis 25:22*).

Question: During Rebecca's pregnancy, she constantly felt embroiled motion inside her body. She went to ask the Almighty what it meant. The reply she was given was, "Two nations are inside you...one shall become strong from the other regime, and the elder will serve the younger." What does this mean *(Genesis 25:23)*?

Answer: This verse teaches us that Rebecca will give birth to two sons who will be the source for two future kingdoms but only one could rule at a time. When one rose, the other fell. This symbolizes good and evil, which cannot successfully coexist on an equal plane. This also comes to tell us that traits of good and evil exist in us all. We can draw examples of this from King David and Esau. Both had the same character traits. King David was able to harness his traits for good, while Esau's character became evil (*Rashi, Ohr Hachayim, Ba'al Haturim*).

Question: "The first one emerged red" *(Genesis 25:25)*. What is the meaning of this reference?

Answer: The Bible is referring to the birth of Esau. His complexion was ruddy. Since red is a sign of bloodshed, we learn that Esau had a tendency toward bloodshed.

Again drawing on our comparison of King David and Esau, David was also born with a ruddy complexion. When Samuel expressed worry about this, God reassured him that David had "beautiful eyes," meaning that as the future king, David would only shed blood when the *Sanhedrin* (the Religious Supreme Court) approved. Accordingly, King David's "redness" was harnessed to do well, whereas Esau's "redness" was used for evil. Esau would shed blood whenever he desired.

Question: The Bible says, "Isaac loved Esau" *(Genesis 25:28)*. What caused Isaac to love Esau?

Answer: Isaac loved Esau because he believed his son to be a pious person. Esau scrupulously observed the mitzvah of *kibud av*, honoring one's father. Because Esau truly loved and honored his father, he wanted Isaac to have a high opinion of him. He made sure his father had the best foods available. But yet Esau tricked Isaac into believing that he was a pious person by asking questions that would make him seem so.

Question: The Bible relates, "So He called his name Jacob" *(Genesis 25:26)*. Who is the he referred to, and what does the name Jacob mean?

Answer: The *Midrash* says the He is God (*Tanchuma Shmot 4*); while *Rashi* says that the he is Jacob's father, Isaac.

Yaakov (Jacob) in Hebrew has the same root as the word *ekey* meaning "heel." When Jacob and Esau were born, Jacob grabbed Esau's heel hoping that he might be born first.

Question: The Bible says, "So they named him Esau" *(Genesis 25:25)*. Why was he called by this name?

Answer: In Hebrew, Esau is spelled the same way as the word *esauy*, which means "ready" or "done." It also means "completely developed." In fact the *Midrash* says that Esau was born with as much hair as a child several years older (*Rashi; Yonatan ben Uziel*).

Question: The Bible says, "The lads grew up" *(Genesis 25:27)*. What do we learn from these words?

Answer: Until Jacob and Esau reached bar mitzvah age (thirteen), they were similar in personality. When Esau was mischievous, it was thought to be because he was a child. However, when they reached *bar mitzvah* each child went his own way. Esau became a man of the fields, enjoying hunting and trapping. He enjoyed seeing animals suffer before they died (*Midrash*). He also hunted for the pure sport of it. He did not always eat what he killed. Jacob, on the other hand, was a pious person who spent his time learning Torah. The *Midrash* says he spent most of his time in the *yeshivot* (school) of sages Shem and Aver (*Bereishit Rabba 63:10,15*).

Question: The Bible records this encounter between Jacob and Esau, "Jacob simmered a stew and Esau came in from the field" *(Genesis 25:29)*. What is the connection between these two statements?

Answer: On that very day, Abraham passed away, so Jacob was preparing a meal customary for people who are in mourning, lentil stew. Instead of mourning, Esau was hunting in the fields. It became common knowledge that Esau was not a worshipper of God. Since God had promised Abraham that only one of Isaac's children would follow in God's path, Jacob realized he needed to buy Esau's birthright (*Rashi; Kli Yakar; Ramban; Ohr Hachayim*).

Question: Jacob said, "sell, as this day, your birthright to me" *(Genesis 25:31)*. Why is it written, "As this day?"

Answer: The use of the phrase 'as this day' declared that the sale was to be as clear as the day itself. This was to be a fully binding trans-action. Esau had no morals and saw no use for his birthright; it meant nothing to him. He saw nothing tangible in it. Jacob purchased the birthright with a sum of gold but sealed the deal with the meal. Esau sold his birthright for a pot of red beans (*Sforno; Kli Yakar; Yonatan ben Uziel*)!

Question: Why is the city named *Be'er Sheva*, "seven wells" *(Genesis 26:33)*?

Answer: Seven wells were found there (this is not the same *Be'er Sheva* named by Abraham) (*Rashbam; Sforno*). Abraham gave seven pledges to King Avimelech (*Ibn Ezra*). Abraham and Isaac swore on this well. *Be'er* means well, and *sheva* means oath (*Ramban*).

Question: The Bible says, "Isaac became old, and he did not see well" *(Genesis 27:1)*. Why all of a sudden does Isaac's vision weaken?

Answer: One response is that Esau and his wives lived with Isaac. They were idol worshippers and were constantly making sacrifices. The smoke from these sacrifices diminished Isaac's vision (*Tanchuma 8*). The constant sacrifices caused Isaac to weep so much that he eventually was unable to open his eyes (*Psikta Raba 12*). When Isaac realized that he blessed Esau wrongly, he cried, and became physically ill, and felt old (*Midrash*). The Midrash tells us that this is one of the tests that God gave Isaac.

Question: How does the *Ohr Hachayim* interpret the interactions of Isaac and Rebecca and Jacob and Esau?

Answer: I heard this answer from my rabbi, Rabbi Gershon Kitzis,*shlitah*. *Ohr Hachayim* explains "the Bible describes that Isaac became old from sorrow, and Rebecca was the cause of his sorrow. Without her actions, that of her switching the blessing's of Jacob and Esau, Jewish history might have been very different."

What does the *Ohr Hachayim*, mean by this interpretation? Rabbi Israel Ba'al Shem Tov, founder of the hasidic movement, interpreted this explanation by telling a parable. A father had only two children. One was a good son who sat and learned. The other son was a troublemaker and a drunkard, not a good person. The father had money and also owned a pub. The father decided to write his will. The children were sure that the good son would inherit all the money and that the bad son would inherit the pub. After the father passed away, the sons read the will and found to their amazement that the good son had inherited the pub and the bad son had inherited the money. Nobody could understand the father's purpose in doing this. Two months after the father's death, the bad son had spent all of his money at the pub, so in the end, the good son got all the money.

Isaac planned to give the blessing to Esau on the condition that he follow the way of God and observe the commandments. Failing to fulfill the conditions everything would then revert to Jacob. Initially Jacob probably would complain, saying to his father, "Why are you not blessing me?" Isaac would then tell Jacob that the blessing that he gave to Esau was conditional. Rebecca heard that Isaac was planning to give the blessing to Esau instead of Jacob. She was unaware of the conditions to be set forth. Rebecca right away thought that something was wrong with Isaac. She therefore persuaded Jacob to trick his father, and Jacob received the blessing instead of Esau. When Esau came he screamed to Isaac, "What about my blessing?" Isaac tells Esau, "You live by your sword; all the blessings that I have given to Jacob are on the condition that he observe the commandments and follow the way of God" (*Genesis 27:40; Yonatan ben Uziel; Yerushalmi; Unkelus*).

Consequently, if the plan had gone Isaac's way, Jacob would have inherited everything. However, because Rebecca was unaware of Isaac's intentions, she switched the blessings around with the pure intention of having Jacob receive the appropriate blessing. Rebecca simply did not understand Isaac's reasoning in giving the blessing to his evil son, Esau. Now we can understand why the holy sage *Ohr Hachayim* says, "The Bible describes the fact that Isaac became old with a lot of sorrow. The reason for this is because without her actions (Rebecca's switching the blessings), much of our nation's affliction would be avoided."

Question: Regarding what verse does *Rashi* comment, "I do not know what it means"?

Answer: *Rashi* makes this comment about *Genesis 28:5*, "he went...to Laban, son of Bethuel, Rebecca's brother, mother of Jacob and Esau." Why does the Bible say "mother of Jacob and Esau," since this fact is clearly stated previously. The *Ramav* suggests that this is evidence of *Rashi's* honesty and humility. The answer is that *Rashi* knew many explanations but was unsure as to which one was the true answer.

Question: What is the connection between *Parshat Toldot,* and the *haftorah* reading from the *Book of Malachi?*

Answer: *Parshat Toldot* portrays Jacob's turning point. Jacob chose to receive the Torah while Esau did not. Since Esau was the firstborn, however, Isaac's blessings should rightfully have gone to Esau. Rebecca, seeing Esau's character, devised a way to fool her husband into blessing Jacob first. The reading from the prophet Malachi reiterates God's love for Jacob and his anger and disappointment in Esau. Malachi states that because of God's hatred of Esau, the nation of Edom, Esau's descendants, would never prosper and would be doomed to destruction.

Vayeitzei
Chapters: 28:10 - 32:3

Synopsis:

Jacob had a dream vision; Jacob established evening prayer; Jacob and Rachel met; Laban and Jacob created a marriage contract; Laban fooled Jacob by switching his daughters; Rachel and Leah had jealousy between them; Jacob planned to leave Laban; Jacob left Laban; Laban ran to catch Jacob; Jacob and Laban fought; Jacob and Laban reached an agreement; God's angels escorted Jacob to the Holy Land.

55

Question: The Bible states, "Jacob departed from Be'er Sheva and traveled to Charan" *(Genesis 28:10)*. Why does the Bible make a special point of telling us this?

Answer: Jacob spent fourteen years in Be'er Sheva studying the oral Torah (Bible) with the holy sages Shem and Aver. According to tradition, the oral Torah was given to Adam, and then orally passed on to the leaders of the later generations (Introduction to the book *Raziel HaMalach*). This was to prepare Jacob for his personal struggles. Shem and Aver taught him how to remain a pious person even when living among dishonest and sinful people. Tradition tells that Shem was from the generation of the Flood; while Aver had lived with the people who built the Tower of Babel.

Jacob was a righteous person. The Bible points out that when a righteous person is residing in a city, the city takes on the splendor, brilliance, and charm of that righteous person (*Talmud Ta'anis*). When Jacob departed Be'er Sheva, all the splendor, brilliance, and charm the city had acquired left with Jacob. That is why the Bible words his departure and travel in the manner it does (*Rashi*).

Question: What did Jacob do in Charan that he had not done in 14 years?

Answer: Jacob lay down and slept a full night (*Bereishit Rabba 28:11*).

Question: The Bible states, "He encountered the place" *(Genesis 28:11)*. What do our sages teach us from this verse?

Answer: "The place referred to in the verse is Mount Moriah, the holy site where Isaac lay ready to be sacrificed to God. It is also the place where the Temple would be built (*Talmud Pesachim 88a*). This is the source from which we learn that Jacob established *Ma'ariv*, the evening prayer service (*Talmud Brachot 26b*).

Question: According to the holy sages of the *Talmud Yerushalmi* and *Yonatan ben Uziel*, how many miracles occurred when Jacob left Be'er Sheva, and what were they?

Answer: Five miracles occurred: The hours of the day became shorter and the sun set earlier because God wanted to speak with Jacob. Second, the four stones that Jacob took to use as a pillow miraculously became one stone. Third, Jacob was able to lift a stone by himself that had proven too heavy for all the shepherds together. Four, after Jacob removed the heavy stone from the well, the water flowed abundantly and freely for the entire time that he was in Charan (twenty years).

Five, when Jacob left Be'er Sheva, God shortened the distance and Jacob suddenly found himself in Charan.

Question: What was Jacob's vow to God *(Genesis 28:20)*?

Answer: Jacob vowed that if God would protect him from danger, hunger, and cold and return him safely to his father's house, he would reciprocate by building a temple. Jacob also promised to carefully write down his earnings and to faithfully give a tenth of his wealth each year to charity. From this vow, Jacob established the precedent of sharing one's good fortune by giving a percentage of one's annual earnings to the needy.

Question: Why did our patriarch, Jacob, make a vow to God that seems to be conditional on God performing certain actions?

Answer: Jacob's vow was not meant to be conditional. According to *Rashi*, Jacob urged God to protect him and his descendants forever, just as God had promised his grandfather, Abraham. According to the sages *Sforno* and *Ramban*, Jacob was filled with doubt and uncertainty about his life's direction and purpose. He was not sure if he should pack up and leave in order to seek a wife as his mother had instructed him to do, or stay as his dream about angels signifying a holy place seemed to imply. Jacob's vow, therefore, was a way of soliciting the Almighty's guidance. Jacob was appealing to God for reassurance and guidance to the right path.

The commentator *Haktav v'haKabbalah* explains Jacob's vow this way. "If God will be with me…then this stone…will become a house of God." The Hebrew word for if was used to imply Jacob's desire that the wish should come true. Haktav derives his impression from the fact that the Hebrew word for if, *im*, comes from the Hebrew word *amen* (may it be His will).

Question: What meaning does Jacob's dream hold *(Genesis 28:12)*?

Answer: The sages teach us that Jacob's dream holds special importance to his life as well as to future generations. In the dream, Jacob sees a ladder standing firmly on the ground. The ladder signifies a person's life. The implication is, therefore, that an individual must have his feet planted firmly on the ground (i.e., working and attaining his physical needs). The ladder reaches into the heavens. This signifies the need for man to strive for spirituality. God watches over every little detail both in man's physical and spiritual life, and as long as an individual follows in the way of God, God will always protect him.

Question: Where in the *parsha* of *Vayeitzei* do we learn of Jacob's unique piety?

Answer: Jacob's piety is reflected in his vow to God. Jacob asked only for food and garments *(Genesis 28:20)*, the bare minimum one needs to survive *(Ralbag; Radak; Talmud Succah 48b)*. Other commentators add that righteous people ask only for "righteous prosperity." We are, therefore, taught to ask God only for what we truly require. Further, we learn that having more than we need could become a burden rather than a blessing *(Kli Yakar; Maharal; Avot: 4)*.

Question: Why did Jacob rebuke the shepherds *(Genesis 29:7)*?

Answer: Jacob felt that the shepherds were not honest with their employer. Since the owner was not watching them, they stopped working. This occurred even when it was early in the day (*Ramav*).

Question: How do we learn about Laban's wicked character?

Answer: Laban expected that Jacob would come with a great deal of wealth, as had Eliezer on behalf of Jacob's father, Isaac. When Laban found out that Jacob had no money, he required him to work seven years in order to procure Rachel as his wife. Jacob loved Rachel and agreed to this. Jacob knew that Laban was a dishonest man who twisted truths. In order to prevent Laban from substituting another in Rachel's place, Jacob made it clear to Laban that he wanted Rachel, Laban's youngest daughter. There was no room for Laban to get out of the deal by pretending that he misunderstood and offer his older daughter. When faced with no way out of the agreement, Laban resorted to outright trickery to get Jacob to marry Leah (*Rashi, Genesis 29:18*).

Question: Why did Jacob weep when he saw Rachel (*Genesis 29:11*)?

Answer: Jacob fell totally in love with Rachel at first sight but foresaw that he would not be buried next to her (*Rashi*). He also felt bad that he had no wealth to offer her, like his grandfather, Abraham, had sent to encourage Rebecca's family to allow her to marry Isaac. Isaac and Rebecca sent their son, Jacob, to the same house, with presents and money, to fulfill the same custom. On the way, Esau's son, Eliphaz, found Jacob and wanted to kill him on his father's instructions. Jacob persuaded Eliphaz to take the material wealth that he carried with him instead of taking his life. According to the *Talmud*, an impoverished person is considered a dead person; therefore, Jacob wept when he saw Rachel.

Ralbag explains that this is an example of settling a claim (i.e., birthright) by paying damages. Eliphaz, instead of killing Jacob, took his property and spared his life. As it is written in *Exodus 21:24* "Eye for Eye, Tooth for Tooth..."

Question: How do we learn of Jacob's work ethic?

Answer: Jacob worked for Laban for fourteen years. Throughout that period, Laban agreed to various terms of employment, each time managing to break the contract. Despite this, Jacob felt honored to perform his work in the best possible way. He never allowed Laban's trickery and dishonesty to diminish the quality of his work. For this reason, Jacob is a perfect example of a proper and honest work ethic (*Talmud*).

Question: How many times did Laban change Jacob's salary and working conditions?

Answer: The Bible teaches us that Jacob's wages were changed a hundred times (*Genesis 30:7*).

Question: Why does Rachel deserve to be called "one of our holiest matriarchs"?

Answer: Rachel exemplified righteousness by unselfishly giving her sister, Leah, the secret sign which Jacob gave to her. Jacob gave Rachel this sign to be assured that it was Rachel he would marry. Once the switch was made, Rachel gave the sign to Leah, to spare her sister insult and embarrassment. Laban forced Leah to marry first so that Jacob would continue to be his servant for another seven years (*Babylonian Talmud Megilah 13b; Bava Batra 123a*).

Another example of this quality was how Rachel feared for Leah. There was fear that Leah would be forced to marry Esau, a man for whom Leah surely did not have feelings.

Rachel suffered many years of infertility. Nonetheless she still maintained her unconditional devotion to God (*Tanchuma 20*).

Question: What is the special reward that Rachel received for her righteousness?

Answer: Rachel had her own gravesite, situated between Jerusalem and Hebron. Rachel foresaw that future generations would be forced into exile and that her gravesite would become the center for prayers for these generations. To this day, many people come to pray at Rachel's holy gravesite.

Question: The Bible states, "Leah's eyes were tender." What do we learn from this?

Answer: Leah cried constantly because she feared that she would be forced to marry Esau.

Question: What excuse did Laban use when he fooled Jacob by switching his daughters?

Answer: Laban reminded Jacob that tradition dictates that the eldest daughter marry first.

Question: Rachel called her firstborn son Joseph because she stated that, "God has taken away my disgrace" *(Genesis 30:23)*. To what disgrace was Rachel referring?

Answer: Rachel had feared that Jacob might divorce her for being childless for many years. She also feared that Jacob would become satisfied with Leah, and Rachel would be forced to marry Esau *(Rashi, Ramav)*. To dispel those fears the Almighty allowed her to become pregnant and give birth. She named the child, Joseph. This according to *Rashi* in the following verse *(Genesis 30:24)* is a prayer from Rachel that the Almighty allow her one more time to become pregnant and give birth to a son.

Question: What were the names of the twelve sons of Jacob? What was Jacob's daughter's name *(Genesis 30:5)*?

Answer: Jacob's sons' names were Reuven, Simeon, Levi, Judah, Issachar, Z'vulun, Dan, Naphtali, Gad, Asher, Joseph, and Benjamin. Jacob's daughter's name was Deena.

Question: "Reuven went out and found dudaim in the field" *(Genesis 30:14)*. What does the word *dudaim* mean? What is the significance of this statement?

Answer: *Dudaim* has many possible translations, one of which is jasmine (*Babylonian Talmud, Sanhedrin 99b*).

The statement "Reuven went out and found *dudaim*" signifies what a devoted son Reuven was to his mother, Leah. It was said that *dudaim* is an "herb" that, among other things, increases fertility. Reuven knew that his mother wanted more children, so he went out and gathered dudaim for her (*Ohr Hachayim*).

Question: Why did Rachel steal her father's idols?

Answer: Rachel wanted her father to stop worshipping idols.

Question: How do we know that when a righteous person curses, the curse will be fulfilled, even if he does not mean to curse that person?

Answer: When Laban saw that one of his idols was missing, Jacob was so certain that no one had taken them that he angrily said to Laban: "Whoever took your idols will not live," obviously not knowing that Rachel (his wife) had stolen it. We read that shortly after that, Rachel died because of this curse.

Question: The Bible states, "Laban called the place *Yagar Sahadusa*, but Jacob called the place *Galed*" *(Genesis 31:47)*. What did that mean?

Answer: *Yagar Sahadusa* is an Aramaic phrase meaning "well of testimony." Jacob used the Hebrew, while Laban the Aramaic, to convey the same thought (*Rashi; Targum; Sforno*).

Question: Why did the angels escort Jacob when he returned to the Holy Land *(Genesis 32:2)*?

Answer: The angels were sent by God to protect Jacob from his enemies (*Yonatan ben Uziel*). These angels can only be found in the Holy Land (*Zohar*).

Question: What is the connection between *Parshat Vayeitzei* and its corresponding reading from the Prophets?

Answer: In *Vayeitzei*, Jacob meets, works for, and lives in the home of Laban. Jacob then marries Laban's two daughters, Leah and Rachel. Laban had a scheming, cheating personality, especially when dealing with Jacob. Laban constantly cheated Jacob, first by tricking him into marrying Leah and then with regard to his wages.

Honesty is the basis of many Jewish laws, both in the home and in business. We are told that, "Truth is the tree of life whose fruits you shall eat all your days."

The prophet Isaiah explores the contrast in characters between the honest and moral (Jacob) and the corrupt (Laban). In the reading, Isaiah laments that people sold their bodies and souls for material gain and forgot their inheritance, the morality and values that our ancestor Jacob passed down to us.

A story is told in the *Talmud* that relates to this. It tells about Rabbi Saffra who owned a store. One day, while the rabbi was in the midst of prayer, a man entered and wanted to buy something in the store. Not noticing that the rabbi was in the midst of prayer, he offered a certain price for the item. When the rabbi did not reply, the man presumed his offer was too low, and he kept raising the price. Finally, Rabbi Saffra finished his prayers and said to the man, "Sir, I will accept your original offer because that was the price I had in mind for this item. The only reason I did not respond to you was because I was talking to God. If I accepted any more money from you, I would be dishonest, and then what could I possibly say to God?"

Vayishlach
Chapters: 32:4 - 36

Synopsis:

Jacob prepared himself to meet his brother Esau; the angel and Jacob fought; the commandment against eating the animal's tendon; Jacob and Esau met; the incident involving Deena and Shechem; the reaction of Jacob's sons; God blessed Jacob; Benjamin's birth; Rachel's death; Isaac's death; the separation between Jacob and Esau; the genealogy of Esau's descendants.

Question: How did Jacob prepare himself for his meeting with Esau?

Answer: Jacob prepared himself by praying and selecting gifts to be given to Esau. He also planned to set up his camp strategically. He divided his party into two camps. In one camp, he put his wife and children. This camp was to the rear, and out of immediate danger. The other camp would serve as a buffer between his family and Esau (*Abarbanel*).

Question: What do we learn from the way Jacob prepared himself?

Answer: We see from this episode that it is preferable to resolve conflict by praying for a peaceful resolution, acting amicably toward your opponents, and presenting them with a gift. If these do not work, there may be no choice but to go to war (*Tanchuma*).

Question: What do we learn from Jacob's words, "I have lodged with Laban" *(Genesis 32:5)*?

Answer: Jacob did not learn Laban's wicked ways. The numerical value of the Hebrew word *garti*, "lodged" is 613. The total number of *mitzvot* (commandments) in the Bible is 613. *Rashi* says we see that even though Jacob lived with Laban for a significant length of time he observed all 613 commandments.

This word *garti* also means "foreign," indicating that Jacob was in reality like a foreigner to Laban. Although his physical being resided with Laban, his spirituality was foreign to Laban's way of life (*Ramav*).

Question: Why was Jacob "left alone"?

Answer: After thirty-four years of being away from home, Jacob heads back toward the Holy Land. He plans to return to the home of his parents, Rebecca and Isaac. En route, Jacob takes his entire family and entourage across a river. Then, according to Rashi, Jacob realizes that he forgot something (small earthenware pitchers) and goes back across the river to retrieve his belongings. Therefore he is "left alone." The *Midrash* says that a *talmud chacham* (scholar) who goes out at night alone is in danger of being attacked by demons.

According to *Chizkuni*, we learn that since Jacob's family let him go back alone, the entire family was punished. This action showed disrespect and is considered to be against the Bible. Therefore, God wants us to learn from this mistake and not to repeat this action again. Also, the Bible wants us to learn that Jacob exemplified to us that leaders are Godly people who are often lonely due to the circumstances in which they find themselves (*Malbim*).

There is also a tradition that once one leaves on a journey, and if something was left behind the person should not return to retrieve the item, but rather continue on the journey and retrieve the item at a later time.

Question: The Bible relates a story about Jacob and a man fighting *(Genesis 32:25-33)*. What was this all about?

Answer: When Jacob was left alone he encountered a "man" who wrestled with him until the break of dawn. This man, according to our sages, was the guardian angel of Esau in the form of a man. Just as Esau epitomized evil, his angel was the prime spiritual force of evil, Satan himself. In the end, Jacob wins. We learn that Satan, the evil inclination, and the Angel of Death are one and the same (*Rashbam; Rabbi Samson R. Hirsch*).

Question: Although the battle takes place one-on-one between Jacob and the angel, what is the universal message for mankind?

Answer: The fight represents the eternal struggle between good and evil, between man's capacity to perfect himself and Satan's determination to destroy (*Ramban; Rabbeinu Bechayei*).

Question: What significance does Jewish mysticism attach to the fact that this fight occurred at night?

Answer: Jewish mysticism equates night with the evil inclination. According to the *Kabbalah*, the *Zohar*, God created the world with opposing forces: white and black, dark and light, good and evil, and so forth. We are cautioned by our tradition to be careful in how we approach the night. We refrain from certain activities out of fear of awakening the other side, the evil inclination. In this *parsha*, the kabbalists explain Esau's angel as the representative of evil.

Question: What are angels, and what purposes do they serve?

Answer: Jewish mysticism teaches us that the Almighty created angels for many different purposes, some positive, some negative. For example, the kabbalists tell us that the angel of healing is Raphael, the Angel of Death is Satan. The sages explain that we have to accept angels as part of God's creation (*Kitvey Harizal, Rav Chaim Vital*). Angels are 100 percent pure. According to the *Talmud* in *Avodah Zorah 76a*, it says if God sends an angel on a mission, the angel is told in advance all of the specifics of his task. You might see an angel as something akin to a robot. Each is programmed for a specific purpose and that purpose only. They blindly obey their Creator. Unlike man they have no freedom of will. They are not responsible for their actions. They are neither good nor bad.

In Jacob's case, the angel was sent to test him, to measure his strength and resolve. God gave the angel until daybreak to battle with Jacob. At daybreak, the angel was to return to heaven and report his accomplishments and sing a song to the Almighty (*Sura; Revash; Tur*). In verse 26, when the angel saw that he could not defeat Jacob in the appointed time, he still wanted to return to God with some accomplishment. The angel sought to do significant damage to Jacob by dislocating his hip joint, perhaps preventing him from having more children.

Rabbi Eliezer Harofeh in *Maasey Hashem*, suggests that there was another reason the angel grabbed Jacob's hip joint. In those days, the hip pocket was a place to store important personal belongings. This is where Jacob kept the contract he made with Esau obtaining the birthright (which Esau had signed over to him). The angel, a defender of Esau, tried to repossess this document. He did not achieve his goal.

There is also a lesson about perseverance to be learned from this struggle. We are taught that regardless of the odds against us, one must continue to struggle, always maintaining one's faith and trust in the Almighty. So too, the Jewish people would suffer, but would emerge with even greater blessings and victories (*Abarbanel*).

Question: How do the sages interpret the meaning of this "wrestling match"?

Answer: The fight that lasted until daybreak is a sign for generations to come that the angel of evil will continue to fight with Jacob's descendants until the dawn of salvation, the coming of the Messiah. The sages also tell us that mankind, like Jacob, will recover from persecution and battle, emerging victorious in the end (*Ramban; Siftei Amet*).

Question: What was a consequence of Jacob's hip injury?

Answer: The *Midrash* says that this injury is a forecast to future generations that during periods of exile, Jacob's descendants will be persecuted to such an extent that they will be near extinction, yet would never be annihilated.

Question: Why did Jacob refuse to let the angel leave?

Answer: Before allowing the angel to leave, Jacob demanded a blessing from him. Jacob knew that angels are spiritual entities. According to *Rashi*, the blessing by Esau's guardian angel would be an acknowledgment that Jacob was truly entitled to the blessing he had received from his father Isaac.

The Hebrew word *beirachtani*, "blessed me," is written in the past tense. The commentators explain that Jacob is looking for affirmation of a previous blessing. He wanted Esau, through this angel, to reaffirm once and for all that the blessing from Isaac to Jacob was legitimate and binding (*Siftei Amet*). The *Zohar* in *Parshat Tazria* says that Jacob's demand for a blessing was important.

Question: Why is Jacob's name changed to Israel?

Answer: After acknowledging defeat the angel asked Jacob what his name was. Jacob told him. The word *jacob* means "heel" or "deceit." The angel told him his name would change because no longer would it be said that he had come upon his blessing with treachery (*Rashi*). The angel admitted that the blessing originally received from Isaac was received by Jacob fairly. Since Jacob had prevailed in an open struggle, this should be reflected by a new name, an inspiration for generations to come.

Finally, where Jacob represented one man, now Israel survived to perpetuate the future of a nation.

Question: Why didn't the angel want to tell Jacob his name?

Answer: The angel tried to say that he was just a servant doing his job. When angels are created, they are given names that describe their missions. The angel tried to keep Jacob off guard, "not giving him any clue or competitive edge" about his true intentions (*Rambam; Tur*).

Question: Why does Jacob call the location where the fight took place *Peniel* "God's face" *(Genesis 32:31)?*

Answer: Jacob acknowledged that he saw the angel face to face and his soul was saved. Therefore, he called the name of the place *Peniel*, "God's face." However, we read in the Bible, *Numbers 12:8*, and *Deuteronomy 34:10* that only Moses saw God face to face. The sages explain that the word elokim refers to "God's judgment" (*Exodus*

70

20:5). So the sages say what Jacob really saw was Elokim, "God's judgment," face to face, through the strength of the angel fighting with him. In the end, God's judgment was one of compassion and mercy (*Zohar Vayahel 209; Rabbi Chaim Vital Sa'ar 44:3; Tanya Sa'ar Hyichud 5*).

Question: What commandment appears in relation to this struggle with the angel?

Answer: The commandment is called *Gid Hanashe.* This is a negative commandment that prohibits us to eat from the hip socket of an animal. The reason for this prohibition comes from the struggle Jacob had with Esau's angel. When sensing defeat the angel sought to injure Jacob. He struck him in the hip socket. We are prohibited to eat the meat from this section of an animal (*Talmud Chulin 91a, 92b; Sefer Hachinuch*).

Question: Why does the Bible devote a full chapter *(Genesis 34)* to the story of Deena, and were the actions of Jacob's sons justified?

Answer: We know that the Bible never wastes words and that there is a reason for each and every word. The sages tell us that this chapter about Deena contains important lessons for future generations and therefore a detailed explanation is necessary. It is extremely important that we listen to what the Oral Torah and the commentators say concerning this account so that we may fully understand the Written Torah. Otherwise we might, at first glance, think that the actions of Jacob and his sons were too extreme.

Deena, Jacob's only daughter, went on an outing and was abducted by Shechem, son of the Hittite leader, Hamor. Shechem repeatedly raped Deena, who was only nine years old (*Seder Hakorot*). The word *hayalda* in Hebrew means "little girl." She was held captive in his house. Shechem's compatriots knew what had happened but did nothing to help Deena (*Malbim*), despite the fact that the *Noahite* law prohibited such acts.

The punishment for rape was death. Each city was responsible for establishing courts and appointing honest judges to administer the laws. By not establishing an effective court system, the Hittites were liable for the same punishment as Shechem.

Jacob heard that his daughter had been violated and was being held in the house of Shechem. If the violation of Deena had not already occurred, Jacob would have risked everything to rescue her (*Alshich*). Before he could consult with his sons about a proper response to this heinous act, Shechem's father, Hamor, came to Jacob to arrange for Deena's marriage to Shechem. Hamor did not apologize, nor did he offer to immediately return Deena to her home or to compensate Jacob for damages. Hamor was afraid that Jacob's people would punish the Hittites. He also wanted to satisfy his son's desire to make the beautiful Deena his wife (*L'vush*). Hamor was also motivated by the belief that closer relations with Jacob's nation would be very profitable for the Hittites (*Ramban*).

Jacob's sons kept their anger in check, pretending to negotiate with Hamor (*Akaida*). Uniting with the Hittites into a single nation would only come about if all the Hittite males agreed to circumcision. *Ramban* says that Jacob's sons did not believe that their offer would be accepted seriously, that the circumcision would be done as a convenience only. This would justify their rescue of Deena. *Abarbanel* says that the offer was made in the belief that once accepted, the Hittites would be physically weakened by the procedure, thus making them vulnerable to attack.

Hamor and Shechem accepted the offer and persuaded all the male Hittite to voluntarily undergo circumcision. Shechem and Hamor persuaded the people by telling them they would share in Jacob's wealth and possessions. Lust and greed basically motivated the Hittite men.

On the third day following the circumcisions, the Hittites were in great pain. It was then that two of Jacob's sons, Simeon and Levi, entered the city, attacked and slaughtered all the Hittite men, and rescued Deena. *Tosafot Hadar Tkanim* says that by the third day, the Hittite regretted agreeing to circumcision, and Jacob's sons expected that the Hittite would attack them and kill Deena. *Sforno* says the sons of Jacob planned from the outset to kill the Hittite in revenge for Deena and knew the Hittite would be weakest on the third day. After killing all the males, Simeon and Levi placed the bodies of

Shechem and Hamor at the entrance to the city (*Yalkut*) as a sign for all to see. Upon their departure, the brothers took Deena and the Hittites' possessions and returned to Jacob.

Jacob was disturbed by his sons' actions. He was afraid of what the surrounding nations would do. The *Rashbam* says that Jacob felt the murders of Shechem and Hamor were justified but that there was no need to kill all the other Hittite males. *Haktav v'haKabbalah* says that Jacob was repulsed by the idea of plunder and would not accept any of the Hittite possessions. Jacob believed in the spiritual value of worshipping God. Even though he felt the killings of Shechem and Hamor were justified, killing in and of itself has a negative spiritual value (*Ramban*).

The last word on this matter belonged to the sons of Jacob, Simeon and Levi. They asked "should they treat our sister as a harlot?" *Rabbi S. R. Hirsch* explained their response this way: "Just because we are Hebrews does not allow the Hittite to victimize us." From this comes the expression: "Our blood is not worthless." *Rabbi Hirsch* and *Abarbanel* both explain that a Jew's reluctance to kill is not a sign of weakness but is based on ethical and moral considerations.

At the end of the *Book of Genesis*, Jacob punished Simeon and Levi by dispersing their households among all the tribes. Before Jacob died, he wanted to make it clear to future generations that the sword is to be used only in extreme situations.

Question: What did Jacob do with the idols and possessions that Simeon and Levi brought from Shechem?

Answer: Jacob buried them under a tree near the city of Shechem (*Rashi*).

Question: According to *Rashi*, why did the incident with Deena happen?

Answer: Before Jacob went to meet Esau, Jacob hid Deena in a casket so that Esau would not see her, and want to take her. Instead of trusting God to protect her, Jacob depended too much on his own cunning, and was thereby punished (*Rashi, Genesis 32:23*).

The Bible commands us that if we promise something, we must keep our word, especially if it is something we swore to. Jacob delayed keeping his vow to build a house of God in Beth El, which he had sworn on the way to Charan (*Genesis 28:20; Rashi; Tanchuma 35:1*).

Question: In *Genesis 35:2* Jacob tells his family, "Change your clothes." Why does Jacob command his family to do this, and who else did the same?

Answer: Jacob insists that the entire family change their clothes because some of them had carried Hittite idols in them. A similar incident happened when Moses, before the revelation at Sinai, also commanded the people to change their garments. The changing of the garments signified that they were making significant personal lifestyle changes. They wanted to rid themselves of any hint of their previous lifestyle.

Question: God blessed Jacob: "kings shall issue from your loins" (*Genesis 35:11*). What do the sages see in this verse?

Answer: *Rashi* on this verse states that "and kings shall issue…" refers directly to Saul and Ish Bosheth, both descendants of Benjamin. Even though Benjamin had yet to be born the Torah declares that this blessing of kingship would include his descendants as well. In the *Book of Judges* (*Chapter 21*), Avner appointed Ish Boshet to succeed his father Saul as king (*Rashi; Bereishit Rabba*). However, as we know, Ish Boshet's rule was not to be. Samuel, the prophet, had taken the kingship away from Saul for his failure to fulfill his duty wipe out Amalek. In Saul's place Samuel appointed David as king, thereby setting aside the normal line of inheritance.

Question: Where do we find an example that the Bible was not necessarily written in chronological order?

Answer: Isaac's death is mentioned before the selling of Joseph. In fact, Isaac lived 12 more years after the selling of Joseph (*Rashi, Genesis 35:27*).

Question: How old was Isaac when Joseph was sold by his brothers?

Answer: Isaac was 168 years old.

Question: What were the names of Esau's wives?

Answer: Esau had a number of wives. One was Ada, daughter of Eilon, but Esau called her *Bosmat*, meaning "incense," because she burned incense before her idols. Esau also married *Oholibamah* whom he called Yehudit to make Isaac believe that she had rejected idolatry (*Rashi*). He also married a daughter of Ishmael, also named *Bosmat*, whom he called *Mahalat*, because when she got married all of her and her husband's sins were forgiven (*Rashi, Genesis 36:2-3*).

Question: Why does the Bible enumerate the descendants of Esau in great detail?

Answer: The Bible wanted to emphasize the magnitude of evil that descended from Esau, such as Amalek and Haman. Counted among Amalek's descendants were Agog, who fought against King Saul, and Haman, who tried to exterminate the Jews during the time of Queen Esther (*Ramav*).

Question: What is the connection between *Vayishlach* and the haftorah reading from the *Book of Ovadiah?*

Answer: The *Book of Ovadiah* is read in its entirety. The prophet Ovadiah was a direct descendant of the Edomites, descendants of Esau (*Zohar*). Ovadiah lived among evil people, yet he remained righteous. Esau lived among righteous people, yet remained evil.

Vayeishev
Chapters: 37 - 40

Synopsis:

The genealogy of Jacob; Joseph's dream; jealousy between the children; Jacob sent Joseph to meet his brothers; the brothers planned to kill Joseph; Reuven saved Joseph; Joseph was sold to Ishmaelites, who then sold him to the Egyptians; Judah and Tamar; Joseph refused to be seduced by Potiphar's wife; Joseph was imprisoned; Joseph interpreted the dreams of the baker and the wine steward.

Question: The Bible states: "These are the offspring of Jacob: Joseph was..." *(Genesis 37:2).* Why does the verse call particular attention to Joseph?

Answer: The *Midrash* says that Jacob and Joseph looked identical. Joseph was Rachel's son. Rachel was considered Jacob's primary wife. Joseph's life was to parallel Jacob's life *(Bereishit Rabba 6).*

Question: Why did Joseph's brothers hate him so much?

Answer: The brothers felt that their father, Jacob, preferred Joseph over them. We see that Jacob gave Joseph a beautiful coat of many colors. Joseph was seen by his siblings as a tale bearer and reported all of his brothers' actions to Jacob. Joseph had the ability to interpret dreams. The manner in which he interpreted his own dreams damaged his relationship with his brothers. Some of these dreams foretold of his future relationship with them and how he would rule over them. This incensed them, arousing anger and jealousy within them.

Question: Why does the Bible describe the brothers' conflict in so much detail?

Answer: The Bible shows us an example of how far needless jealousy and hatred can be carried *(Ramban).* The details are a foreshadowing of events to come. This is an example of prophecy. The story shows that many things are predetermined *(Abarbanel).*

Question: What was the significance of the coat of many colors *(Genesis 37:3)?*

Answer: It was Jacob's way of showing his love for Joseph. Jacob made the coat because an inner voice was telling him that Joseph would have many sufferings and transitions in his life (*Rashi, Bereishit Rabba 84:8*). Jacob selected Joseph to be the leader of the family and the coat was a sign of this leadership that his brothers were expected to follow (*Sforno*). The coat symbolized the transference of leadership from Reuven, Leah's first son, to Joseph, Rachel's first son. Reuven discredited himself by tampering with Jacob's bed, by placing it in his mother's room. The other brothers recognized the coat as the symbol of the change in authority (*Kli Yakar*).

Question: What kind of reports did Joseph bring to his father? Why?

Answer: Joseph was a pious but naive young man. He thought his brothers should correct their bad behavior. Jacob felt responsible for his sons' actions, but was unaware of their deeds. Joseph considered himself obligated to report to his father that his brothers were misbehaving (*Rashi*). They were eating the flesh of living animals, having illicit sexual relations, and mocking the sons of Bilah and Zilpah by referring to them as slaves (*Rashi*). Joseph also reported any tales he heard from others about his brothers (*Rabbi Samson R. Hirsch*).

Question: The *Talmud* says that a person should mourn the death of another for no more than one year. Why did Jacob mourn the death of Joseph for so many years?

Answer: Jacob did not accept condolences from anyone after he was informed that Joseph was dead. The sages say that he knew deep down that Joseph was still alive. Therefore, after one year, the pain over his "loss" was still very strong.

Question: When Joseph was sold, where was Reuven, Joseph's eldest brother?

Answer: Reuven was in his father's house (*Genesis 37:29*).

Question: Who sold Joseph to the Egyptians?

Answer: There is much discussion about who exactly sold Joseph to the Egyptians. *Rashi* says it was the brothers themselves. The *Rashbam* believes that Joseph's brothers put him into a well where the Midyanites found him. The Midyanites were the ones who ultimately sold Joseph to the Ishmaelite.

Another view has Joseph being sold to the Midyanites by his brothers, who sold him to the Ishmaelites, who sold him to the Egyptians (*Ibn Ezra*). The *Midrash* says that Joseph was bought and sold four times before he ended up in Egypt.

Question: Who is the "man" who found Joseph straying in the field *(Genesis 37:15)*?

Answer: The "man" who found Joseph was the angel Gabriel sent by God. This was no chance encounter (*Tanchuma; Yonatan ben Uziel; Malbim; Ha'amek Davar*).

Question: Did Isaac (Jacob's father) know what had happened to Joseph?

Answer: Isaac knew that Joseph was still alive, but he also mourned because he saw his son Jacob suffering (*Genesis 37:35; Bereishit Rabba 84b*).

Question: What is the story of Judah and Tamar?

Answer: Judah was a son of Jacob and one of the important Jewish leaders. He was seen as a power behind the twelve tribes of Israel. Judah had three sons: Err, Onan, and Shelah. Err married Tamar. Instead of fulfilling the commandment to be fruitful and multiply he made the Almighty angry, by spilling his sperm, therefore he did not have children with Tamar. As a punishment God killed him. According to Jewish law, if a married man dies childless, and has male siblings who are not married, this man's widow now is obligated to marry a sibling (known as the *mitzvah* of *yibum*). Err had two brothers so Tamar become obligated to one of the brothers. She married Onan. Onan married Tamar only because of her beauty. Feeling that pregnancy would detract from her beauty he behaved like his brother, wasting his sperm as well. The same punishment befell him as his brother. Tamar then became obligated to marry Shelah, the third brother. Judah felt this was not good. He told Tamar that she could not marry Shelah, for he was much too young. She was sent to her parents' house to wait until Shelah became of age. This was his only excuse (*Rabbi Samson R. Hirsch*). Judah feared for his son because two sons had died while married to Tamar. She left and resided in her parents' home. Tamar needed either to marry Shelah or be released in order for her to marry someone else (*Rambam; Morch 3:49*).

It came to Tamar's attention that her mother-in-law passed away. When Judah came to her neighborhood, she disguised herself and Judah thought her to be a prostitute. The two of them had a physical relationship. Judah did not recognize his daughter-in-law. As payment, Judah offered her sheep, but he had none with him. She asked for collateral until payment could be made. He gave her some of his things. She later disappeared. Judah's servant returned with the sheep to collect the collateral, but Tamar was not there. Three months later, Tamar realized she was pregnant. She sent a message to her father-in-law to tell him she was pregnant but did not reveal to him that he was the father. Upon hearing the message Judah said to give her the death penalty and burn her. As she was being taken out to killed, she sent a message to Judah asking him if he recognized his things. Judah was amazed. He got back his belongings and realized that the children (she had twins) were from him.

Rambam (Moreh Nevuchim, vol. 3, ch. 49) explained that only later, after Sinai, was the law of *Yibum* (the obligation to marry a childless, widowed sister-in-law) delivered to the children of Israel. It states that when a man dies and leaves his wife childless, if he has an unmarried brother, it is that brother's obligation to marry the widow, so that there will be a continuation of the line. However, this only refers to a brother of the same father, not a brother of the same mother, who has a different father.

Question: What is the name of Tamar's father? How do we know that?

Answer: According to *Rabbi Meir,* one of the sages of the *Talmud,* Tamar was Shem's daughter. Shem was a priest (*kohen*). According to Biblical law, if a priest's daughter becomes a harlot, she is deserving of the death penalty (*Leviticus 21:9, Bereishit Rabba 85b*).

Question: How do we know that Judah repented?

Answer: Judah confessed and admitted his guilt: "I am wrong and she (*Tamar*) is right" (*Genesis 38:26*).

Question: Why did Tamar deserve to have the highest kings descend from her *(Genesis 38:26)*?

Answer: Her behavior and her modesty merited this reward (*Babylonian Talmud, Sotah 10b*).

Question: What is the story of Joseph and Potiphar's wife?

Answer: Joseph was sold to Egypt and became a servant in Potiphar's house. Potiphar put him in charge of the prison. Joseph was very loyal and made Potiphar a successful leader in Egyptian society. According to the Bible, Joseph became so trusted by Potiphar that he left everything in Joseph's hands. Potiphar's wife consulted astrologers, who predicted that she would "have" children from Joseph. Potiphar's wife wanted a physical relationship with Joseph. However, her consultants did not tell her exactly where the children would come from. Years later, Joseph would marry Potiphar's daughter, Asnat.

Potiphar's wife attempted to trick Joseph by hosting a party. During the party she managed to get hold of some of his clothing. When he ran away from her, she ripped part of his clothing. Then she twisted the story around and said that Joseph attempted to rape her. Consequently, Potiphar sent Joseph to prison.

Question: Why does the story about Joseph and Potiphar's wife immediately follow the story of Judah and Tamar?

Answer: The Bible wants to show that both Tamar and Potiphar's wife believed that their actions were necessary (*Bereishit Rabba 85b*).

Question: The Bible states, "Potiphar perceived that God was with Joseph" *(Genesis 39:3)*. How did Potiphar see that?

Answer: *Rashi* says that Joseph frequently mentioned God's name in his daily speech.

Question: Why was Joseph thrown into the royal Egyptian prison?

Answer: According to *Ramban*, Potiphar knew that his wife's charges against Joseph were completely false. Potiphar had Joseph jailed just to satisfy his wife. Potiphar put Joseph in the royal prison so he would not suffer as much as he would have in the regular jail. While he was in prison he shared a cell with the royal baker and wine steward.

Question: How many years were the baker and wine steward in prison *(Genesis 40:4)*?

Answer: According to the Talmud it was one year (*Babylonian Talmud, K'tubot 57b*).

Question: Why did the baker and wine steward become prisoners?

Answer: The wine steward was imprisoned because a fly was found in the king's goblet. The baker was imprisoned because a rock was found in the king's bread (*Bereishit Rabba 88b*).

Question: The Bible relates, "Joseph came and saw the two prisoners who looked quite upset" *(Genesis 40:6)*. To what does this refer, and why were the men upset?

Answer: The two prisoners referred to here are the royal baker and the royal wine steward. Joseph saw that his fellow prisoners seemed troubled. They both had had a dream that caused them distress. He took an interest in them. Joseph cared enough to want to help lift their spirits. As a result of Joseph's concern, he helped them by interpreting their dreams. Eventually these two men, after their release from prison, told Pharaoh about Joseph's ability to explain dreams. Joseph was released from prison as a result of his unique ability. Joseph later became Viceroy of the entire kingdom of Egypt.

This chain of events comes to teach us that one never knows what will occur when one person cares enough to inquire about another person's life or feelings.

Question: Why did the baker believe Joseph's interpretation of the wine steward's dream?

Answer: According to the sages (*Babylonian Talmud, Brachot 55b*) the baker also saw in a dream the exact interpretation that Joseph had given to the wine steward's dream.

Chanukah

Synopsis:

*The holiday of Chanukah always occurs after we read
the Torah portion of Vayeishev.*

Question: What are the customs of the festival of Chanukah?

Answer: The festival of Chanukah is celebrated for eight complete days. The lighting of the menorah is the symbol most commonly associated with Chanukah. The flames should burn for at least a half hour after it gets dark. In many communities, it is customary to eat dairy foods on Chanukah. We also eat foods cooked in oil–potato pancakes or doughnuts, for instance. Children play the dreidel game. It is customary to give money to children. We say an additional prayer during this time telling of the miracle that happened at this time of year. *Al haNissim* "For the Miracles," is added in the Amidah prayer and in the Grace after meals. A full *Hallel* is said every day during the festival. The Bible reading is that which tells of the dedication of the Tabernacle by Moses in the wilderness. It is also customary to give charity on the festival of Chanukah.

Question: What is *Hallel?*

Answer: *Hallel* is an additional service that the prophets instituted by the prophets. It is comprised of a series of psalms and praises to the Almighty. It is a service that is to be recited on the festivals, *Sukkot, Passover, Rosh Chodesh,* and times when Israel is saved from harm. It was recited at the splitting of the sea, at the defeat of the king of Canaan by Joshua, after the defeat of Haman by Mordechai and Esther. These psalms contain five fundamental concepts of Jewish faith: the Exodus, the splitting of the sea, the giving of the Torah, the future resuscitation of the dead, and the coming of the Messiah. It is not recited on days of judgement like *Rosh Hashanah* or *Yom Kippur.* It is not said on Purim because despite the victory the Jews still remained servants. However on Chanukah the victory was complete.

Question: What happened on Chanukah?

Answer: Over 2,000 years ago the Syrian-Greek king Antiochus IV refused to allow the Jewish people in the Holy Land to observe the commandments. Antiochus defiled and disgraced the holy Temple in Jerusalem. The Maccabees, a small band of families, fought against the Greek tyrannts. Matityahu, leader of the Maccabees, and his sons, led a successful revolution against Antiochus. Our tradition describes the many miracles that occurred on the day the Maccabees won. When the Maccabees entered the Temple, they found only a one-day supply of pure oil. The miracle was that this cask of oil, which held only a one-day supply, lasted for eight days. This was enough time to produce new pure oil.

Question: When does the festival of Chanukah begin?

Answer: The festival begins on the twenty-fifth day of Kislev (the third month of the Jewish calendar). We kindle the first flame at nightfall. On the night of the twenty-sixth, we light two flames, and so on, for eight nights.

Question: What is a *shamesh?*

Answer: According to Jewish law, we are not allowed to use the Chanukah candles for any purpose, to provide light for reading, for example. Therefore, a separate candle, not one of the eight, is set aside to light the others. The shamesh may be used for all purposes. The word *shamesh* means "helper."

Question: We light candles every Friday night. Which candles do we light first on Sabbath Chanukah, the Chanukah candles or the Sabbath candles?

Answer: The lighting of the Sabbath candles marks the beginning of the day of rest. If we were to light the Sabbath candles first, we would not be permitted to light the Chanukah candles. Therefore, prior to sunset on Friday we first light the Chanukah candles and then we kindle the Sabbath candles.

Question: On Saturday night, at the conclusion of the Sabbath, which do we light first, the Chanukah candles or the *Havdalah* candle, which symbolizes the separation between the Sabbath and the rest of the week?

Answer: The *Havdalah* candle represents the Sabbath past, while the Chanukah candles each night represent the following day. At the Sabbath's end, we first light the *Havdalah* candle, and then the Chanukah candles.

Question: Where do we light the Chanukah candles?

Answer: Our sages teach us that every household should have at least one menorah. It is customary to light a Chanukah menorah in the synagogue. Lighting Chanukah candles in the synagogue does not remove ones responsibility of lighting Chanukah candles in his home as well.

Question: What is the meaning of *pirsume nisah?*

Answer: *Pirsume nisah* is an Aramaic phrase that the sages in the *Babylonian Talmud* tell us is to "Proclaim in public the miracles" that occurred to our forefathers on Chanukah. This is why we put the menorah in the window, so that anyone who passes by will see it. This accomplishes the intent of *pirsume nisah*, which means publicly proclaiming the miracles.

Question: How do we light the candles?

Answer: We begin by placing our oil wick or candle to the far right. The "newest" candle or wick always should be added to the left of the candle we lit the previous night. The candles or wicks should be in a straight line, not in a circle; one may not be higher than the other. This excludes the *shamesh* candle, which is placed either higher or lower than the others. The Chanukah candles are lit using the *shamesh*. We always light the new wick or candle first, lighting from left to right.

Question: What do we do first, recite the blessings or light the candles?

Answer: Two blessings are recited first, then we light the candles.

Question: What is the difference between the first night and the rest of the Chanukah festival?

Answer: On the first night we add the *Shehechiyanu* blessing, reciting three blessings instead of two. The *Shehechiyanu* is said to offer thanks to the Almighty for sustaining us and allowing us to reach this occasion.

Question: Why is it customary to eat dairy food on Chanukah?

Answer: Dairy dishes are eaten during Chanukah to recall the story of Judith and *Holofernes*, a Greek general. According to tradition, Judith gave *Holofernes* milk to drink and cheese to eat. This caused him to fall asleep, and while he slept, Judith killed him, thereby saving the Jewish people from Nebuchadnezar, king of Assyria.

Question: Why is it customary to eat foods cooked with oil on Chanukah?

Answer: To remind us of the miracle of Chanukah that was the oil that burned for eight days instead of just one. We eat potato pancakes or doughnuts fried in oil. We hope and pray that God's kindness and grace will be with us always.

Question: What is a *dreidel?*

Answer: A *dreidel,* in Hebrew a *se-ve-von,* is a four-sided top. Each of the four sides has a Hebrew letter: *nun, gimel, hay, shin* (or pay).

Question: Why do some *dreidels* have a *shin* while others have a *pay?*

Answer: In Israel, *dreidels* have a *pay,* which stands for the word *po* meaning "here." So the phrase attached to the Israeli *dreidel* is *Neis Gadol Hayah Po* or "a great miracle happened here." While in lands outside of Israel, the *shin* is used which stands for the word *sham* meaning "there." So the phrase would be *Neis Gadol Hayah Sham* meaning "a great miracle happened there (Israel)."

Some communities use both types of *dreidels.* The one with the *shin* referring to events that happened in the past (there) while the *pay* refers to events in our days and the fact that we live by the grace of God and His miracles.

Question: What was the inspiration for the *dreidel* game?

Answer: King Antiochus forbade the Jewish people from following Torah law. Refusing to obey Antiochus's decree, Jews studied the Bible in secret. Whenever a soldier would come by, the holy books were quickly hidden away and *dreidels* taken out so that the students appeared engrossed in a game of tops.

The word *Chanukah* comes from the Hebrew word *chinuch* meaning "education." We educate children even when they play. When they ask us what the Hebrew letters on the *dreidel* mean, we recount the miracle of Chanukah.

We cannot predict on which letter the *dreidel* will land. Much like life, sometimes we feel that we are going in circles, with no direction, unable to predict an outcome. It is our belief in God that gives direction and purpose to our life.

Question: Why do we light candles for eight days instead of seven?

Answer: The priests said that only pure olive oil was to be used to light the *Menorah*. If there was no other choice then one could use impure oil. There was only enough pure olive oil for one night, and they were planning to use impure oil the second night. The miracle was that the pure oil burned for an additional seven days, equaling eight. Therefore, instead of lighting for seven nights, we add an eighth candle to symbolize God's grace. (*Babylonian Talmud, Sabbath 24; P'net Yehushuah*).

Under the Greeks Jews were forbidden to circumcise their sons. When the Maccabees emerged victorious from their war with the Greeks, the Jews once again began living their traditions, in the open. Circumcision was one of those commandments that was banned. As we know, circumcisions are done on the eighth day. So in commemorating the fact that we were again doing circumcisions at their correct time, we light the Chanukah candles for eight days.

Question: Why is it customary to give money to children during the festival of Chanukah?

Answer: Money is given to children as a reward for their learning Torah. At the time of the Maccabees, children learned in secret at great risk to their personal safety. The money given is referred to as Chanukah *gelt*, money of Chanukah. It usually is given on the fifth night because there are more candles lit than unlit.

Chanukah is an educational festival. We give our children money so they may buy games and books that teach them about our history, heritage, and tradition.

Question: Why and when do we say the additional prayer *Al haNissim*, "For the Miracles"?

Answer: The sages established this special prayer to thank the

Almighty for the miracles He performed in the Temple. The prayer briefly describes the story of the Maccabees. It is inserted in the *Amidah* prayer of the three daily prayer services. It is also included in the blessing after the meal.

Question: What exactly do we say in this prayer?

Answer: "For the miracles, for the liberation, and for Your special actions and for the conquest which You performed, for our ancestors in those days and in our time. In the time of Matityahu, son of Yochanan, the Hasmonean. When the evil Greek kingdom forbade, through a royal decree, the people of Israel from studying their Bible, to make them forget their teachings and thereby force them to stray from the law of God. You, God, with full compassion and mercy helped them in the time of their agony and torture. You heeded their complaint, made justice, and took revenge upon their enemies. You gave the wicked hand into the pure hands, the hands of the numerous to the hands of the few. The hand of the unclean into the hand of the uncontaminated. The evil into the hand of the pious. And the careless into the hands of Your disciples of Your Bible and this made You great Lord and holy in the universe and for the people of Israel You made a great redemption and victory as You did from there through our days. After that, the Hasmonean came to the Temple, cleansed Your house, and purified the Holy of Holiness and Your children light the candles in Your shrine. And from that day they instituted the festival of eight days, which is called Chanukah, to signify special appreciation and thanks for Your grace and holy Name."

Question: Why is it customary on Chanukah to give charity?

Answer: The giving of charity, *tzedakah,* shows that we are truly grateful to God for all that he has done for us. Children should be encouraged to give some of their Chanukah gelt as *tzedakah* so that they can be instilled with the desire to give charity.

Question: Jewish history is full of wars and miracles. Why do the sages decree that we celebrate the festivals of Chanukah and Purim?

Answer: Both these holidays celebrate the defeat of our enemies, who tried to totally destroy our past and future. The sages want us to learn from the past and to teach future generations about the unique miracles performed for us. We are to appreciate these miracles as if they occur in our own day.

Question: What are the main differences between Chanukah and Purim?

Answer: Both festivals recall attempts to destroy the Jewish nation. Chanukah represents victory in a spiritual and cultural war, when the Greeks wanted to convert Jews and worship multiple gods. Purim represents a physical victory over Haman's plot to kill the entire Jewish population.

Mikeitz
Chapters: 41 - 44:17

Synopsis:

Joseph interpreted Pharaoh's dream; Pharaoh made Joseph Viceroy over all Egypt; due to a famine Jacob sent his sons to bring food from Egypt; interaction between Joseph and his brother.

Question: Why did Joseph not immediately reestablish contact with his father Jacob, when he rose to power in Egypt?

Answer: According to the biblical commentator *Da'at Zekanim Miba'alei Hatosfot* (*Genesis 37:35*), when Jacob sent Joseph to check on his brothers and their flocks in the field, they became angry at the sight of Joseph and thought of killing him. Reuven persuaded them not to kill Joseph but rather throw him into a pit. The brothers then made a binding pact, swearing not to reveal this deed to their father, Jacob. The pact was so binding because it was made by a quorum of ten men. According to Jewish law, this is the strongest and most binding oath possible. Such an oath can be canceled only if the entire group assembles to cancel it. Since Joseph was present at the time, he also was bound by the oath of his brothers. Joseph was so righteous a man that he maintained his silence as long as the pact was in effect.

Question: What do we learn from "...and his father Jacob cried" (*Genesis 37:35*)?

Answer: We learn that only Jacob cried over Joseph's "death." The brothers knew that Joseph did not die.

Question: The Bible states, They [Egyptians] called Joseph *avrech* (*Genesis 41:42*). What does *avrech* mean?

Answer: This word has three possible meanings: *Av* in Hebrew means father and *rech* means youth. The Egyptians saw Joseph as a "father of wisdom and youth in age" (*Sifri Davarim 1*). Another definition is the "king's father"; and still yet "Everybody bowed down to him" (in Hebrew *berech* means "knee") (*Rashi*).

Note: Today we refer to Torah scholars by this term *avrech*.

Question: Why is it stated twice at the end of the previous *parsha*, *Vayeishev*, that Pharaoh's wine steward forgot Joseph, and why is it two years later that Joseph was called from prison?

Answer: According to *Rashi*, the number two is significant in the sense that we are speaking "measure for measure" or quid pro quo. Twice while in prison Joseph asked the wine steward for help. Instead of depending on God alone, Joseph looked to another person for help. The result was that the wine steward "forgot and did not remember," and Joseph remained in prison for two more years. Years were chosen by God as the unit of time because one year is the time of remembrance. As the *Babylonian Talmud, Brachot 58* says, "The dead are not forgotten in the heart for at least twelve months."

Question: What is the Jewish attitude toward asking others for help?

Answer: This issue is a wide-ranging one in the *Babylonian Talmud* and in Jewish philosophical works. When is it permissible to ask others for help, and when should one depend on God alone? The sages emphasize repeatedly that a person must help himself as much as possible and not rely on miracles. However, we know that God is the ultimate power and source of all the good in our lives. The righteous Joseph's problem was not that he asked for help but that he picked the means of getting help (that is, the wine steward). It was as though he was telling the Almighty how to save him by means of the wine steward (*Rabbeinu Bechayei*).

When the Jews wandered the desert after leaving Egypt, Moses asked God for help for the starving Israelites. God, not Moses, decided on manna to feed them. Similarly, the prophet Elijah begged God for food, and it was brought by crows. Elijah never dreamed of crows bringing him food; God decided the means. The famous *Rabbi of Dubna* imparted this parable: a king once told someone he loved that he could live in any of the king's cities without paying taxes. The man foolishly chose a city that had a local minister that the king did not totally control. The promise of the king could not be entirely fulfilled even though the man freely chose where to live. Joseph did a similar thing by depending on a man who could change his mind.

Question: How did Joseph react when Pharaoh asked him to interpret his dream?

Answer: Joseph said to Pharaoh, "I cannot interpret your dream. Only God can do that. However I will try..." (*Genesis 41:16*).

Question: What is the goal of Joseph's interpretation of Pharaoh's dream?

Answer: There were three possible goals:

According to the sages *Sforno* and *Abarbanel,* Joseph was successful in interpreting Pharaoh's dream because he was inspired by the presence of God. His interpretation was like a prophecy. Joseph tried to explain to Pharaoh that he was God's messenger (*Rashbam*). He constantly made reference to God because he did not want Pharaoh to think that he was a fortune teller who interpreted dreams for money. Joseph showed that he continues to follow in the ways of his father and grandfather (*Akaida*).

Joseph was God's emissary, although he did not clearly understand the mission. Joseph had to bring his family to Egypt and save them from starvation. This was achieved by his interpreting Pharaoh's dream (*Sforno; Rashbam*).

We learn that history continually repeats itself. Joseph was loyal to Potiphar; Potiphar rewarded Joseph by putting him in jail. Later, by interpreting Pharaoh's dream, Joseph became Viceroy in Egypt and saved the country and his own family from starvation and annihilation. Joseph and his family were rewarded by being enslaved for over two hundred years. They were so loyal to Pharaoh, yet they were treated badly (*Ramav*).

Question: Why did Joseph treat his brothers so harshly and accuse them of spying?

Answer: Joseph did this in order to cancel the pact they had made to not reveal anything to their father. Joseph had to arrange for them to be assembled together and to experience regret and repentance so that the pact could be canceled. He accused them of spying to frighten them. They started to think that they were being punished for the way they had treated Joseph. They felt regret and began to repent their action. Joseph heard them say, "We are guilty for what we did to our brother." However, Joseph did not hear his brothers repent for the anguish they caused their father. Joseph required them to leave one brother, Benjamin, in Egypt while the rest returned to get Jacob. He had to be sure that they would return with the father. He felt that otherwise they would return to Canaan with the food and not say anything to their father.

Question: How did Joseph arrange to have Jacob come to Egypt?

Answer: As the brothers planned to head home with Benjamin, Joseph had his servant hide some silver valuables in Benjamin's food sack. After the brothers departed, Joseph sent his servant after them to accuse them of stealing and to "search" their possessions. On this pretense, Joseph said he would keep Benjamin as a hostage, requiring Jacob to come to Egypt. The brothers were afraid to return home without Benjamin, especially Judah, who had personally sworn to his father to be responsible for Benjamin. Judah begged Joseph to remain in Benjamin's place, saying that he could not face his father otherwise. Joseph saw that Judah, whose idea it had been to sell Joseph as a lad, was remorseful for the grief he had caused Jacob and that the brothers repented completely. As a result, Joseph revealed his identity to Judah and sent all of them to bring Jacob.

Question: Joseph recognized his brothers, but the brothers did not recognize him. Why?

Answer: Joseph left them when he was seventeen years old. His face was still that of a lad's, with no beard. His brothers, however, were much older, with fully grown beards, yet their appearance had not changed over the past thirteen years. Now, Joseph was thirty years old, with a beard and a deep voice (*Babylonian Talmud K'tubot 27b; Yevamot 88a*).

Ramban explained that Joseph covered his face so that his brothers could only see his eyes.

97

Vayigash
Chapters: 44:18 - 47:27

Synopsis:

Judah negotiated with Joseph; Joseph revealed himself to his brothers; Joseph's brothers went back to Jacob to tell him that Joseph was alive; Jacob/Israel went down to Egypt; God appeared to Jacob in his night vision; the meeting between Jacob/Israel and Joseph; Joseph convinced Pharaoh to give his family the city of Goshen.

Question: The Bible states, "Judah went to Joseph and said…'To me you are like Pharaoh'" *(Genesis 44:18)*. What did Judah mean?

Answer: First, Judah indicated his willingness to give to Joseph the respect due Pharaoh. He told Joseph that if he kept treating them badly, and kept Benjamin captive, he (Joseph) would suffer from leprosy like Pharaoh. Judah was very insistent that Joseph keep his word to protect Benjamin. "That if you annoy me, I will kill you along with your king" *(Rashi, Genesis 44:18)*.

Question: Judah says to Joseph, "If you do not let us take Benjamin back with us, our father will be extremely sad, and he will die of sorrow" *(Genesis 44:34)*. Why?

Answer: Jacob had four wives. Of all his wives, he loved Rachel the most. Rachel died at a very young age, 34. When Rachel died, Jacob took it very hard. He was brokenhearted. Jacob had worked for Rachel's father for many years before he was permitted to marry Rachel. Jacob had two sons with Rachel, Joseph and Benjamin. When Joseph's brothers put him in a well and returned to Jacob with a bloodstained shirt saying this was all that remained of Joseph, Jacob was beside himself with pain. He would not accept any consolation from people during his period of mourning. Jacob never recovered from the pain and sadness of losing this son, and he aged almost overnight. So now, because Joseph kept Benjamin as his hostage in Egypt and did not let him return home to his father with his brothers, Judah begged Joseph to release Benjamin. He tells Joseph that his father told him, "If Benjamin does not return, disaster will come to me and my sadness will carry me to my grave" *(Genesis 44:29)*.

Question: The Bible states, "Joseph could not restrain himself" *(Genesis 45:1)*. What does this mean?

Answer: The *Ohr HaChayim* explains that Joseph could no longer control his feelings. He could not hold on to his secret any longer. Joseph's emotions erupted like a volcano. He could no longer tolerate the pain or hold back his tears; he could no longer keep up the charade.

Question: Joseph yelled, "Remove everybody from this room, only this group of Hebrews may remain" *(Genesis 45:1)*. Why did Joseph command the Egyptians to leave the room?

Answer: Joseph did not want anyone to know how his brothers had treated him *(Abarbanel)*. The righteous Joseph did not want anyone to know that his brothers had sold him. According to *Rashi*, the Torah wanted to emphasize that Joseph removed everybody from the room not because he was ashamed of his brothers. Joseph was careful not to humiliate his brothers because of their past deeds.

Question: Joseph said to his brothers, "I am Joseph. Is my father alive?" His brothers could not answer him because they were frightened, and they jumped away from him *(Genesis 45:3)*. Why did Joseph ask if his father is still alive if he already knew the answer?

Answer: There are many views to this question. Among them are: the *Malbim* sees this question as Joseph's strong rebuke to his brothers. Asking, "Is my father alive?" implying "How dare you let our father suffer for so many years? Where is your compassion? How dare you withhold the truth from him that I am alive?"

The *Sforno* says Joseph asks his brothers, "How do you explain that our father is still alive after so many years of struggling and suffering?"

The brothers interpreted Joseph's question as stern criticism. They were shocked and attempted to run away *(Babylonian Talmud, Chagiga 2b)*.

The *Torah T'mimah* and *Bet Halevy* both suggest that this rebuke is directed at Judah, because it was Judah who was the one responsible for selling Joseph and showing Jacob the bloodstained shirt. Judah is the one responsible for Jacob's thirteen years of agony and sadness. It was Judah who had the audacity to ask Joseph to let Benjamin go

100

back to his father! Joseph responds to Judah by saying, "Why do you ask me for compassion and mercy? Why? In all this time you have never thought about your father's broken heart, your father's suffering and anguish over the thought that I was dead."

Joseph's dialogue is more than a rebuke. His intention is to make the brothers feel guilty and repent for the wrongs that they had done (*Chizkuni*).

Joseph knew that his father was alive. His question was in regard to their father's mental faculties. Thus Joseph had touched upon a very sensitive subject. Jacob had very powerful prophetic abilities. He was concerned as to whether Jacob still had the same capabilities (*Ramav*).

Joseph asked, "Is my father still alive?" Joseph says my father to make the point, I behaved like a son, but not you. This rebuke frightened the brothers (*Kli Yakar*).

By asking this question Joseph caused his brothers to become suspicious that he planned to take revenge, especially when he said *my* father. According to the *Ramav* this is what frightened them.

Question: The Bible states, Joseph said to his brothers, "come to me." They came to him. Then Joseph said to them, "I am Joseph your brother whom you sold to Egypt" *(Genesis 45:4)*. How did Joseph prove his identity to his brothers?

Answer: Joseph showed his brothers that he was circumcised (*Rashi; Bereishit Rabba 8; Tanchuma 5*).

Question: Joseph was very tactful in his approach to his brothers. What do we learn from this?

Answer: Joseph tried to calm his brothers by telling them that everything that happened was for the best. God planned everything to help the family. Joseph and his brothers were only God's tools for fulfilling the dream (*Revash; Sforno*). Joseph reassured them that they would not be punished for selling him or be rebuked by their father (*Abarbanel*). Man has freedom of choice but sometimes God leads a person on a mission to fulfill a special goal (*Sfat Emmet*). Joseph viewed the events as being orchestrated by God and thanked his brothers for carrying out God's plans.

Question: Joseph sent his brothers back to their father. He said to them, "On your journey do not be upset with each other" (*Genesis 45:24*). What specific advice did Joseph give to his brothers?

Answer: Joseph wanted to prevent emotional pain to his brothers, so he advised them not to discuss issues that would make them upset with each other (*Rashi*). Joseph wanted his brothers to have a good life. He told them: "Do not be so impatient to return home..." (*Babylonian Talmud, Ta'anit 10b*).

Joseph asked his brothers to promise him in advance that they would not discuss their having sold him on their journey home. Joseph wanted to avoid any conflict among his brothers (*Unkelus; Yonatan ben Uziel*). He did not want to create ill will among his brothers since he himself had experienced the negative consequences of sibling rivalry.

Joseph knew that his brothers lived by the commandments. As it is written, "You shall study the Bible, in your home, on the way, when you lie down and when you wake up" (*Deuteronomy 6:7*). One can study something lightly or in depth. Joseph suggested to his brothers that they discuss issues that would not bring them to dispute (*Kli Yakar*).

Joseph asked his brothers to practice moderation in their thoughts and actions. Always take a middle position, avoid the extremes (*Ramchal*).

Question: What do we learn about Joseph's character from the way in which he led his brothers to bring Jacob to Egypt?

Answer: Joseph sought to make peace with his brothers regardless of previous events. Joseph wanted to make sure that peace existed between the brothers, especially while traveling back to Jacob's house. Joseph also wanted to be certain that they would deliver the news to Jacob. *Rashi* and *Unkelus* interpret the verse "Do not fight on the way" to mean that the brothers must not argue about who was responsible for selling Joseph.

Other commentators translate Joseph's advice as "Do not worry on the way." Telling the brothers not to worry about the amount of food they were bringing back, which was much more than an average person would take. Joseph knew that there was a possibility that the authorities might stop his brothers and may even arrest them for suspicion of theft. For that reason Joseph placed his seal on the packages, which granted permission for the food to be transported (*Ramban; Chizkuni; Rashbam*).

Another explanation given the *Ba'al Haturim* says that Joseph gave his brothers extra food to feed their cattle so that they would not graze in fields that did not belong to them.

Rabbi Samson R. Hirsch explains that Joseph was trying to calm his brothers by saying, "Do not worry about the future; if you follow my direction you will be successful."

Other biblical commentators like *Tosafot* and *Abarbanel* explain that Joseph blessed his brothers because they were on a holy mission and the blessing would protect them from harm.

Still other commentators interpret that Joseph was trying to urge his brothers not to procrastinate in their tasks–that they should just go and do it. On the contrary, *Rabbi Sa'adya Gaon* said, "Do not rush. Everything is from God, everything in its time. Even if you run you may have to delay."

Question: What sign did Joseph give his brothers to convince their father that he was still alive?

Answer: When Joseph left his father, they had been studying the complicated issue of slaughtering a calf. Now Joseph said to his brothers, "Tell father that I am still studying this issue, and I have come up with some answers about our discussion." Joseph sent a few calves with his brothers as further proof (*Rashi, Bereishit Rabba 94:3, 95:3; Tanchuma 11*).

Question: What is the source of the sages' ruling that one has to show more respect for one's father than to one's grandfather?

Answer: Because the verse (*Genesis 46:1*) says that when Jacob went to the city Be'er Sheva, he offered a sacrifice to the God of his father, Isaac (*Rashi, Genesis 46:1*).

Question: How do we know that Jacob did not want to leave the Holy Land, especially to go to a place like Egypt?

Answer: Jacob wanted to stay in the Holy Land forever. He forced himself to go to Egypt only because of his son Joseph. When he reached the border, he became frightened. He saw in a prophecy that something bad would happen in Egypt, thus making him fear for his descendants both physically and spiritually. God therefore blessed Jacob and encouraged him not to be fearful regarding the trip to Egypt (*Rashi, Genesis 46:3*).

Question: Which of Jacob's granddaughters came to Egypt? How do we learn this?

Answer: *Rashi* says that it was Serach, daughter of Asher, and Yocheved, daughter of Levi. The sages also say that Serach sang to Jacob and informed him that Joseph was still alive. We learn this from the verse "his son and grandson with him. His daughters and grand-daughters...Jacob brings to Egypt" (*Rashi, Genesis 46:7*).

Question: How many people went to Egypt?

Answer: Seventy.

Question: The Bible states that on the way to his son Joseph in Egypt, Israel/Jacob "offered a sacrifice to the God of his father,

Isaac" *(Genesis 46:1)*. Why does the Bible say, "to the God of his father, Isaac"?

Answer: There are two ways to worship God. Abraham worshipped by reaching the highest level of understanding in every detail of the Bible and fulfilling the intention of God's will. Isaac did it differently. His was a simple faith as seen by his own self sacrifice, by being bound to the altar without any question or investigation. Isaac accepted God's will without any reservations whatsoever! Our forefather Jacob prays to the "God of his father Isaac" in order to show us which direction we must take in exile. If we look at Jewish history, we see that only those who live by simple and total faith survive (*Berzen Gaon*).

Question: Why did Jacob/Israel have to bring a sacrifice?

Answer: Jacob saw in a prophetic vision that this trip was the beginning of the exile, which meant that his descendants would be servants to the other nations (*Ramban*). Therefore, he brought a sacrifice and prayed to God, hoping to spare his future generations any suffering.

Question: God spoke to Jacob in a night vision. Why did God come to him at night?

Answer: The darkness of night symbolizes the coming exile. The exile will be a spiritual darkness and there will be no more "daily connection" or "direct communication" with God (*Ha'amek Davar*). God never appeared to Abraham or Isaac at night; God wanted Jacob to understand that although he and his descendants were heading for a long, dark exile, God would be with them. As our sages said: "Every place that they went in exile, God went with them" (*Babylonian Talmud, Ma'ilah 29; Meshach Chachmah*).

Question: Why did God call him Jacob, since earlier God had changed his name to Israel?

Answer: It would appear that the Almighty is reaching back to a time when He and Jacob were closer, when Jacob experienced "direct contact" with God.

Question: The Bible states, "God says to Jacob...do not be afraid of going to Egypt. I will make you a great nation.... I will go down with you to Egypt, and I will bring you up again and Joseph shall put his hand upon your eyes" *(Genesis 46:34).* What does this mean?

Answer: Jacob was extremely fearful of the exile. God encouraged and reminded him that in the end, he would be a great nation. God told Jacob that as much as you suffered, your reward would be great (*Chizkuni*).

Abarbanel says that Jacob was afraid of leaving the Holy Land for four reasons. He thought perhaps the Egyptians would kill him, his children, or his grandchildren. Since Egypt was a land full of idols and magicians who performed black magic, that perhaps he would lose his direct connection to God.

Jacob thought he might die and be buried in Egypt, and his dream of burial in the Holy Land would not be fulfilled. Jacob thought that maybe Joseph would die before him, and thus their only protection in Egypt would be forfeit.

The *Abarbanel,* therefore, says the Almighty gave Jacob four promises. First, go to Egypt and I will make you a great nation there. Second, The Almighty told Jacob He would be with you all the time and in every place. Third, the Almighty told Jacob that He would see to it that his body would be brought back to the Holy Land for burial. Finally, God told Jacob that Joseph would take care of them.

Question: Why was Jacob so fearful of going down to Egypt?

Answer: The sages give us a few explanations. They tell us that Jacob worried that his children would assimilate into the Egyptian culture. He believed that only in the Holy Land could his children exist as a nation. God promised him that they would become a nation and not assimilate with others. This is the reason why Joseph wanted a separate place, the city of Goshen (*Ha'amek Davar*).

The *Ma'avam* explains that God told Jacob not to worry because in the Holy Land he lived in peace with so many other nations, and his children did not assimilate. In Egypt, the Egyptians would be so hostile to the Hebrews, "the Egyptian cannot eat bread with the Hebrew" (*Genesis 43:32*), that there is no way the Hebrews would be allowed to assimilate.

It is difficult to understand the last explanation because it is written that when the Children of Israel left Egypt, many non-Hebrews left with them (*Exodus 12:38*). It is likely that the Hebrews did not assimilate with the Egyptians at all. However, some Egyptians asked to convert in order to become part of the Hebrews and be allowed to marry with them.

Question: Twice it is written that Jacob blessed Pharaoh. What did Jacob say and why?

Answer: The first time, Jacob simply greeted Pharaoh. The second time, Jacob prayed that the river would always come to Pharaoh. We see that Egypt would have an abundance of water. As long as Pharaoh lived Egypt never suffered from a lack of water. Once he died water became a valued commodity (*Rashi; Tanchuma 47:10*).

Question: Why did the Egyptians dislike shepherds?

Answer: Animals were as gods to the Egyptians (*Genesis 46:34*). So the thought of anyone working, or mishandling an animal was tantamount to sacrilege.

Question: Where was the first Jewish ghetto? Why was the ghetto established?

Answer: The first Jewish ghetto was Goshen. Historians say that the Hebrews created this ghetto to separate themselves from the Egyptians. They also did not want to offend the Egyptian culture that made gods of some animals. If the Israelites were seen working animals this might appear offensive to the Egyptian populace. The Egyptians also did not adhere to the Noahite law which prohibited one from cutting off the limb of a living animal and eating it.

Question: How did Joseph explain to Pharaoh his family's decision to live in the city of Goshen?

Answer: Joseph told his brothers to tell Pharaoh that they were shepherds. Although Goshen was far away, it was a special place that had excellent grazing land for animals (*Genesis 46:34*).

Vayechi
Chapters: 47:28 - 50:26

Synopsis:

Jacob asked his son Joseph to bury him in the Holy Land; Joseph swore to Jacob that he would; Jacob blessed Joseph's children Menasha and Ephraim; Jacob blessed the twelve children; Jacob died; the Egyptians mourned for Jacob; Joseph promised that he would continue to support his brothers; Joseph died.

Question: Jacob and Israel are the same person. Why does the Bible sometimes refer to him as Jacob and at other times as Israel?

Answer: When he was born, he was named Jacob. Jacob worked hard, studied, and prayed to the Almighty. He suffered the abuse of Laban, who tricked him continuously. Later, he fought against the wicked angel of Esau. When Jacob defeated the angel, God changed his name to Israel. Because of this victory, Israel became a name of protection. Jacob's descendants are known as the Children of Israel. When Israel became bitter over the loss of his son, Joseph, he lost his ability to prophecize and reverted to the name Jacob (*Genesis 45:2,28*). When his sons finally told Jacob that Joseph was still alive, God's Presence returned to Jacob. Israel was very happy and immediately wanted to go visit his son, but Joseph was in Egypt. Jacob/Israel was conflicted. On the one hand, Jacob/Israel wanted very much to see his beloved son Joseph. On the other hand, God had previously forbidden him to leave the Holy Land. God appeared to him in a night vision and called, "Jacob, Jacob." God encouraged Jacob to go down to Egypt by repeating to him the promise that he made to Jacob's grandfather Abraham, "I am your God and the God of your fathers. Do not fear descending to Egypt...I will go with you and I will bring your future generations back to the Holy Land." In this way, it became clear that Jacob and his family were not going just to visit Joseph. Jacob and his family were directed into exile by God. At the beginning of Genesis, God had told Abraham that his children would be strangers in a foreign land. They would be enslaved for 400 years but ultimately would return as a nation to the Holy Land. Jacob/Israel is described by the Bible as a great world leader. Israel was considered a victorious name and became the name of the entire nation.

Question: Right before Jacob was about to die, he called Joseph and told him, "Put your hand under my thigh .... Don't bury me in Egypt *(Genesis 47:29)*. Please, bury me in Israel with Abraham and Isaac." Why?

110

Answer: Jacob wanted Joseph to make a vow to which he would be strongly bound. At that time, placing one's hand under another's thigh was the most serious way of making an oath. The angel damaged Jacob's hip when they wrestled because the angel was trying to get at the birthright agreement made between Jacob and Esau; the agreement was kept in Jacob's hip pocket. In both instances we are talking about the continued existence and continuity of Israel as a people and as a nation.

Question: According to the Bible, what is the highest level of kindness?

Answer: The highest level of kindness is to do something for a deceased person. Such an act comes purely from the heart; there is no reward involved. Even by attending the funeral service of an unknown person you perform this *mitzvah*. We find a parallel between this and the righteous Joseph's behavior. Jacob asked his son Joseph before he died, "Do me a favor of true kindness and promise that you will bury me in the Holy Land and not leave me here in Egypt" (*Genesis 47:29*). After Jacob died, there would be nobody to verify this deed and no reward to be gained.

Question: Why did Jacob not want to be buried in Egypt?

Answer: There are two major reasons why Jacob did not want to be buried in Egypt. First, Jacob believed Israel to be the holiest land on earth (*Rashi, Genesis 47:29*). Second, the Egyptians had a tradition to worship the dead. Jacob did not want his body to be worshipped like an idol (*Rashi*).

Question: Why did Israel/Jacob bow down to his son Joseph (*Genesis 47:31*)?

Answer: The sages say in the *Talmud*, "When the fox was in his glory, all the animals bowed down to him." Jacob wanted to demonstrate that we must show reverence, respect, and recognition to a leader even if the leader is one's own son (*Babylonian Talmud, Magillah 16b*).

Question: Why does Israel/Jacob not recognize Joseph's sons?

Answer: In the simple meaning of recognition, Israel/Jacob's eyesight began to fail in his old age. Jacob had seen in a prophecy that wicked kings would descend from Joseph's sons. In shock he said: "From where did these children come that they are not suitable for blessing?" (*Yonatan ben Uziel; Rashi*). Jacob did not know Joseph's wife and was not sure of the legitimacy of his grandsons since the marriage had taken place in Egypt. Joseph showed his father their marriage documents, thereby reassuring Jacob of his sons' legitimacy (*Rashi; Masechet Kallah 3:15*).

Question: When Jacob blessed Joseph's sons, why did Jacob put his right hand on the head of Ephraim, the younger son, and his left hand on the head of Menashah, the older son, when it should have been reversed, as the right hand gives a stronger blessing?

Answer: Jacob saw in a prophecy that Ephraim would be greater than Menashah and therefore deserved the stronger blessing.

Question: Twice in this parsha, Jacob has a prophecy and plans to tell it when the prophetic message suddenly disappears. When and why?

Answer: The first instance occurred when Joseph brings his sons Ephraim and Menashah to their grandfather Jacob to be blessed. Jacob begins to bless them but stops when he sees in a vision that wicked people will descend from them. This initially kept Jacob from blessing them. From the descendants of Ephraim would come the evil kings Yeruva'am and Ach'av. From Menashah would come the wicked Yahu and his sons (*Rashi, Genesis 48:8*).

Just before Jacob passed away, he wished to bless his children. He started by saying "come near my bed and I will tell you the future." He began to disclose to them the future, the coming of the Messiah, but before he could reveal those secrets he lost his train of thought, was unable to continue and then he died (*Rashi, Genesis 49:1*).

Question: What special blessing did Joseph's sons eventually receive from their grandfather Jacob?

Answer: They received the blessing of *Vayidgu Larov*. "May you be like fish. May you be fruitful and multiply. May the evil eye never touch you." Therefore, it became customary that when someone wants to bless his children he says, "May you be like Joseph's sons Ephraim and Menashah" (*Rashi, Genesis 48:16, 20*).

Question: Why did Jacob gather all his sons together before he died?

Answer: First, he wanted to unite all his sons. Second, he wanted to bless or rebuke each son individually.

To *Reuven* he gives only rebuke. He was told he would lose his kingdom, the priesthood, and his birthright. All of this because he acted in haste.

To *Simeon*, a rebuke and a blessing. His tribe would be dispersed among the other tribes. This was the result of his desire to kill Joseph and the slaying of the people Shechem. The blessing was that he would be a teacher of children.

To *Levi*, rebuke and blessing. His tribe also would be dispersed among the tribes of Israel. This was a result also of his desire to kill Joseph and the massacres of the people Shechem. His blessing was he would be called to do service in the Temple, and collected of the tithes.

To *Judah* came a double blessing. His tribe would receive the kingship of Israel. The tribe would also receive the most fertile lands in Israel. This came about because he truly repented for his past actions.

To *Z'vulun* a blessing. His tribe would become successful in seafaring. This came about because he supported his brother Issachar in his learning.

To *Issachar* a blessing. Because of his dedication to Torah learning his tribe would include many of the great scholars and leaders of Israel. This came to fruition because he applied himself to Torah learning.

To *Dan* a blessing. Because of his tribe's bravery in the war with the Philistines, he was given the distinction that the great judges of Israel would descend from him. Samson is a descendant of Dan.

To *Gad* a blessing. This tribe was the first to volunteer to defend Israel from any enemy. The blessing was that its members would return home from battle safely.

To *Asher* a blessing. They would receive the land of olive groves. They received this because they supported Gad in defending Israel.

To *Naphtali* a blessing that their lands would ripen quickly and beautifully and be plentiful. This came about because they would be the tribe that would protect the burial rights of Jacob to the *Cave of Machpelah.*

To *Joseph* five blessings. The first would be that the evil eye would not affect the tribe. Second, that the land he inherited would never lack water. Third, his land would produce bountifully. Fourth, the tribe would be fruitful and multiply. Last, he would be the one to inherit the blessings of his forefathers Abraham, Isaac, and Jacob. All of this came about because he was of a high moral caliber. He overcame many obstacles yet remained true to the Will of the Almighty. He also overcame the animosity and antagonism of his siblings.

To *Benjamin* a blessing. He would defeat his enemies. He was fearless in battle against Israel's enemies.

Question: How does *Rashi* prove that Simeon and Levi were the brothers who planned to kill Joseph?

Answer: When Jacob blessed his children he said to Simeon and Levi, "You are too violent. I will separate the two of you, and your tribal descendants will be far apart" (*Genesis 49:7*). When Joseph was in the field with his brothers, the Bible says that one brother said to the

114

other, "Here's the dreamer, let's kill him" (*Genesis 37:19-20*). We know that Reuven and Judah did not want to kill Joseph (*Genesis 37:22,26*) and that Dan, Naphtali, Gad, and Asher were friendly with Joseph. Issachar, and Z'vulun never spoke up before their brothers, so that leaves only Simeon and Levi. (*Rashi, Genesis 49:5*).

Q**uestion:** What were Jacob's commands related to his burial?

A**nswer:** He wanted to be buried with his ancestors in the *Cave of Machpelah*. He did not want Egyptians to carry his coffin, because they were idol worshippers. He also did not want his grandchildren to carry the casket, because some of them married Canaanite women, and he did not want to embarrass them. He had a specific order for the funeral procession. The tribes along with their flags had to be in a specific order: to the east Judah, Issachar and Z'vulun; to the south Reuven, Simeon, and Gad; to the west Ephraim, Menashe, and Benjamin; to the north Dan, Asher, and Naphtali. Jacob also declared that Levi should not carry the coffin, which foreshadowed the tribe's service in the Temple when they would be the ones to carry the Ark. Joseph also was not to carry the coffin because of his status as second to Pharaoh. Ephraim and Menashah would substitute for Levi and Joseph. Although they were technically grandchildren, Jacob saw them as his children.

Q**uestion:** While Jacob's final words to Simeon and Levi may seem harsh, how do we see that they contained prophecy?

A**nswer:** The Torah says, "I will separate and disperse them among the tribes." Jacob saw the dangers presented by Simeon and Levi when they were together (e.g., they killed the entire city of Shechem, they planned to kill Joseph...) so Jacob helped them. Levi will be separate from the rest of the tribes; as it says in the Bible, when Moses divided the Holy Land, the tribe of Levi did not inherit any part of the land. Moreover, Jacob, in order to avoid any more overzealous actions, put Simeon among the tribes, assuring that Simeon would be separated from Levi.

Jacob, in his wisdom, prayed that Simeon and Levi would use their special natures, their toughness, for good. Levi served in the temple. One of his duties was to collect the tithes (ten percent of a person's salary or property). Simeon's descendants would be teachers. A good teacher sometimes has to be very strict with his students. From this Jacob hoped to demonstrate how Simeon and Levi could use their character traits for good purposes (Rashi, *Genesis 49:7*).

Question: What are the similarities between the blessings Jacob and Moses gave to the tribes?

Answer: To the tribe of *Asher* the blessing from Jacob was "His nourishment will be riches" (*Genesis 49:20*). From Moses the blessing is "His feet will be dipped in the be richest oils" (*Deuteronomy 33:24*).

To *Joseph* Jacob said, "A charming son is Joseph. He will stand above all his brothers" (*Genesis 49:26*). While Moses blessed him with this, "A special blessing upon the crown of Joseph, who was isolated from his brothers" (*Deuteronomy 33:16*).

To *Z'vulun* Jacob blessed "He will dwell at the shore and sail ships" (*Genesis 49:13*). Moses blessed "Z'vulun, enjoy your travels and your shipping business" (*Deuteronomy 33:18*).

To *Gad* Jacob blessed "Your enemy will be under your heel" (*Genesis 49:19*). While Moses blessed him by saying "Tearing off the arm and head of your enemy" (*Deuteronomy 33:20*).

Question: Jacob blessed one of his children by having his descendants be great scholars and judges. Which one of his children was this? How did we learn this?

Answer: *Issachar* received this blessing. Jacob blessed the tribe with *L'mas Oved* (*Genesis 49:15*), which means that they would be blessed in the future as spiritual leaders, taking responsibility for the rules. They would become decision makers regarding matters of the Bible (*Rashi, Exodus 49:16*). It is said that two hundred of Issachar's children became heads in religious courts.

116

Question: What did Jacob prophesy to the tribe of Dan?

Answer: Samson was a grandson of Dan. Jacob prophesied that Samson would knock over the pillars and bring down everyone who was sitting on the roof, like the snake that encircles the leg of a horse, causing the rider to be thrown off, even though the snake does not bite him directly (*Rashi, Genesis 49:17*). We learn this from the prophetic words of Jacob: "Dan will be a snake on the main road ... that bites a horse's heel so that its rider would fall backward."

Question: How did Jacob predict Samson's life would end?

Answer: "For your redemption do I long God..." Jacob prophesied that the Philistines would poke out Samson's eyes "please remember me, and please give me strength this time" (*Rashi, Genesis 49:18*).

Question: "Joseph, son protective of the eye" (*Genesis 49:22*). What did Jacob mean by this?

Answer: According to the sages, this statement describes Joseph's actions when he was only six years old. Joseph stood in front of his mother, Rachel, in order to protect her from the gaze of Esau, who wanted to take her from his brother Jacob to be one of his wives (*Rashi, Genesis 9:22*).

Question: According to Unkelus, why did Joseph merit a prophetic dream?

Answer: Joseph followed the way of God and observed God's commands as a prisoner and later as a minister in Egypt (*Unkelus, Genesis 49:24*).

Question: Did Jacob bless all of his children?

Answer: Yes. Even though Jacob rebukes his children, he still blesses all of them (*Rashi, Genesis 49:28*). The Bible says: "Jacob finished blessing his sons and put his feet up on the bed. He departed and was joined to his people" (*Genesis 49:33*).

Question: What do the sages teach us from this verse "he departed and was joined to his people" *(Genesis 49:33)*?

Answer: Because it is not written explicitly that Jacob died, the sages say it means that Jacob never tasted death (*Babylonian Talmud, Ta'anit 5b*).

Question: Why did Joseph need permission from Pharaoh to bury his father in the land of Canaan?

Answer: Although Joseph was Pharaoh's decisionmaker he still thought it would be difficult for Pharaoh if he left the land of Egypt. Pharaoh was worried that maybe Joseph would stay in the land of Canaan (*Chizkuni*). In order to go to Canaan, Joseph would need a horse and wagon. No horse or wagon was allowed to leave Egypt without the permission of King Pharaoh (*Mincha Balula*). On the day that Jacob died, the Egyptian exile began. Consequently, Joseph did not have the same authority he had had before, so he needed Pharaoh's permission (*Yalkut Ma'am Loez*).

Question: When Jacob blessed his children, which ones did he compare to other species?

Answer: Jacob compared some of his children to other species because they seemed to have similar traits. He saw Judah as a lion cub; Issachar was compared to a strong-boned donkey; Dan was as a serpent; Naphtali like a deer; Joseph was compared to an ox; and Benjamin was seen as a wolf.

Question: How did Jacob's funeral and burial proceed?

Answer: Joseph sent messengers to Pharaoh informing him of his father's death. Joseph asked and received permission from Pharaoh to go to the land of Canaan to bury his father. The funeral procession was to be as follows: Joseph was to lead, followed by Pharaoh's dignitaries and the elders from the house of Jacob. Then came the elders from Egypt, Joseph's people and his servants. Jacob's sons followed with their flags in the order specified above. Jacob's people and his servants came next, followed by wagons carrying his belongs and horsemen befitting a man of distinction.

In a place called *Goren Haatad*, the mourners lamented for seven days, and all the Ishmaelite princes and kings took their crowns and put them on Jacob's casket (*Talmud Sotah 13a*).

As we answered above only Jacob's sons were to carry the casket with Menashe and Ephraim substituting for Levy and Joseph.

Jacob was buried in the *Cave of Machpelah*.

After the funeral and the mourning period, the whole procession returned to Egypt.

Question: After Jacob's death, why did Joseph's brothers become fearful that Joseph's attitude toward them had changed?

Answer: Before Jacob's death, Joseph frequently invited his brothers to dine with him at his table, but after Jacob's death the invitations ceased. The invitations ceased not because Joseph had changed his feelings toward his brothers but because he chose to protect them from the Egyptians who would feel that the Hebrews were gaining in power and influence. However the brothers felt Joseph would now seek revenge on them. *Rashi* says that even had Joseph wanted to do this the Almighty would have prevented this from happening.

Question: How long did it take from the time that Jacob passed away until they buried him in the *Cave of Machpelah*?

Answer: Seventy days. They spent forty days embalming his body and thirty days crying for him (*Rashi, Genesis 50:3*).

Question: What special orders did Jacob give regarding his funeral?

Answer: Jacob gave his children specific instructions on how the funeral procession should proceed. He told his sons how his casket should be held, where they should stop along the way from Egypt to his grave site in the Holy Land, and on which side each tribe should stand and plant its flag (*Rashi, Genesis 50:13*).

Question: After Jacob died, why did Joseph's brothers become afraid of him, and how did Joseph calm their fears?

Answer: After Jacob passed away, Joseph stayed away from his brothers. The brothers worried that Joseph planned to take revenge. Joseph told them that they had nothing to fear: If I wanted to do something I would have done it years before. I am not God. Even if I wanted to hurt you I could not do it. If I did something to harm you, the Egyptians would think that I had lied to them by telling them that you were my brothers. How can one brother kill another (*Babylonian Talmud, Magilah 16b*)?

Question: Were Joseph's brothers' fears justified?

Answer: Joseph stopped inviting his brothers to dine with him because when Jacob was alive, he insisted that Joseph sit at the head of the table. Now with Jacob's death and his having blessed Judah with the future kingdom, and with Reuven as the firstborn, Joseph felt uncomfortable sitting at the head of the table. On the other hand, the Egyptians still recognized Joseph as an authority figure, so it would not be right for him not to sit at the head of the table. Following Jacob's death, the Egyptians' animosity toward the

Hebrews began. Joseph knew that if he invited his brothers to dine with him, it would only increase the Egyptians' ill will.

Question: The Bible states, "Raised on the knee of Joseph" (*Genesis 50:23*). What does this mean?

Answer: It means that Joseph was blessed to be given the opportunity to raise his grandchildren (*Rashi*).

Question: How old was Joseph when he died?

Answer: Joseph was 110 years old (*Genesis 50:26*).

It is a worldwide custom that when the Torah reader finishes the last sentence of each one of the five books of Moses, the entire congregation stands and encourages one another with the following proclamation:

"CHAZAK CHAZAK V' NITCHAZEK!"

(STRENGTH...STRENGTH...AND BECOME STRONG)

II

The Book of Exodus

Shemot
Chapters: 1 - 6:8

Synopsis:

*A new Pharaoh ruled Egypt and subjugated the
Children of Israel; the Egyptians enslaved and tortured
the Hebrews; Pharaoh decreed that every new Hebrew
male baby born should die; Moses' birth; Moses retrieved
from the Nile; Moses raised in the house of and raised as
a Prince of Egypt; Moses killed an Egyptian; Moses
escaped to Midyan; Moses married a daughter of
Midyan; God appeared to Moses in the burning bush;
the three miracles; circumcision of Moses' son; Moses
and Aaron go in front of Pharaoh; Pharaoh remained
stubborn and refused to allow the Hebrews either to into
the wilderness to worship their God or to leave Egypt
entirely; Moses warned Pharaoh.*

Question: The Torah says "These are the names of the Children of Israel who came to Egypt...Reuven, Simeon, Levy, Judah, Issachar, Z'vulun, Benjamin, Dan, Naphtali, Gad, and Asher. And all the people who came from Jacob's loins were seventy souls, and Joseph was in Egypt" *(Exodus 1:2-5)*. Why is Joseph's name mentioned separately from his brothers?

Answer: According to the biblical commentators Joseph is counted as one of the "seventy people..." *(Exodus 1:5)*, although he came to Egypt several years before his family. The Torah mentions Joseph separately because his behavior was extremely unique and established him as a righteous man. When Joseph was a servant in Potiphar's house, or a prisoner in an Egyptian jail, or during the time that Joseph's family was starving and came to Egypt, Joseph behaved righteously. He was not vengeful, nor did he hold a grudge against his brothers. Without question, he gave them food and the supplies that they required. Later, in order for them to live as they had previously lived in Canaan, Joseph asked and received from Pharaoh the city of Goshen as their safe haven. In that way, they would avoid living among the Egyptians, and thus not be susceptible to their corrupt manners and customs. Contrary to the fear of his brothers, who anticipated Joseph's retribution when Jacob died, there was no change in Joseph's compassionate treatment toward them (*Rashi, Ramav*).

Question: "The Children of Israel were fruitful and multiplied prodigiously, they increased and became strong very, very much..." Why the need to describe the Israel's population increase in such terms *(Exodus 1:7)*?

Answer: *Rashi* explains that this use of words is deliberate. The Torah wants to emphasize the miracle by which the Children of Israel increased so incredibly. When a woman gave birth she did so with multiple births, sometimes six at a time. The sages teach us that six children came from one womb, seen by the Torah's use of six words: (a) fruitful, (b) multiply, (c) increased, (d) growing, (e) very, (f) very much (*Tanchuma 5*).

Question: "The Egyptians enslaved the Hebrews with extreme cruelty." What type of work did the Egyptians impose upon the Hebrews?

Answer: The Egyptians used the Hebrews for incessant hard labor that literally broke down the bone structure of the human body (*Babylonian Talmud, Sotah 11b*).

To destroy the Hebrews' body but also their spirit, the women were chosen to do hard labor that normally would have been done by the men. This included preparing boulders for use in the building process. This physical strain affected their ability to bear children, diminishing the Hebrews' birth rate, which was the goal of the Egyptians. Men were allocated jobs normally associated with women, like sewing, housework, and cooking. An added result of this allocation of work was to cause resentment among the women towards their men.

There was no end to the Hebrews' work. When a project was completed, new projects were started without valid reasons. Many times what they built was to be torn down immediately and then rebuilt.

At times the Egyptians appointed Hebrew overseers. This also added to the ill feelings, having their own impose such harsh conditions on them. These overseers were often crueler than their Egyptian counterparts. The more productive their slave crew, the more the overseers were rewarded.

Question: Why did Pharaoh only want to kill the male newborns *(Exodus 1:17)*?

Answer: Pharaoh's court astrologers told him that a redeemer would be born among the Hebrews. This redeemer would be male. The Egyptian wizards prophesied to Pharaoh that the Hebrew leader would come from water and would be punished by water.

The wizards guessed correctly but interpreted incorrectly. Moses did come from water and was punished because of water. He was set adrift by his mother in a basket into the Nile only to be saved by Pharaoh's daughter. Later in Moses' life he would receive punishment from the Almighty due to his behavior over water.

Question: What does the name Moses mean?

Answer: The name Moses means, "For I drew from the water" (*Exodus 2:10*).

Question: What did Pharaoh ask from the Hebrew midwives?

Answer: Pharaoh asked the midwives to kill every newly born male child. The midwives feared the Almighty more than they feared the wrath of Pharaoh. They risked their own safety and failed to carry out Pharaoh's decree. They would say that the Hebrew women gave birth so quickly that it was impossible for them to attend to all of the deliveries. They therefore were unable to carry out the decree.

Question: What were the names of the midwives?

Answer: One was named *Shifrah*, meaning "fertile." She was so named because she made sure the babies were born healthy.

The other was *Puah* meaning "open-mouthed." She was so named because she calmed and soothed all the newborns with her voice (*Babylonian Talmud, Sotah 11b*).

Question: According to the sages, who were *Shifrah* and *Puah?*

Answer: Our sages tell us that *Shifrah* was Yocheved, the mother of Moses and *Puah* was Miriam, Moses' sister (*Sotah 11b*).

Question: What reward was given to the Hebrew midwives?

Answer: The sages tells us "God made them houses" (*Exodus 1:21*). God rewarded the Hebrew midwives by blessing them that their descendants would be the leaders of the "House of Israel." The sages explained that in the future, the structure of the Temple would be as follows: the *Kohanim* (Priests), *Leviem* (musicians in the Temple), and Israel, the ordinary Hebrew, the majority of individuals who brought offerings. The blessing was that the *Kohanim* and

Leviem would descend from the Hebrew midwife Yocheved (Shifrah) and Israel would descend from the Hebrew Miriam (Puah) (*Babylonian Talmud, Sotah 11b*).

Question: When Pharaoh saw that the midwives did not follow his orders what did he do?

Answer: He relied upon his own people to kill the newborn Hebrew males. See the *Talmud* (*Rashi, Sanhadrin 101b*) which describes the holocaust and the tragedy of the death of numerous male babies.

Question: "A man left from the house of Levi and took a Levite daughter" *(Exodus 2:1)*. What is the meaning of this verse?

Answer: *Rashi* explains that this verse is discussing the relationship of Moses' father and mother, Amram and Yocheved. With Pharaoh's decree to kill newborns Amram chose to divorce his wife thereby having no children at all. *Rashi* states that Miriam chastised her father telling him his choice was worse than Pharaoh's decree. Amram remarried his wife and subsequently Moses was born.

Question: Pharaoh's daughter found Moses in a basket in the Nile and adopted him. Was this coincidence or the Hand of the Almighty?

Answer: The Almighty is telling us by this incident that He alone controls events. Pharaoh issued a decree to drown every newborn Hebrew male. It is ironic that the daughter of the very person who wished to eradicate a threat to his throne should be the one who saved the one who has destined to oppose that power. Not only that, but the threat would be raised within the very walls of his house and be protected by him (*Ozniem L'Torah*).

Question: According to the biblical commentators, why did God have Moses grow up in Pharaoh's house?

Answer: The *Ibn Ezra* says that it was God's intention to have Moses grow up and learn the customs and manners of the Pharaoh's house. This would provide Moses with the knowledge of the inner workings of the Egyptian political and cultural system. Moses, as a future leader, would need the courage and knowledge to rise up against the evil Pharaoh and his wicked kingdom. God put Moses in Pharaoh's palace so Moses would not be fearful of Pharaoh. Moses could then see Pharaoh as only flesh and blood, not as a god as his people did.

The *Abarbanel*, and others, reason that the Almighty's goal in having Moses grow up in Pharaoh's palace was so the Children of Israel would identify Moses as someone experienced with authority.

Question: How old was Yocheved when she gave birth to Moses?

Answer: Yocheved was 130 years old when she gave birth to Moses. The commentator *Rashi* proves it by telling us that Yocheved was born when Jacob/Israel went to Egypt. The Children of Israel left Egypt 210 years later when Moses was 80 years old. Therefore, Yocheved gave birth to Moses when she was 130 (*Rashi, Exodus 2:1*).

Question: How did Yocheved hide the baby Moses for three months?

Answer: According to *Rashi*, Moses was born prematurely, six months and one day into the pregnancy. The Egyptians counted nine months from the time that Moses' father Amram remarried Yocheved. They assumed a full term pregnancy, so they were not looking for a child until three months later.

Question: "Moses went out to his people and saw their burden" (*Exodus 2:11*). What significance does this verse hold?

Answer: The Torah wants to explain that Moses was the greatest redeemer of the Israelites. Moses devoted himself to alleviating his people's suffering (*Chatam Sofer*). The sages say in *Bereishit Rabba,* "God said to Moses, 'You left your business, and went to see how your people were suffering, and you behaved like a real brother. I, the Lord, will leave the heaven and the earth, and speak with you.' As it is written, 'God came to him in the bush.'" Thus, the Lord showed Moses that He was concerned for the Children of Israel just as Moses was (*Shevet Sofer from Prashburg*).

Question: Why did Moses kill an Egyptian?

Answer: Moses saw injustice when an Egyptian, for no valid reason, was severely beating a Hebrew (*Rashi*). Moses used the name of God to slay the Egyptian (*Zohar*).

Question: How does the Torah show the exemplary nature of Moses?

Answer: The Torah describes Moses' life in three phases. During the first phase he resided in the house of Pharaoh. During the second, Moses had to leave Egypt and move to Midyan. Later he became God's messenger.

Throughout his life Moses is seen as a compassionate and righteous person. Moses saw an Egyptian beating a Hebrew. Immediately, Moses came to the person's aide. He helped that person and killed the Egyptian, risking his standing and prestige in Pharaoh's court.

Moses saw two Hebrew men fighting. Again, Moses got involved and helped the weaker man. He asked the stronger man, "Why are you hitting your brother?" The stronger man replied, "Are you planning to kill me the same way you killed the Egyptian?" Upon hearing this Moses realized that there were witnesses to his killing of the Egyptian. Moses stopped the fight, regardless of the risk he was taking.

An informer reported the two incidents to Pharaoh. Moses was forced to flee to Midyan to save his life. When Moses came to Midyan, he again came upon a situation where he involved himself to help the weak. Moses saw Yitro's daughters trying to give their animals water from a well. The Midyanite's shepherds refused to allow Yitro's daughters to give their animals water. Moses saw this and rescued Yitro's daughters from the shepherds, and Moses gave their animals water.

From these three instances, we see that Moses was a compassionate and understanding man and had the character to be the leader of the Children of Israel (*Rambam, Moreh Nevuchim 11:45*).

Question: Which test did Moses pass in order to gain the ability to be the prophet and leader of the Israelites?

Answer: Moses was a humble man. After he was forced to leave Pharaoh's house he became a shepherd. The sages say that we see the potential for Moses' leadership in the way he treated the animals. Moses' compassion and mercy toward sheep in the desert is the background to events in the future. The ability to prophesy did not come to Moses when he was in Pharaoh's house. According to *Abarbanel*, the ability to prophesy can only be achieved through humility. Moses achieved this level little by little. First, God made Moses a shepherd in order to isolate him from people and master the skills of tending to "one's flock" (*Rabbeinu Bachayei*). Moses also worked as a laborer. By understanding the concept of work in its pure form and his humility Moses was able to fully understand human behavior and suffering (*Chatam Sofer*).

Question: If somebody raises his hand to hit somebody, he is called evil and wicked. Where did we learn this?

Answer: We learn it from the story in which Moses sees a man lifting his hand to strike another (*Exodus 2:13*).

Question: Why did Moses run away from Pharaoh?

Answer: Pharaoh sent his ministers to kill Moses. Moses had been accused of killing an Egyptian who had beaten a Hebrew slave (*Yerushalmi Talmud, Brachot 9b*).

Question: How did Yitro, a Midyanite, recognize that Moses was a Hebrew?

Answer: Yitro's daughters told him that the water rose up to Moses as it had done to Jacob. This was how Yitro recognized that Moses was a descendant of Jacob (*Exodus 2:20*).

Question: According to the sages, what advice did Pharaoh's doctor give him to cure himself of leprosy?

Answer: The doctor advised Pharaoh to use human blood. Pharaoh was told to kill Hebrew infants, then take their blood and bathe in it *(Rashi; Yonatan ben Uziel)*.

Question: What was the name of Moses' wife?

Answer: Moses married Tziporah, one of Yitro's daughters.

Question: What were their sons' names?

Answer: Their first son was named Gershom. *Ger* in Hebrew means "stranger." Moses felt that he was a stranger in a foreign land. Their second son was named Eliezer, in Hebrew meaning "with God's help." Moses gave his second son the name Eliezer as gratitude to the Almighty for having saved him from Pharaoh's sword (*Exodus 2:22, 18:4*).

Question: What happened when Moses was first approached by God?

Answer: Moses, the shepherd, was in the wilderness when he saw a bush on fire. He saw that the bush was not being consumed by the flames. As Moses came closer, he heard a voice call to him to take off his shoes, because he was approaching holy ground. It was then that Moses had his first encounter with the Almighty.

Question: Why did God choose the bush to meet Moses?

Answer: The Almighty was demonstrating that He too suffers with the Children of Israel. The Almighty was feeling the pain of His children. Also appearing in a place like a bush tells us that the Almighty is everywhere, that there is no place so low that God's Presence is not there (*Midrash*).

Question: Why did Moses ask God to show the people of Israel signs and miracles?

Answer: There are some positive and some negative explanations for this.

The Children of Israel suffered and struggled for many years. They were at the lowest level of impurity. Moses felt that if he were to go to them and present himself, they would not believe that God spoke to him. He did not believe that his people would follow him. He felt that the children of Israel needed a sign and/or a miracle from God.

The miracles could be viewed as a rebuke to Moses because he gossiped against the Children of Israel to God by saying that they would doubt him and not believe him (*Rambam*).

Abraham, Isaac, and Jacob were prophets, yet they did not address the general public. Moses was the first prophet of Israel who spoke publicly. He asked God, "how should I talk to these people?" (*Rambam, Moreh Nevuchim, 63, First Part*).

Question: Why did Moses originally turn down God's mission?

Answer: The answer is twofold. First Moses did not feel confident that he would be able to convince a king to release a people. Moses asked, 'Who am I to talk with the king?' Second, Moses asked why the Children of Israel were entitled to miracles and deserving of being brought out of Egypt (*Rashi*).

Question: How did God reply to Moses?

Answer: God replied that the way the bush burns and is not consumed is the way I will save the Children of Israel from Egypt. The Children of Israel are entitled to My miracles and to be brought out of Egypt because in the future they will receive the Torah.

Question: Moses felt that the Children of Israel would not believe him. How does the Almighty rebuke Moses?

Answer: The Almighty rebuked Moses three ways. He reminded Moses of the snake in the Garden and the sin of evil speech. The Almighty tells Moses that by speaking ill of Israel he is committing this offense. The sign of leprosy, that Moses temporarily received, also was God's rule. "He who speaks gossip would get leprosy." This disease was also given to Miriam, the sister of Moses, for speaking such gossip.

God asked Moses what he had in his hand. Moses responded that he held his staff. God told him the staff would be an instrument of punishment. We know during his leadership of Israel in the wilderness Moses hit the rock with this stick instead of speaking to the rock as instructed by God. Because of this failure in trust Moses would not lead the Children of Israel into the Holy Land.

The Almighty told Moses that he should take water from the river and it would turn to blood.

Question: What is the meaning of the miracles that Moses showed the Children of Israel?

Answer: One takes away from this story the fact that it is the Almighty Who controls all. It is only the Almighty Who can change staffs to snakes, make water turn to blood, make an inert object into a living being. We also see that it is the Almighty Who provides healing, or God forbid brings on disease.

These miracles exemplify the Children of Israel's destiny. According to the *Chatam Sofer* it was the Almighty who turned a staff into a snake, a lowly creature destined to crawl along the earth. In another instant that same snake returned to its original status as a staff. All of this signified the Children of Israel's fall to slavery and rise to become *the Chosen*.

Moses posed three questions to the Almighty. The first, how could such a large group of people, enslaved for hundreds of years, under tyrannical subjugation, overcome adversities and be redeemed? The second question posed was how would the Children of Israel be purified and able to retain blessings while in their impure state? The final question was how would it be possible for the Children of Israel to be able to escape from the Egyptians, who were by far more physically and mentally superior and had an army that could most assuredly keep them from leaving Egypt?

The Almighty answered Moses with three miracles. The first miracle was the staff turning into a snake symbolizing the end of Pharaoh. The history books say that this pharaoh did not come from a lineage of kings but was able by force to overthrow the previous pharaoh. Initially Moses ran when the staff became a snake. Moses represents the Children of Israel. The end will be their return to God at Mount Sinai. The second miracle showed the future of the nation of Israel. In the dark days when Egypt symbolized the fact that they left the Holy Land and went into exile, they got leprosy, which is an impure state. In the end, they returned to the righteous path, which is symbolized by the healing of the leprosy. The third miracle was the water, which turned to blood. This symbolized the Egyptians, who were drowned in the Red Sea (*Abarbanel*).

Question: Which signs did God give the Children of Israel so that they might believe Moses' role?

Answer: The Almighty made Moses' staff turn into a snake. Second, Moses' hands turned leprous. Third, the water in Egypt's rivers became blood.

Question: Why did Moses have so many doubts regarding the Children of Israel? Why did he need so much encouragement to assume a leadership role?

Answer: The *Shemot Rabba* states that Moses still did not believe that Israel would believe him even after all the assurances the Almighty had given him. The miracles shown to Moses would be a stern warning to him. The *Sforno* suggests the people would believe that a true emissary of the Almighty would not fail in his attempts to convince Pharaoh. Moses felt he lacked the appropriate prophetic abilities, like wealth, wisdom, and physical perfection. He had thought, wrongly, that the Almighty would have transformed him into a perfect person capable of meeting this role. That did not happen.

Question: How many days did Moses discuss with God his role as leader of the Children of Israel?

Answer: Moses spent seven days with the Almighty discussing his role. The role of his brother Aaron was also discussed.

Question: How did God punish Moses for his refusal?

Answer: The *Midrash* says that Moses had been destined to be *Kohen*. Aaron was to become a *Levi*. Because of this refusal, the Almighty punished Moses by giving Aaron the *Kehuna* the line of priesthood, and Moses became *Levi*.

Question: God says to Moses "Go back to Egypt for the people who pursue your life have died" *(Exodus 4:19)*. Who were these people and what did the sages learn from this verse?

Answer: The two people who hated Moses were Datan and Aviram. They witnessed Moses killing the Egyptian, and had informed on Moses to Pharaoh. According to the sages they did not really die but suffered tremendous hardship to show that they were no longer a threat to Moses. They were seen as being actually dead (*Babylonian Talmud, Nadarim 64b*).

135

Question: Why does the Torah tell us that Moses' wife, Tziporah, circumcised their son?

Answer: Tziporah circumcised Eliezer because she feared for her husband who was struggling with an angel sent by God to kill him (*Rashi, Exodus 4:25*).

Question: "When he was on the way, at the inn, the Almighty encountered him [Moses] and sought to kill him" *(Exodus 4:24)*. Why does the angel of the Almighty seek to kill Moses?

Answer: There are many opinions surrounding this interesting occurrence. *Rashi* says that this is a show of the Almighty's anger toward Moses because he did not circumcise his son Eliezer. The sages (*Babylonian Talmud, Nadarim 31b, 32a*) see Moses as a totally righteous person who weighed the issues before him and decided that it was more important to redeem the Children of Israel rather than take care of his personal obligation. That personal obligation was the circumcision of his son. He calculated, perhaps incorrectly, the distances which had to be traveled. Being remiss in his obligation was punishable by death according to one opinion in the *Talmud.* Moses reckoned that if he circumcised his son in Midyan he would have to postpone his journey three days or risk his son's life on the journey back to Egypt. He hoped to reach a place, like the inn mentioned in the parshat, where he would do the circumcision. However, once at the inn the family encountered the angel of the Almighty. The angel did battle with Moses. *Rashi* sees Moses as the intended victim for not performing the *mitzvah* in its appointed time. The *Ramav* points out that "The messenger fulfilling a *mitzvah* will never be hurt." So according to this view Moses was showing a lack of faith. The *Tur* suggests it is Tziporah who insists upon the delay at the inn to perform the *mitzvah.* Moses hesitated, but only until the encounter with the angel. Still other commentators, the *Ibn Ezra* and the *Ramban,* say Moses was warned earlier about his route. He was told to leave his wife and son at the inn after the circumcision was done, but Moses refused. This forced the angel of the Almighty to battle with him.

The view that the son was the intended victim of the angel is held by the *Rashbam* who suggests that bringing along his family, wife and son, Moses was hampered or slowed down on his journey. Therefore Tziporah thought by circumcising her son she would be offering a sacrifice just as the prophets would do at a later time in Israel's history. The *Shemot Rabba* says Moses wanted his family to be recipients of the Torah as well, and that is why they were brought on this journey back to Egypt.

Regardless of which opinion one holds it is evident that it is the angel's appearance at the inn which instigates the previously neglected circumcision.

Question: According to the commentators, what special merit brought the redemption to the Children of Israel?

Answer: "And the children of Israel believed" (*Exodus 4:31*). This simple but apparently powerful act of faith made them worthy of the redemption (*Ramav*).

Question: What happened to the Hebrew elders who promised to go with Moses and Aaron to see Pharaoh?

Answer: *Rashi* on this verse (*Exodus 5:1*) says that the elders, of which there were seventy, gradually slipped away one at a time. They feared the wrath of Pharaoh.

Question: How were these elders eventually punished?

Answer: For their cowardice it says "Moses alone shall approach [the mountain] and receive the Torah" (*Rashi; Shemot Rabba 5:14*).

Question: How did Pharaoh react when Moses and Aaron came to him?

Answer: Pharaoh refused from the outset to even consider Moses' and Aaron's request. Even the request to go into the desert to pay homage to God and return was outright refused. The Hebrews were too large a group to let go en masse. Pharaoh considered the Children of Israel too valuable an asset to be let go. This would be a definite loss of manpower to the work force. He told them to stop their troublemaking and return to their responsibilities.

Question: In *Exodus 5:6* the Torah uses two words which seem similar, foreman and taskmaster. What is the difference between foremen and taskmasters?

Answer: The taskmaster can be viewed more like a supervisor who supervised a number of crews with their guards, where a foreman was in charge of a crew of laborers (slaves). It seems from *Rashi's* comment on this verse that the foreman or guard was the more rigorous and concerned with meeting quotas.

Question: According to *Rashi* what differences are there between Moses and Abraham?

Answer: Moses talked out of turn, Abraham did not. Abraham never complained, even when God told him to sacrifice Isaac. Moses refused to accept the leadership of the Children of Israel. Abraham was very patient and accepted everything. Moses wanted a fast resolution and always questioned (*Babylonian Talmud, Sanhedrin 111a*).

Va'eira

Chapters: 6:2 - 9:35

Synopsis:

God commanded Moses to go to Pharaoh; Moses and Aaron went to Pharaoh; seven plagues.

Question: Why does the Almighty tell Moses "I am the Lord" (*Exodus 6:2*)?

Answer: *Rashi* explains that each time the phrase "I am the Lord" appears in the Torah, the Almighty is saying that He is faithful to His word. He promises to reward those who do His will, to exact punishment from those who do not. By believing that the Almighty is Lord and by doing His will, a person can feel that the Almighty's protection surrounds him.

Question: Every Passover (*Pesach*) each person at the Seder drinks four cups of wine. A final cup, the cup of Eliyahu, the prophet, is left untasted. What does the parsha have to say on this?

Answer: The five cups correspond to five promises that the Almighty made to the Hebrews (*Exodus 6:6-7*). They are: (a) "And I will take you out...," (b) "And I will save you...," (c) "And I will redeem you...," (d) "And I will take you as a nation...," and (e) "And I will bring you to the land..."

A simple answer to the question is that since the last promise was made to all Hebrews for all generations it has yet to be fulfilled. Therefore the cup remains untasted.

Another explanation is that throughout history, over thousands of years, the Jewish nation has survived many threats to its existence. The threats include: Egyptian exile, Babylonian exile, Greek exile, the Spanish Inquisition and the Holocaust. This has tested the Jews' strength as a nation. When times are easier for Jews, it is an even stronger test of their resolve. They are not being forced to be together and they can easily assimilate if they want to. Jewish history has shown that it is more difficult for Jews to survive as Jews in friendly environments than in a hostile one. The fifth cup of wine therefore corresponds to the intact survival of the Jewish nation through times of ease and lack of suffering.

Question: What were the names of the children of Levi?

Answer: Gerson, Kehat, and Merrari.

Question: Why did Moses try to run away from his mission as a leader of Israel?

Answer: This *parsha* revisits Moses' concern about his leadership abilities. This time the reason was Moses' physical defects. He told the Almighty that the Children of Israel would not listen to him because of "shortness of wind and hard work" (*Exodus 6:9*), and Pharaoh would not heed him because "I have a blocked lip" (*Exodus 6:12*). He was a stutterer.

Question: How does the Torah teach us that before one becomes engaged, one has to investigate the prospective spouse's family?

Answer: The Torah tells us the story of Aaron, Moses' brother. "Aaron took Elisheva, daughter of Aminadav and sister of Nachshon, as his wife" (*Exodus 6:23*). *Rashi* says: The names of the father and brother(s) are specifically mentioned to show that Aaron had to consider the family in choosing a wife. The *Talmud* tells us that no matter what one may feel for a person, one is not only marrying a partner, one is also marrying the family of his/her partner.

Question: How old were Moses and Aaron when they first met with Pharaoh?

Answer: Moses was 80 and Aaron was 83 (*Exodus 7:7*).

Question: Does either Moses or Aaron have more importance than the other?

Answer: The fact that either brother may be mentioned prior to the other does not imply the importance of one brother over the other (*Rashi, Exodus 6:26*). Each brother had his own particular strengths and weaknesses which he brought to the tasks he was supposed to perform. There was no jealousy between them.

Question: How did God instruct Moses regarding his approach to Pharaoh?

Answer: The Almighty begins by telling Moses that Pharaoh is not a supreme ruler and cannot hold the Children of Israel captive for all time. The Almighty then tells Moses to expose Pharaoh's true character, which had been kept hidden even from his own people. Pharaoh had always prided himself in his ability to convince everyone he was all powerful and above human weakness. He went so far as to tell people that he did not have bodily functions. There was no bathroom in the palace. The Almighty told Moses to go early in the morning to the river to see Pharaoh and confront him. Then to tell him, "Let My people go" (*Rashi, Exodus 7:15*).

Similarly, Pharaoh had a reputation of being supreme among the magicians. Pharaoh would rise early and meet with wizards to learn their tricks (*Babylonian Talmud, Moed Katen 18a; Sabbath 75a*). Moses was told by God to go out early and spy on Pharaoh and to reveal his secrets (*Maharshah*).

Question: Why did God say to Moses, "I will make Pharaoh's heart strong and he won't send you out even after he receives the plague, only after the tenth plague will he let you go"?

Answer: The biblical commentators explain that God was not just punishing an individual. He was punishing a leader and the nation he led. God punished Pharaoh and his nation, measure for measure for all the wicked actions inflicted upon the Hebrew people. For example, Pharaoh wanted every Hebrew baby boy that was born to be drowned in the river; so the first plague was blood, which filled the nation's river. This went on until all ten plagues had been inflicted upon Pharaoh and his nation. God made Pharaoh's heart stubborn so he would not give in to Moses until he received all the punishment he deserved. God was showing the world that Pharaoh received just punishment.

Question: What kind of competition did Aaron have with Pharaoh's top magicians?

Answer: Magic was known in those days and was practiced extensively. Moses and Aaron went to Pharaoh and told him they were sent by God. To prove this, Aaron threw down his staff and it turned into a serpent. Pharaoh called his top magicians and told them to do the same. The magicians were able to do exactly the same thing. But Aaron's serpent was superior in that it ate all of Pharaoh's magicians' serpents.

Question: How do the sages explain the event with the serpents?

Answer: Jewish mystics explain that when God created the world, He created it in balance. He created forces in opposition to one another, good and evil, dark and light, heat and cold, and so forth. These forces are always opposing each other.

Our sages see this episode with Aaron and the staff highlighting this balance. Aaron represents good, Pharaohs' wizards represent evil. On Aaron's staff were written the Names of God. When Aaron concentrated on the Names, the staff changed into a snake. The wizards, using their powers of magic, transformed their staffs into snakes as well. The snakes fought. God caused Aaron's snake to swallow up all of the wizards' snakes. The fight was really between good and evil (*Kitvey Hasulam*). From this we learn that even though it may take a long time and a great deal of effort, good shall triumph over evil. When we have to face adversity in our personal lives, we must persevere and have faith that God will help us in the proper time.

Question: God told Moses in advance that Pharaoh's heart would be stubborn. Furthermore, Pharaoh would give empty promises and show no remorse for his harsh treatment of the Hebrews. Why?

Answer: Maimonides (*Rambam*) in his book M*ishna Torah, Hilchot T'shuva 6:3* said that there are people so wicked that the doors in heaven remain closed to them even if they later choose to repent. Maimonides uses Pharaoh as an example of pure evil for which there is no forgiveness.

Question: If there was no way for Pharaoh to repent, why did Moses come to warn him to stop his evil behavior?

Answer: *Rambam* explained that Moses came on behalf of God to teach the world that the door of repentance is not always open for everybody. There are sinners so corrupt that they would never be forgiven until they are punished not only in this world but in the next world as well. But this is not a judgment man can make. Giving one every opportunity to repent is a fundamental tenet within Judaism.

On this question the *Ramav* asks, does putting someone to death contradict the principle of giving everyone the opportunity to repent for their sins? He concluded that as long as the sin is not utterly sinister in nature, there is always room for repentance. The *Ramban* explained that Pharaoh, like all men, had the freedom of choice to be any kind of man he wanted to be but his choice was evil. The fact that Pharaoh, against his will, finally decided to let the Children of Israel go was not due to any repentance on his part, but that he wanted to save himself from the last plague (slaying of the first born). The *Abarbanel* said that there are two ways to repent for any iniquity. If a person commits a sin because of a lack of faith, one's repentance is simply to regret what was done, confess and promise never to do it again. For example, if a person steals money from his fellow man, his repentance is not acceptable until he returns the money. However there are much more severe forms of sin not stemming from a mere lack of faith but from an innate sense of self over others, that a mere regret, with an act of compensation and a resolve not to repeat again will not suffice. Such was the need for the tenth plague when Pharaoh and his nation committed the sin of spilling Hebrew blood. For this, the Egyptians had to pay dearly with their own blood. One may say the fact that Pharaoh's heart remained strong, that he refused even against unusual acts was because he represented not only himself but his entire nation and therefore any real atonement had to take into account the need to receive full punishment via ten plagues for the ten sins committed against the Hebrew people.

The *Shlah* explains that God made Pharaoh's heart strong in order to show everybody that he deserved his punishment, especially when he proclaimed "Who is God that I should listen to Him!" Pharaoh deserved punishment "measure for measure" for disgracing the Name of God. He and his nation were punished in a way that would clearly show the world that there is a God.

Question: From where do we learn that God always gives the warning before the punishment?

Answer: Moses, under God's directive, warned Pharaoh to free the Hebrew people or suffer the consequences. Moses would tell Pharaoh in advance exactly what the plague would be if he failed to let the Children of Israel go.

Question: What were the ten plagues inflicted on Pharaoh and the Egyptians?

Answer: The first plague was that of Blood. Moses and Aaron held a staff, and God commanded them to strike the river. It turned to blood. Pharaoh ordered his magicians to do the same. His heart hardened. All water within the borders of Egypt turned to blood. All animal life in the river died as a result of this plague. There is a discussion among the commentators as to the length of the plague. It either lasted one week or three.\The second plague to strike was the Frogs. Aaron stretched his arm over the river and frogs came forth. They crept into homes and bodies all over Egypt. Pharaoh summoned Moses and Aaron and begged that this plague be removed. Once the plague was lifted Pharaoh hardened his heart. Moses cried out to the Almighty and the frogs died but the land smelled of decaying frogs.

The third plague was one of Vermin or Lice. Aaron took his staff and struck the ground. Swarms of lice were everywhere. Pharaoh summoned his magicians to remove the lice but they failed. The magicians admitted that the "finger of God" was at work. Pharaoh's heart was hardened. Everyone and everything was affected by this plague. Living conditions became unbearable.

The fourth plague God sent was in the form of Wild Beasts. Herds of wild beasts roamed at will destroying whatever grew on the land. Pharaoh again summoned Moses and Aaron begging for an end to the plague, suggesting they make an offering to the Almighty. God stopped the plague. Pharaoh's heart was hardened. This was the first plague that made Pharaoh agree to Moses' demands.

The fifth plague was Cattle Disease. With this plague God fulfilled a promise to bring disease to the cattle. Still Pharaoh's heart was hardened. This plague highlighted the power of God in that the plague only affected the livestock of the Egyptians, while leaving Hebrews' animals unharmed.

The sixth plague inflicted on the Egyptians was Boils. Moses was commanded to toss soot from a furnace into the air. From this boils erupted over all of the Egyptians and their animals. Again Pharaoh's heart was hardened even more. This plague effected the magicians so that they were unable to stand before Pharaoh to perform their magic.

The seventh plague to come was Hail. Moses is commanded to stretch his hand toward Heaven and God sent forth heavy hail and thunder. With this plague Pharaoh admitted he sinned. He once again begged Moses to intercede with the Almighty to lift the plague. He promised once again to let the Hebrews leave. Once the plague was lifted his heart once again was hardened.

The eighth plague was that of the Locusts. Moses stretched his staff over the land of Egypt and the Locusts swarmed. Again there was an admission of sin on the part of Pharaoh. Again he asked Moses and Aaron to pray that the plague should cease. The Locusts covered everything, and ate everything. Again, once the plague was removed by a great blast of wind Pharaoh hardened his heart again.

The ninth plague to strike was one of Darkness. Moses was again commanded to stretch out his hand towards Heaven and there was a Darkness that could be felt. It was tangible. It is with this plague that Pharaoh decided to let the Israelites leave but without their belongings. This was unacceptable to Moses. This plague lasted three days. With this plague the people were unable to move physically.

The last plague, the tenth one, was perhaps the cruelest. This was the plague of the Slaying of the First Born of Egypt. At midnight the Almighty sent the Angel of Death throughout Egypt. This plague even affected the house of Pharaoh. Pharaoh himself became frightened since he too was a first born. With this plague Pharaoh summoned Moses and Aaron and told them the Israelites must leave immediately with their belongings.

Question: How many of the plagues that the Egyptians received are recorded in *Parshat Va'eira*?

Answer: There are seven plagues listed in this *parsha*: Blood, Frogs, Lice, Wild Beasts, Cattle Disease, Boils and Hail.

Question: How did the blood plague occur?

Answer: Moses hit the water of the Nile with his staff and the water turned to blood. This turned the rivers and wells to blood, and even urns that held previously drawn water. The *Midrash* says that even the fruit yeilded blood when squeezed. This particular plague lasted seven days.

Question: Why did God tell Moses in advance that Pharaoh would say he would free the Children of Israel and then change his mind?

Answer: The simple explanation is to show the greatness of God. God knows all past, present and future. He knows how things will turn out (*Rashi*).

It also showed Moses how man operates. God gave Pharaoh ten opportunities to repent. According to *Rambam*, God gives every human being freedom of choice. Unfortunately, Pharaoh always chose the wrong way. When Pharaoh was feeling the torture of the plagues he promised Moses "If you pray and God stops this plague, I promise that I will immediately send away the Children of Israel." Then, as soon as the plague was over and Pharaoh was no longer feeling the torture, he changed his mind (*Ramav*).

Question: How did the plague with the frogs begin?

Answer: *Rashi* says that it started with only one frog. When an Egyptian went to kill it, it multiplied into many when he hit it with a stick (*Midrash*). One frog multiplied into more. According to the *Talmud,* one frog whistled and all the rest came (*Babylonian Talmud, Sanhedrin 67b*).

Question: Prior to the warning about the plague of locusts, the eighth plague, Pharaoh tells Moses he will release the men. What is Moses' response?

Answer: Pharaoh agrees to release only the Hebrew men, but Moses insists that everyone must go, men, women, children, even their livestock. Moses told Pharaoh that as the Hebrews had all served him as slaves so all of them would now serve God. Moses, the loyal messenger of God, was under strict orders to take out all the people. Pharaoh wanted the women, children, and animals to stay as hostages in Egypt, to ensure that the men would return.

Bo

Chapters: 10:1 - 13:16

Synopsis:

The last three plagues; the commandment of the new moon; the Passover commandment; Pharaoh forced the Children of Israel to leave; the baking of Matzoh; the commandment of tefillin.

Question: What are the four main ingredients in understanding the Torah?

Answer: There is a system to the study of Torah. It contains four significant elements. The acronym for this system is **P'RDS** (pronounced "*pardess*"). Each letter stands for something. The "P", *Pshat*, to understand or look at the Torah in a literal way, word for word. The "R" for *Remez*, or hint, is a unique way which asks the reader to understand the implications of what is being said. The "D" for (Mi) *drash* gives us the stories within the Torah written by the sages adding to our knowledge and understanding. Finally the "S" for *Sod*, the secrets hidden deep beneath the surface holding the keys (*kabbalah*) which unlock the mysteries the Torah holds.

Question: Different commentators on the Bible appear to rely on one or another of the above elements. How does their preference affect their commentary?

Answer: *Pshat* — Many commentators explain the Torah word by word because they believe that what is written is literal and one must follow the law exactly as it is written. However, one must be careful in attempting this. The best-known biblical commentator was Rabbi Shlomo Yitzchaki (*Rashi*), a twelfth-century French biblical scholar who used this method. However, there are many instances when one just cannot explain the Torah in a simplistic way; one needs more.

    Remez — This is used to explain when the Torah implies something, and it is needed to help clarify questions which occur in *Pshat*. For instance, the holy Rabbi Chaim Ben Attar (a famous Sephardic Rabbi who wrote the biblical explanation called *Ohr Hachayim*) states that although he respects the *Pshat*, we cannot take everything at face value. He said that one must look at the underlying circumstances in order to understand the complete picture, which may be totally different than what appears at first glance. Therefore, in his explanations, he tells us a lot of what the underlying meaning is. For example, we ask in Genesis, why did not Joseph reestablish contact with Jacob, his father, after he became a powerful man in Egypt? According to the Biblical commentator *Da'at Aanim Miba'alei*

150

Hatosfot (Genesis 37:35), when Jacob sent Joseph to see his brothers and their flocks in the field, they became angry at the sight of him and thought of killing him. Reuven convinced them not to kill him but to throw him into a pit. The brothers made a strong binding pact swearing not to reveal this deed to their father Jacob. The pact was binding because it included ten men. According to Jewish law, this is the strongest and most binding oath possible. In order for the entire group to cancel such an oath, they must assemble and, in unison, cancel the pact. The *Remez* technique in this case leads us to conclude that since Joseph was present at the time, he was also bound by the oath of his brothers, and since Joseph was so righteous a man, he maintained his silence as long as the pact was in effect.

We call Joseph a righteous man, but there are people who might think he was not because he did not contact his father during all those years, especially when Joseph was in such a high position. However, when we look at the underlying situation (by way of *Remez*), the picture is clarified such that Joseph merits to be called our righteous forefather.

(Mi) *drash* — Numerous sages and historians brought us many stories and interpretations, which fine tune the Torah and give us further biblical details. Sometimes these stories lead to further questions and analyses.

Sod — Many commentators believe that a great many mysteries and hidden meanings lay in each Torah word or even a single letter. The most prominent of the sages who dealt with the mysteries in the Torah (*kabbalah*) was Rabbi Shimon Ben Yochai who lived approximately 1,928 years ago. He wrote a famous series of books called the *Zohar* which is recognized as the main source of Jewish mysticism. Add to this numerous books which seek to interpret and explain the meaning of the *Zohar*, which discuss mystical aspects of life. Other famed sages who looked into and wrote concerning *kabbalah* were the *Ha'ari* and his disciples, Rabbi Chaim Vital and Rabbi Yehuda Leib Ashlag, who wrote the series *Hasulam* on the *Zohar*.

Question: What concept is the Torah emphasizing in the verse: "...relate in the ears of your son and your son's son...my miraculous signs and that you will know I am God" *(Exodus 10:2)*?

Answer: The Torah is telling us the importance of transmitting information. We are told that if information is to be transmitted, it should go from one person's mouth to another person's ear. There is active exchange taking place. For continuity it is essential that information be passed from generation to generation in this manner. The Torah teaches that parents are obligated to teach their children and their grandchildren about the ways of God. By talking to one's family, one strengthens the attachment to God and has a greater understanding of God's actions. This idea reinforces the necessity of speaking to one's children and grandchildren.

Question: What dangers and warnings does Pharaoh tell Moses and Aaron they will suffer if they leave Egypt and go into the wilderness?

Answer: The *Midrash* tells of the verbal exchange between Pharaoh and Moses and Aaron. Pharaoh as we know had some abilities in regard to magic and astrology. Pharaoh told Moses and Aaron that if the Children of Israel were let go "I predict that your people will experience a lot of bloodshed in the wilderness." When Pharaoh saw this star, *Ra'ah* (evil), in the heavens he saw it as an omen of blood and killing. He interpreted this sign to mean that the Children of Israel would suffer bloodshed and murder in the desert.

Rashi explained that Moses took note of Pharaoh's prediction. He prayed to God to prevent this vision of bloodshed from coming true. When the Children of Israel were in the desert, they committed the sin of the Golden Calf, an act so terrible that the Almighty wanted to destroy the Children of Israel. However, Moses prayed to God and told Him that if the Israelites would die by His hand then all generations would believe that God did take them [Israel] out in evil *(ra'ah)*. Instead, the Children of Israel were circumcised in the desert, thereby transforming the judgment of blood into one of mercy (*Rashi, Exodus 10:10*).

Question: What is the difference between the plague of darkness and the rest of the plagues?

Answer: Moses activated all the other plagues with his staff. To initiate the plague of darkness, God instructed Moses to raise only his arms to the Heavens and to look at the sky. Then there was darkness.

Question: God commanded Moses before the last plague, the slaying of the firstborn, "Please talk to the people that every individual man/woman has to borrow from his Egyptian fellow man/woman, silver and gold trinkets. And God granted the Children of Israel kindness to the Egyptians..." *(Exodus 11:2-3).* What does this mean?

Answer: God requested of the Children of Israel to collect whatever they could from the Egyptians right before they left Egypt. They had been enslaved to Pharaoh without compensation and were therefore entitled to keep the gold and silver from the Egyptians as payment for their years of work. This was God's promise to Abraham in a previous prophecy. In *Genesis 15:118,* God told Abraham that his descendants would be slaves in a strange land, and they would leave from there with great wealth. Now God was fulfilling His promise to the Jewish nation (*Babylonian Talmud, Brachot 9a*).

Question: Why did God methodically and deliberately bring ten plagues on the Egyptians?

Answer: The *Midrash* suggests that the Almighty was employing a strategy employed by countries attempting to defeat their enemy. You cut off the enemies' water supply (blood); then use loud noises such as drummers (frogs); then archers (lice); then look for allies to join the battle (wild beasts); then attempt to dwindle the food supply by causing a pestilence; then deplete the enemies' army (boils); come closer to the enemies' cities, hurling missles to destroy the walls; then looking to conquer the city, finishing off what the missles did not (locusts); once inside the city taking prisoners, (darkness), and finally killing the leadership of your enemies' camp (slaying of the firstborn).

The Almighty brought ten plagues to punish Pharaoh for his denial of God's existence as Creator of the universe, which was brought about by *Ten Pronouncements*. Also Abraham had withstood ten tests so his enemies should bear ten plagues. These plagues came from the elements: water, earth, air to show that the Almighty is Master of them all.

Question: If God really wanted to fulfill his promise to Abraham by giving his descendants great wealth, why is it done by "borrowing" from the Egyptians instead of acquiring the wealth in a different manner?

Answer: Holocaust survivors told me that when the Allied armies came to the concentration camps and liberated them, they did not want to keep anything. Their only wish was to be freed from slavery. By analogy, the Egyptian exile lasted many more years. Why would the Jewish people want to carry heavy gold vessels while traveling for long distances in the wilderness and then to the Holy Land? As we mentioned above, God promised that He would redeem the Jewish nation and, therefore, God ordered them to take riches and wealth (*Kli Yakar*).

Question: While executing the ten plagues, why did God make a mockery of the Egyptians?

Answer: The Almighty was extracting from the Egyptians measure for measure for the wrongs they had brought upon the Israelites.

Question: Why was it necessary that Moses be shown the new moon?

Answer: The word "month" *chodesh* in Hebrew shares the same root word as *chadash* or "newness." A new moon represents a new beginning. It was on the first day of the Hebrew month of Nisan that the Almighty tells Moses and Aaron that the Children of Israel will be freed during that month. They were told therefore to count this month, Nisan, as the first month of their year.

God wanted Moses to "see" that a new period in Jewish history was taking place. It is at this point in history that the Almighty tells Moses that from this point forward it will be man's obligation to usher in the new month. Moses was given all of the particulars as to how to judge the occurrence of the new moon, which then would usher in the new month. This has been passed down through the Oral Torah.

The Exodus was counted as the first month, and all subsequent months were counted as the second from the going out of Egypt, third…, and so on.

The secular calendar follows the solar year, the sun cycle, and consists of 365 days. The Jewish calendar follows the lunar system, the moon cycle, and is approximately 354 days. To make up the difference of close to 11 days, every few years is a leap year, after which we actually end up a few days ahead of the solar year. The leap year serves as a reminder that everyone has an opportunity from time to time to make up for what one has failed to accomplish in the past.

Question: What was the first *mitzvah* given to the Jewish people as a whole nation through Moses *(Exodus 12:2)*?

Answer: The first *mitzvah* of *Rosh Chodesh,* the blessing of the new moon escorting in the new month. The word *rosh* means "head," the "beginning." Just as we count the days of the week to remember the Sabbath (the creation), we count the months to remember the Exodus or the recreation of the Jewish people.

Question: How is *Rosh Chodesh* celebrated?

Answer: As we have stated *rosh chodesh* is the first day of each Jewish month. Although it is not a holiday per se it does have some added holiness to it. An additional prayer service is added on that day. Some people serve more elaborate meals and dress in a somewhat nicer fashion than they would do on other days. Some people abstain from unneccessary work.

155

Question: Why did the plague of the slaying of the firstborn child and animal occur at midnight rather than during the day?

Answer: There were people who believed that the sun was a god. They would therefore attribute these slayings to the sun rather than to God. Midnight represents a period of total darkness (*Kings 11 25:4*) in which there is no hope except to look to Heaven and pray to God.

Question: According to Jewish history, how many miracles happened at midnight?

Answer: A famous song at the end of the *Passover Haggaddah* is called, "*It Happened At Midnight.*" It describes eleven miracles that the prophet Zachariah called "God's miracles in the *mid of night.*" They were:

Abraham's victory over King Nimrod and the four kings.

God appeared in a dream to Avimelech, king of Garar, and told hi that he would die because he took Abraham's wife Sarah (*Genesis 20:3*).

God appeared to Laban and warned him not to hurt Jacob (*Genesis 31:24*).

Jacob defeated the angel who represented Esau (*Genesis 32:25*).

During the tenth plague, the firstborn of the Egyptian people died (*Exodus 12:29*).

General Sisrah, an enemy of the Jewish people, was destroyed (*Judges 4:15, 5:20*).

Sanhariv, an evil military leader, fought to destroy Jerusalem with a collaborator, Ravshaka. Sanhariv's army disappeared (*Kings II 19:35*).

The statue of King Nebuchadnezar was smashed, including its base (*Daniel 3*).

Daniel interpreted Nebuchadnezar's dream (*Daniel 5:17-30*).

Nebuchadnezar's grandson, Belshtzar was killed after he drank from the temple's vessels (*Daniel 8*).

King Achashvarosh could not sleep, so at midnight, he called for a reading from his chronicles. This consequently redeemed the nation of Israel (*Esther 6*).

Question: Why is the land of Israel known as the land of milk and honey?

Answer: Milk flows from goats and honey flows from dates and figs. These products are found in abundance in the Holy Land. The sages also tell us these are allusions to the knowledge of Torah.

Question: What is the reason that every firstborn Jewish male should fast the day before Passover?

Answer: The reason goes back to the last plague. "It was in the middle of the night, that the Lord struck every firstborn in the land of Egypt, from Pharaoh's firstborn son to the firstborn son of the poorest class..." (*Exodus 14:29-30*). There was chaos when the Almighty sent this tenth plague upon the Egyptian people. This plague caused the most suffering for the Egyptians. In commemoration of this dramatic event and in appreciation to the Almighty for sparing the Hebrew people, firstborn males fast the day before the Passover.

Question: Is fasting the only way for firstborn males to commemorate their rescue by God from the Egyptians?

Answer: One may substitute the completion of studying a Tractate from the *Mishnah* or the *Gemorah* (Oral Torah) for fasting on this day. At the conclusion of the study period, it is customary to have a special party in honor of the completion of the book.

I would like to share with you an important story I witnessed myself seven years ago. It occurred on the eve of Passover when I was called to be the tenth man for minyan in the home of one of the oldest rabbis in Israel. Rabbi Dov Be'er Eliezerov, who is in his upper 90s is known to be a tremendously pious man who studies day and night. His appearance is still vivid to me: a long white beard, a chassidic hat and long black coat, and a face reminiscent of a great Rembrandt portrait. It was a tremendous honor for me to sit with such a great man and witness his *siyum* during the Passover season. It was 2 a.m., and we were learning, when suddenly from outside a knock and moan were heard at Rabbi Eliezerov's front door. A friend of mine opened the door and, to his surprise, he found a large dog sitting there. He closed the door and returned to the table. Moments later, moaning and banging were heard again. Again my friend opened the door and saw the dog. He chuckled, closed the door, and returned to the table. Seconds later, we heard the same intense moaning and banging. This time, I went and saw the dog. He had a strange and woebegone look. I decided to leave the door open and, upon returning to the table, explained to the old rabbi what was happening. He felt that the dog should be allowed to enter the room, and the dog eagerly walked in. The dog immediately focused on the rabbi and sat near him, licking his shoes and rubbing his head against his legs, crying at the same time. The rabbi took careful note of the dog and finished his *siyum.* He then summoned each member of the group to rise. We did not understand the reason for this and thought the whole scene was comical. In a serious tone, the rabbi summoned the group to say "I forgive you" to the dog. In disbelief, but out of great respect for the rabbi, everyone complied. When the group finished, the rabbi told the dog, "Go in peace and rest in peace." Having heard those words the dog picked itself up, left the room, and was not heard from anymore. After the *siyum* and upon leaving the rabbi's house, we discovered the dog lying dead outside the building.

This story illustrated for me what our sages have told us, that the soul given to each person comes directly from God. Sometimes souls can migrate into animals to fulfill their mission in this world. We never know where a soul may be found, and so we are taught never to judge anyone because our concept of the world is sometimes very narrow. In this case, a soul was undoubtedly returned to receive final forgiveness from one of the greatest, most righteous men of our time. Spirituality is all around us; we must only look carefully to see it everywhere.

Question: During the entire Passover holiday, God strongly warns against eating *Chometz*. What is *Chometz?*

Answer: *Exodus 12:15* says "For a seven-day period...but on the first day you shall remove chometz from your homes." *Chometz* is normally a classification of foodstuffs that contain one or more of the five grains, has a leavening agent in it, and has been allowed to rise for a period of eighteen minutes or longer. Jews are not allowed to have in their possession anything containing *chometz*. Examples of these would be breads, rolls, bagels, cheerios, and things of that nature. There are also other items which contain *chometz* and cannot be used or owned on Passover, such as certain types of shampoos, soaps, the list goes on. Competent rabbinic authorities should be consulted on this matter.

Question: What is the main commandment in the *Passover Seder* and why?

Answer: The main commandment during the *Passover Seder* is to teach our children from generation to generation the story of our ancestors in Egypt. The reason is to recall our historical background and to understand events in the Torah.

Question: How many children are described in the Passover story and why?

Answer: There are four sons in the Passover story.

One is referred to as the *wise* son. The second is called the *wicked* son. The third son is called *simple*. And the fourth is referred as *one who does not know how to ask*.

The Torah mentions all four sons in different places, but the Torah stresses the importance of uniting and bringing all the children together at the table, especially those who are far away from religious faith or practice.

Question: When your son says to you, "What does this Passover service mean to you? you shall reply to him, 'this is a Passover offering that God separates between the houses of the Egyptians and the houses of the Children of Israel'" *(Exodus 12:26-27)*. The sages refer this question as being asked by wicked son. Why?

Answer: The *wicked* son is really asking his parents why they are doing these services when they were never there. Why celebrate something in which they never were involved and which belongs to the past? The problem with this son is that he himself does not observe the commandment and, worse, he tries to persuade others to follow his example. This son possesses a harmful personality trait in that he ridicules observant people by asking, What is this Passover service? Nonetheless, part of the Passover commandment is to educate all children, including the evil son, with love and with an outstretched arm to bring closer those who have strayed (*Bnai Yissachar, Ritva*).

Question: Why do we eat *matzah* on Passover?

Answer: When the Hebrews were told by the Egyptians to pack up and leave Egypt, it was the middle of the night. With no time to spare, the Hebrews grabbed their household belongings, food, and drink, and hurried to escape. They made cakes and breads very quickly without time to wait to let the dough rise or bake more than 18 minutes. The end product was flat bread known as a *matzah*. Therefore, to commemorate these events, one eats *matzah* on Passover (*Exodus 12:39*).

Question: The Hebrews were in such a hurry to leave Egypt that they didn't have time to take anything but bare provisions for themselves. What does this mean?

Answer: The Hebrews showed their greatness by demonstrating their tremendous belief in God. When they began their journey to Israel, they did not ask, "How can we go without enough food for the journey into the wilderness?" They trusted that God would somehow provide them with food and always watch over them (*Rashi*).

Question: How many times does God command us to teach our children the story of the Exodus from Egypt, and why are we commanded to teach it to them specifically that number?

Answer: It is written four times in the Torah that God commands us to teach our children the story of the Exodus from Egypt.

"When your children ask you: What manner of service is this?" (*Exodus 12:26*).

"You shall tell your son what happened in Egypt" (*Exodus 13:8*).

"When your son will ask you tomorrow: What is the meaning of this holiday? You shall describe to him how God, with His strong hand, removed us from Egypt" (*Exodus 13:14*).

"If your son asks you tomorrow, 'What are the laws and decrees that our God commands you?'" (*Deuteronomy 6:20*).

This symbolizes the four types of sons described in the *Passover Haggadah*: wise, evil, simple, and ignorant.

Question: What is the meaning of the commandment of *tefillin* (putting small boxes called phylacteries, in which there are holy written parchments, on one's arm and head)?

Answer: This is a sign between the people and God to commemorate the Exodus. The *tefillin*, wrapped around the weaker arm next to the heart, symbolizes that one is binding one's desires and thoughts to do God's will and service. The *tefillin* on the head, which is near the brain, symbolizes that one's soul is motivated to do God's service.

The *tefillin* is a medicinal aide to protect the body from the evil inclination (*Sefer Hachinuch Mitzvah 421*).

The *tefillin* purifies one's body from negative external influences and keeps one safe.

The act of putting on *tefillin* is an educational process that not only reminds a person of the Exodus from Egypt but, at the same time, demonstrates to children the importance of performing mitzvot. When children observe an adult putting on the *tefillin*, they are familiarizing themselves with an important Jewish tradition.

The act of putting on the *tefillin* serves two purposes. Wrapping the *tefillin* straps around the head reminds us of what God did for us by taking us out of Egypt. Wrapping the *tefillin* on the arm reminds us of the physical exodus of leaving Egypt (*Chizkuni*).

Fulfilling this commandment gives one encouragement even in what is sometimes referred to as the weak hand. In exile one feels weak and filled with doubt. The act of putting on *tefillin* gives strength (*Meshach Chachma*).

Question: Why do we put *tefillin* on every day?

Answer: Putting on *tefillin* fulfills a God-given commandment just as each of us have physical/material needs that we fulfill on a daily basis, such as drinking coffee in the morning, daily jogging, watching television, reading the newspaper. It is more important to have a daily dose of spirituality, which putting on *tefillin* provides. Putting on *tefillin* activates the connection between man and God.

Question: Why do we first put *tefillin* on the hand before the head?

Answer: We first put *tefillin* on the hand/arm close to our heart to show that we first physically follow God's commandments and then we try to understand. Thus, we first obey God's commandments, and then we try to understand their purposes and meanings (*Sha'ary Emunah 63: 218*).

Question: Why do we put *tefillin* on the weak hand?

Answer: The strong hand symbolizes power and victory, so to show us that only God is the strong hand, we put the *tefillin* on the weaker hand (*Kli Yakar*).

Question: Is there any symbolism in the construction of the *tefillin?*

Answer: Yes. In the head there are four senses: taste, smell, hearing, and sight. So the *tefillin* for the head has four separate compartments. The hand has only one sensation, touch (*Mairi*), so this phylactery has a single compartment.

Question: What is the connection between the commandment of *tefillin* to slavery endured in Egypt by the Children of Israel?

Answer: The four passages included in *tefillin* are basic to Judaism. Two speak to the exodus from Egypt, and a Jew's responsibility to God. The two passages from the *Shema* express the concept of the *Oneness of God* and His Kingship, reward and punishment, and the responsibility to observe the commandments. All of these concepts must always be with us, upon our arm that symbolizes action and is opposite the head, which is the seat of emotion. And they must be upon our head, the seat of intellect, which enables us to be conscious of our responsibilities. The message of the Exodus is more than basic, it is something that we must be ever vigilant about, so we wear *tefillin* which become those constant reminders to remember what they are and to do the commandments. Whether these *mitzvot* are minor or major is not the issue, because they will forever reinforce our faith.

Question: We are commanded to wear *tefillin*. We wear them on our head and hand. Are we performing one or two *mitzvoth* when we put them on?

Answer: *Rambam* says that each one is a separate commandment. His son Abraham disagrees and says that placing them on your head and hand is considered one action, therefore one *mitzvah*.

Question: How many commandments, positive and negative, are there in *Parshat Bo?*

Answer: There are twenty commandments of which nine are positive, and eleven are negative.

Bashalach
Chapters: 13:17 - 17:16

Synopsis:

The Children of Israel went to the sea; they were trapped between the water and the Egyptians; God split the sea; the Song of the Sea; the manna in the Wilderness; the complainers; the war against Amalek.

Question: How does slavery in Egypt parallel life in modern times?

Answer: The bondage in Egypt symbolizes, on a grand scale, our smaller personal struggles. There are many unpleasant things in everyone's life to which one is "enslaved," for example, health, finances, and family problems. One must learn to deal with these things in the appropriate manner so that one can be emancipated.

Question: Why do we mention the miracle of the splitting of the sea every day in the morning prayer?

Answer: The morning prayers were written and established with the intention that future generations should remember that we live by the miracle of God's grace, which we do not always recognize or appreciate. The sages say "the recipient of a miracle does not always recognize the miracle." Therefore, the sages put the song of the Almighty splitting the sea in the morning prayer to remind us that God's hand performs all miracles (*Babylonian Talmud Nidah 31b*).

Question: When Pharaoh sent the Hebrew people away, why did God not lead them on the shortest route through the desert to the Promised Land?

Answer: As *Rashi* explains, the people might have changed their minds. They could have had second thoughts about leaving and desire to return to Egypt. Therefore, instead of the direct route, God had the Hebrews go on an indirect route. The sages point out that the Almighty wanted the Israelites to be confronted by circumstances where they would see constant miracles in order to survive. The *Sforno* says that the Almighty wanted to keep the people from meeting people who would tell them that Pharaoh was planning to chase them to bring them back, thereby intimidating them into returning on their own to Egypt.

Question: How do the commentators interpret "the Hebrews left Egypt *chamushim*, armed" *(Exodus 13:18)?*

Answer: According to some commentators it meant they left Egypt with army equipment, swords and shields (*Midrash; Old Rashi; Unkelus*).

In Hebrew, the word *chamushim* means one-fifth. Our sages tell us that only one-fifth of the Hebrews left Egypt, while the other four-fifths, because they refused to leave, died during the three days of the plague of darkness (*Rashi*).

Question: How did Moses know where Joseph was buried?

Answer: According to the *Midrash* Sarach, Asher's daughter and Jacob's granddaughter, was one of the elders who was still alive going back to the era of Joseph. When Sarach was a young girl, she informed Jacob that Joseph was still alive. Consequently, Jacob blessed her to live a long life. Now an old woman, Sarach told Moses that she remembered how the Egyptians placed Joseph's bones inside a metal casket, placed the casket in the Nile, and then prayed that the Nile would be blessed. Sarach also said that Pharaoh's advisors told him to put the metal casket in the river in order to delay the Children of Israel's departure from Egypt because they had sworn to take Joseph's bones out of Egypt with them when they left.

The *Midrash* describes how Moses went to the Nile, took a board of gold, and wrote the Name of God on it. Then he put this board in the water and screamed, "Joseph, Joseph, it is time that we take part in God's redemption. We are going to the Holy Land. You must come with us now, or we are released from the oath." The casket immediately rose to the water's surface, and Moses took it easily (*Midrash Rabba*).

Question: How did the Children of Israel survive in the wilderness when it was so hot during the day and freezing at night?

Answer: The *Pillar of Cloud* will not leave them by day and the *Pillar of Fire* will not leave them by night (*Exodus 13:22*). God's miracle was that there were two pillars that went in front of the Children of Israel: one of clouds, the other of fire. When one pillar would leave, the other would appear, thus providing special protection from the elements. The *Pillar of Cloud* would provide protection from the heat and sun of the desert; the *Pillar of Fire* would keep them warm and provide light at night (*Rashi*).

Question: "Pharaoh and his huge army with chariot-driven horses were gaining on them. The Children of Israel saw that the Egyptians were close behind, and they became frightened. They cried out to God. They said to Moses, Were there no graves in Egypt that now you took us here in the desert to die? What are you doing to us by taking us from Egypt?" *(Exodus 14: 10-11)*. How do the biblical commentators explain this situation?

Answer: All of the commentators agree that this was a test of faith: To what extent would the Children of Israel follow the way of God? The test of faith, which God gave the Children of Israel, was that they had to pray to God for help instead of looking to Moses for help. They now needed to place their complete trust in the Almighty because it would only be through their adherence to the commandments that they would survive as a nation.

A relevant story illustrates the situation. Two Arab terrorists, suicide bombers, went to the central market in Jerusalem. After the bombs in their suitcases exploded there was terrible chaos, and many people were left critically injured. A dentist who practiced nearby left his clinic to see if he could help some of the people before the ambulances came. While he was helping people, a woman came to him frantic that her father needed his attention immediately or he would die. Noticing that the dentist was not reacting quickly, the woman got upset and started screaming that it was an emergency, and he must come at once. When still the dentist delayed, the woman finally looked up to Heaven and said, "Oh Lord, you're the only one who could help my father!" At that point, the dentist ran to help her father. After the dentist saved her father, the woman asked him why he didn't react immediately. The dentist replied, "I am only a dentist, and I knew that I was limited in the help that I could give. There were other people who weren't as critically injured, that I knew I could help. You came and depended entirely on me to help your father. So I caused you despair, and only when I heard you cry out directly to the Creator did I run to help your father."

Question: When the sea was in front of the Hebrew people and the Egyptians were behind them, who was the first Hebrew to jump into the water?

Answer: The first to jump into the turbulent water was Nachshon, son of Aminadav. After him followed some of the leaders of the tribes. As they walked further and the water rose to their mouths, the miracle occurred. God split the sea moments before they would have drowned (*Babylonian Talmud Sotah 36b; Yalkut Me'am Loez*). The term *nachshon* is used today in Israeli slang to depict extraordinary courage and strength.

Question: How was Nachshon rewarded for his act of bravery and faith?

Answer: Nachshon became leader of the tribe of Judah, the most distinguished tribe of Israel (*Numbers 7:12*).

Question: "God says to Moses, why do you beg me, speak to the Children of Israel and let them go forward" *(Exodus 14:15)*. What is wrong with Moses begging and crying to God?

Answer: When Moses called to God for help in this situation, God instructed Moses to take action, saying, "I will escort them, and you have to move them forward" (*Rashi*). This teaches us that there is a time and place for prayers, as well as actions.

Question: How is the splitting of the sea a miracle of God?

Answer: The biblical commentators have many different views of this. The simple explanation is that the outstretched hand of Moses brought about the split, which God caused by a strong wind (*Ibn Ezra*). The reason for the wind was to plant doubt in the minds of the pursuing Egyptians that it was merely the wind, not God, and therefore the Egyptians continued their suicidal plunge after the Israelites.

Question: "Israel saw the greatness of God's hand in Egypt. They feared God and they believed in God and his servant Moses" *(Exodus 14:41)*. Is this a positive or negative sentence?

Answer: As was previously discussed there are commentators who interpret it in a very positive way, saying that the Children of Israel sang the *Song of the Sea* as part of their faith in God and his servant Moses.

Some commentators, however, interpret this phrase in a negative way. The Israelites only believed in God after they saw the miracles indicating a previous lack of faith.

Question: Why is it customary to stand up during the recitation of the *Song of the Sea?*

Answer: Moses and the Children of Israel sang the *Song of the Sea* at a time of euphoric gratitude to God. The song was sung with great joy and beautiful melody in appreciation to God for His cumulative miracles. This episode highlighted one of the most unique times, when all the people were united in a spirit of total gratitude to the Creator of the universe. All attention, all focus was on God. In this special moment in history, the egocentricity of each individual temporarily evaporated as a nation became one entity. All people of all socioeconomic backgrounds merged; the lowest servant was on equal footing with a prophet. The biblical commentators explain that all bigotry, jealousy, and negative habits disappeared.

The sages explain that the two sentences that introduce the *Song of the Sea (Exodus 14:30-31)* contain the seventy-two letter name of the Almighty. This is the only place where it occurs; therefore as a sign of respect, recognition, honor, and thanks, we stand when this portion is read on the Sabbath.

Question: What is the general custom regarding standing during the reading of the Torah?

Answer: There are different customs. Some in order to give honor, stand up the entire time the Torah Scroll is open. Every community stands up during the recitation of the list below:

In the *Book of Genesis,* at the beginning of the book (*Chapter 1 to 2:3*) which is read on *Simchat Torah* (the end of the festival of *Sukkot*), and on the Sabbath when reading the last verse of the *Book of Genesis (50:26).*

In the *Book of Exodus (15:1-21)* we stand on the Sabbath when the *Song of the Sea* is read; on the Sabbath that the Ten Commandments are read (*Exodus 20:2-14*); on public fast days when the portion in which Moses begs for forgiveness for the sin of the Golden Calf (*Exodus 32:12-14, 33:12-23, 34:1-10*). Those fast days are the third of *Tishrei,* tenth of *Tevet.* We also stand and on the Sabbath on which the end of book of Exodus is read (*40:38*).

In the *Book of Leviticus (27:34)* on the Sabbath when the last verses of the book are read.

In the *Book of Numbers (36:13)* on the Sabbath when the last verses of the book are read.

In the *Book of Deuteronomy (5:6-18)* on the Sabbath when the **Ten Commandments** are read and the end of the book (and the Torah is completed), which is on *Simchat Torah* (end of the holiday of *Sukkot*).

Question: God punished the Egyptians measure for measure. How do we see this?

Answer: When Pharaoh wanted to kill every Jewish firstborn, he said to throw the male babies in the water. Later, God punished the Egyptians for this evil plan by drowning the Egyptian soldiers in the water instead (*Midrash*). This reinforces the biblical statement that "whoever blesses the Hebrew people will be blessed, and whoever curses the Hebrew people will be cursed" (*Deuteronomy 25; Leviticus 30*).

Question: How did the Egyptians die in the Red Sea?

Answer: The sages tell us the Egyptians died in the Red Sea in three different ways, according to their wickedness toward the Hebrew people. One group drowned immediately. This group inflicted the least amount of suffering upon the enslaved Hebrews, and for this God gave them a less horrible death. Another group got trapped in the whirlpools and died. A third group suffered the worst death. They were thrown very high in the waves and came crashing down repeatedly until they died. They were tortured the most, since that group was cruelest to the Hebrew people. The Midrash says that all the dead Egyptians were flung onto the land in front of the Hebrew people. This was to show the Hebrews the actual evidence of what became of the Egyptians. God wanted to further demonstrate His miracles and eliminate the worry that the Egyptians would come after them (*Midrash Rabba, Yalkut Shimoni*).

Question: What happened to all of the Egyptians' belongings of gold, silver, and clothing, that went into the water with them?

Answer: The *Midrash* says the sea spit them out and it was thrown to the Children of Israel. This is called the *Sea's Loot.*

Question: Who is the only one who did not touch the *Sea's Loot*, and how was he rewarded?

Answer: Moses was the only one who did not touch the *Sea's Loot.* God rewarded him with pieces of sapphire that were mounted on the Tablets of stone on which the Almighty had inscribed the Ten Commandments (*Yalkut*).

Question: From all the Egyptians who chased the Children of Israel to the sea, who was saved?

Answer: Only Pharaoh was saved. Pharaoh went back as a witness to tell his people and the other nations what had happened at the sea (*Yalkut*).

Question: "Your right hand is a strong power, your right hand destroyed the enemy" *(Exodus 15:6)*. Why is "your right hand" repeated twice?

Answer: One hand of the Almighty is enough to save Israel and to destroy the enemy (*Rashi*).

Question: "The enemy says I pursue, I gather the wealth, I satisfy my lust, I brought out my sword, and I became impressed with my hand" *(Exodus 15:9)*. Why is this in an illogical order? It should be, "The enemy says: I pursue; I brought out my sword; I gather the wealth; I divide up the loot; I satisfy my lust, and I became impressed with my hand."

Answer: When the Children of Israel saw the Egyptians chasing them, they dropped their possessions and ran for fear of their lives. Therefore, the order "The enemy (Egyptians) says: I pursue; I gather their wealth; I divide up the loot; I satisfy my lust, and then; I will bring out my sword, and my hand makes me proud" (*Ramav*).

Question: About whom did the sages use the phrase, "He prophesies and he does not even realize what he prophesies"?

Answer: This phrase refers to Moses, who was a holy, special, and powerful leader. According to *Rambam* and the Jewish tradition, Moses is referred to as the highest of the highest prophets. Therefore, every word he says is meaningful. The main part of this *parsha* is the *Song of the Sea*, sung with the Israelites after God split the sea. Moses, along with the Hebrews, sang jubilantly and spontaneously. Right before the end of the song, Moses sang *TeviaMo* which means, "You will bring them" (*Exodus 15:17*) instead of saying *TeviaNu*, which means, "I will bring us." This song suggests that Moses would not enter the land. This song was sung long before Moses was punished for hitting the rock rather than talking to it. As it is written at the end of *Deuteronomy (32:52)*, "You [Moses] will see the Holy Land, but you will not enter with them."

Throughout history, there have been leaders who have exhibited traits opposite from Moses'. They believed that their every utterance was monumental. Clearly, this is not something to strive for. Moses was a humble and honest leader. Biblical commentators explain that this is why he was chosen by God for such an exalted position.

Question: What happened at the place that was called *Marah*?

Answer: After the Hebrews finished the *Song of the Sea*, they traveled from the Red Sea. They walked three days in the desert and could not find water. They finally found water but it was bitter and undrinkable. They rested there regardless and named the place *Marah*, meaning bitter water. The people complained to Moses and said, "What should we drink?" Moses called out to God for help. God then sent a ray of light pointing to a bitter-tasting tree. Moses took pieces of that tree, threw them into the water, and, as explained in the mystical teachings of *The Pardes on the Zohar*, "negative plus negative equals positive," the bitter tree mixing with bitter water made the water sweet.

Question: What do we learn from the story of *Marah (Exodus 15:25)*?

Answer: The biblical commentators have two different opinions: one is that God tested the Children of Israel to see how they would accept His authority in a situation in which they did not feel His Presence, as they did in Egypt during the ten plagues and the splitting of the sea. The result was disappointing. After witnessing so many miracles in the past, the Hebrews still showed impatience and a lack of faith by complaining. The other opinion is that the incident of the tree and the water (bitter + bitter = sweet), reminded the Hebrews that they are dependent upon the Almighty.

Question: What subjects did Moses teach the Children of Israel while in *Marah?*

Answer: Moses taught the Children of Israel the laws of Sabbath, the commandment about the red calf, and the rules and regulations between man and his fellowman (*Rashi*). The *Rambam* says they were learning only to gauge their receptivity, because as of yet they were not bound by the commandments. The nation was to taste Torah to see if they liked the taste and would be willing to accept it.

Question: "If you listen to the voice of the Lord and are honest in the eyes of the Lord, fulfill His commandments, and observe His laws, then any illness that you saw in Egypt I will not bring upon you because I am the Lord who heals you" *(Exodus 15:26)*. What is the meaning of this sentence?

Answer: "If you listen to the voice of the Almighty" refers to people's unquestioning obedience to Torah law. "And you be honest in the eyes of the Lord" means to be honest even without being watched. "Fulfill His *commandments* and observe His *ordinances*" includes all the prohibitions that are not so readily understandable, such as the red cow or eating of pork or mixing of wool and linen (*Babylonian Talmud, Yoma 67b*). "Any ill that you saw in Egypt I will not bring upon you because I am the Lord Who heals you" means that God would give us the Torah and the commandments so that we will not fall into spiritual illness (*Mechilta, Rashi*).

Question: What did the Children of Israel complain about in the Tzin wilderness?

Answer: One group of people complained, "We wish we could go back to Egypt where we had great food." They forgot all the suffering and hard work they were forced to do for the Pharaoh.

Question: What did Moses reply to the desert complainers?

Answer: Moses tried to reassure the people and offer hope. Moses replied on behalf of God, "Every day, everyone will receive a portion of the food (*manna*) directly from Heaven. It will be enough to satisfy everyone's appetite."

Question: How did God use the manna to test the Children of Israel?

Answer: Moses commanded the Children of Israel to take only the quantity of food that they needed for the day. This was a test to see if they believed that tomorrow the manna would come again. On Friday, Erev Sabbath, the people got a double portion, enough for that day and for the Sabbath. Moses warned the Children of Israel not to collect the manna on the Sabbath, for this would constitute work, prohibited on the Sabbath. God commanded the people to rest on the Sabbath.

Question: According to tradition which miracles happened with the manna?

Answer: The *Righteous* found the manna at their door. The *Disbelievers* had a very difficult time finding theirs; they had to go out and search for it.

For the *Righteous*, the manna was ready to eat; for the *Disbeliever*, it had to be ground and baked.

The *Righteous* took what they needed and no more. The *Disbeliever* tried to hoard it, but the saved manna was filled with worms.

It says also when the babies put the manna into their mouths it became liquid and they drank it. When the Children of Israel finished collecting the manna the surplus became liquid and the animals drank it. The manna became whatever the individual desired it to be.

Question: "God said to Moses I give you food directly from Heaven...so I can test them [the Hebrews]" *(Exodus 16:4)*. Which "test" is God giving them?

Answer: *Sforno* explains that their reaction to kindness was also being tested. *Ohr Hachayim* explained that once they got the manna from Heaven and were free from worry, God would see if they would worship him properly. Until this point, the Hebrews had the excuse that they needed to concentrate on their enslavement, and now that they were free, God tested them to see if they would follow His ways. The modern version of this is the test of the rich person: What does such a person do with his wealth – does he use it to enhance selfish or hedonistic drives or does he donate to charitable and community causes?

According to the *Ramban*, however, the test was one of dependence – they had to deal with a foreign food, as well as the lack of settled habitation in the wilderness. It was a difficult test, which required them to have complete faith in God. This is the equivalent to the test of the poor person who has to struggle with hardships and still show faith in God.

Rashbam and *Ibn Ezra* explain that the test is that all people, both rich and poor, should acknowledge their need for God every day. The sages say in the *Talmud (Yoma 76b)*, the disciples of Rabbi Shimon ben Yochai ask him, "Why didn't the manna come just once a year? He replied that since there was a chance that the manna would not fall the next day, the Hebrews were forced to depend on and believe in God's help and thus gain appreciation for and give gratitude to God for all his kindness on a daily basis."

The commentators also ask, what is the goal of the test? Why did God put the people through this test? *Rambam* disagrees with the opinion of many commentators who state that the purpose was to reward the people who passed the test. He says that it is impossible that the Creator of the Universe tortured his creations for the purpose of rewarding them. *Rambam* also does not believe that God would want to test the people to see how much they would follow Him. He says that God knows human nature. Therefore *Rambam* explains, the manna proves to every human being that whoever worshipped God with a full heart would be rewarded with prosperity and nourishment, even in the wilderness.

Question: According to the story of the manna, what is the right direction that God wants the people to follow?

Answer: *Rabbi Elazar HaMudai* says "Whoever has food for today and asks 'What am I going to eat tomorrow?' has a lack of faith." His conclusion is do not worry about tomorrow, just work hard enough to make a living today and make each day meaningful.

Rabbi Shimon ben Yochai says "The Torah was given to the manna receiver, those who sit and learn Torah and do not pay attention to where they get their nourishment." His conclusion is when people do exactly what the Creator wants, they are prosperous through someone else's labor and without any worry.

Rabbi Yehoshua says I bless you in whatever you do. The conclusion drawn is that a person has to work for money and worry about tomorrow and not wait for miracles.

Question: Was the phenomena of manna a positive event or not?

Answer: The Hebrews' reliance on God's delivery of manna is complex. The reliance on God's generosity is a contradiction because on one hand, it makes people seem to be doing nothing and receiving a free handout. This may foster laziness and the negative trait of ingratitude over time. When one is idle or has unlimited free time, one can become sinful. The fact that a person works hard can be a good thing. However, when a person is busy working, he is occupied with making a living. Thus, one may be saved from sin, but one may be so busy that one neglects to study the Torah or think about God (*Chovat Halevavot*).

Additionally, since the manna was divided equally for all, competition and jealousy among the people was minimal (*Tifaret Shlomo*).

Question: How do we know that Moses was the most humble man who ever lived?

Answer: The *Babylonian Talmud (Chulin 88a)* describes how our ancestors were humble people.

When Abraham begged God not to destroy the evil cities of Sodom and Gomorrah, he said, "Please, my Lord, let me speak to you even though I am only dust" (*Genesis 18:27*). This is a very humble statement, but still Moses is more humble than that. While Abraham is considering himself dust, he is still considering himself something. Dust might not be much, but it is still something. Moses does not even credit himself with that. Moses would ask the people, not just God, "Who am I?" (*Exodus 16:8*), meaning that Moses considered himself a nobody. Therefore, the Torah called Moses "The most humble from all of mankind on the earth."

Question: What was the purpose of God commanding Moses to put some manna into a jar and to keep it?

Answer: The jar kept the manna fresh through the time of the Temple. It is a miracle that it did not spoil. This jar was meant as a reminder to always have trust in God.

Question: "They did not obey Moses and people left it over..." Who is the they the Torah is referring to?

Answer: The quote is from *Exodus 16:20*. The *they* is Datan and Aviram. They were members of the Hebrew community who tried to create hostility among the people. Their goal was to destroy the Hebrew community from the inside. For example:

When Moses left Pharaoh's palace he saw an Egyptian trying to kill a Hebrew. Moses used the Name of God to stop the Egyptian from murdering the Hebrew. Consequently, the Egyptian died. Later, Datan and Aviram informed the Pharaoh that Moses killed an Egyptian. Pharaoh pursued Moses to kill him. Moses fled to Midyan (*Exodus 2:11-16*). In the wilderness, when the Hebrews complained to Moses about the lack of food, Moses begged God to help them. God decided to send them manna straight from Heaven, but there were a few rules regarding the manna. For example, God commanded that on the Sabbath, one must not carry outside of one's tent, travel far, gather food from the earth or trees, and other rules, because the Sabbath is supposed to be a day of rest. Datan and Aviram violated God's commandments of the Sabbath by leaving the tent and trying to find extra manna in the fields. This they did even though Moses clarified all of God's rules of the Sabbath with all the Hebrews in advance. One of the miracles God gave to the Hebrews was that the manna gathered on Friday for the Sabbath remained fresh until after the Sabbath was over. Datan and Aviram also disobeyed Moses by taking more manna than they needed, so at the end of the day it spoiled and was filled with worms (*Exodus 16:27*).

The Torah also related the story of *Korach* (*Numbers 16:1-35*). He belonged to the highest tribe of Levy and, therefore, had high honor and recognition. Even though Korach was a relative of Moses, he was jealous of Moses' leadership, and so he took with him 250 followers and made a disgraceful campaign against Moses (*Numbers 16*). Datan and Aviram were the campaign managers. They insulted Moses publicly and verbally abused him. Datan and Aviram's lives ended in an earthquake. The earth swallowed them up, while Korach and his followers, the 250 who offered the incense, were consumed by fire (*Numbers 16:24-33*).

Question: What do we do today to remember the miracle of the Hebrews in the desert and the manna that sustained them?

Answer: In the desert, the manna was covered on the top and bottom by dew. This moisture is what preserved its freshness until the end of the day. To commemorate this event today, on the Sabbath, Jewish people put two *challahs* (braided breads) on a *challah* board and covered them with a decorative cloth.

After the morning prayer, it is customary for many communities to recite the portion in the Torah about the manna, to remind one to have absolute faith that all one's nourishment comes directly from heaven.

Question: How many years did the Hebrews eat the manna in the desert?

Answer: Forty years (less thirty days).

Question: The Bible states, "See God gave you the Sabbath, therefore he gave you on Friday a double manna portion. A man will not travel from his place on the Sabbath day" *(Exodus 16:29)*. What did the sages learn from that?

Answer: The sages (*Eruvin 17b, 48a*) learned that we are not allowed to travel beyond a certain point.

Question: Why did God ask Moses to use his staff when performing miracles?

Answer: In the book *The Ethics of the Fathers (Pirkei Avot 5:8)*, it is written that the staff was created by God at the end of the six days of Creation. The staff was transferred from Adam through many ancestors until it reached Moses. On the staff were carved many of the names of God, which showed that God alone was responsible for miracles. Moses was chosen by God to be the middleman. God asked Moses to use the staff so it would be clear to everyone that it was God Who was performing the miracles (*See Exodus 4:17; Sforno*).

Question: For which purposes did Moses use the staff?

Answer: The staff was utilized for many purposes. When activated, Moses used it to bring forth the plagues as well as to initiate the parting of the sea. It was also used in bringing water out from the rock.

Question: The Torah states: "*Amalek* came and fought with Israel in the place called *Rafidim*" *(Exodus 17:8).* Why did *Amalek* come suddenly?

Answer: The Children of Israel showed a lack of faith when they faced a water shortage for a second time. They asked, "Is God with us or not?" God said, "I will send you a dangerous beast that will bite you." The sage *Rashi* tells a fable about a man who took his son on his shoulders and went away into the forest. On the way, the son said, "I want this item," and the father devotedly bent down and gave it to him many different times. One day, while the son was still sitting on his father's shoulders, they met someone. And the son asked this person, "Did you see my father?" The father was upset and said, "You don't know where I am? Soon you will know." The father took his son down from his shoulders, and an animal came and bit the son.

So too, the evil *Amalek* came when the Israelites asked "Where is God? Is He with us or not?" (*Rashi*).

Question: Why did the strong Amalekite army lose the war against the Children of Israel?

Answer: Against all odds, the Children of Israel won the war. They were tired and worn out from Egyptian slavery. The journey into the wilderness further exhausted them. In addition, the Children of Israel were slaves just set free. They had no recent military experience or professional training. On the contrary, the Amalekites were experienced fighters with excellent military skills and equipment. So, why did *Amalek* lose? The *Babylonian Talmud (Rosh Hashanah 29a)* explains that this is an excellent example of God's intervention. God showed everyone that Moses was the only emissary of God. Only when Moses raised his arms to Heaven, and his eyes followed to where his arms pointed as if he were looking to Heaven for God's help, did the Children of Israel win.

In addition, *Rashi* explains that Amalek worked with a wizard, Bilam. Bilam's magic worked at only certain times of the day. Therefore, Moses, who was the prophet of prophets, understood how Bilam performed his evil magic. Moses kept his hands up so that the sun would not move, thereby changing the time of day and undermining Bilam's plans. Amalek lost the war.

Question: Why did God make the war with Amalek last all day?

Answer: If the war had lasted only an hour or so, there would have been people who were skeptical. They may have said, we won the war without the help of God. However, when the war dragged on and they saw that Moses' arms fell and they started to lose, they began to understand that they needed Moses' help. When Moses raised his arms, they started to win again. Only then did they begin to realize that they were absolutely dependent on God and his messenger, Moses. When they honored God by seeing Moses with his arms raised, they won the war against Amalek (*Mishnah Rosh Hashanah 3:8*). As a result of this outcome, honor was brought to God's majesty in front of all the nations surrounding the Israelites (*See Ramban; Rashi; Ohr Hachaim*).

Question: Why did the sages decide that we should read the story of Deborah, a famous Jewish judge (*Judges 4-5*) in the same week that we read the story of God splitting the sea?

Answer: In this *parsha* after God split the sea for the Children of Israel, Moses sang a song to God for the victory won over Pharaoh. By comparison, in the *haftorah*, the prophetess Deborah wrote a song about the wicked General Sisra after he had drowned in the Kishon River. The sages chose that we should read a story from the *Book of Judges* that was similar to the Torah portion of the week.

Yitro
Chapters: 18:1 - 20:23

Synopsis:

Yitro, Moses' father-in-law helped and advised Moses' leadership; Moses went to Mount Sinai; Moses brought down the Ten Commandments.

Question: Who was Yitro?

Answer: Yitro, a Midyanite, was the father of Tziporah, Moses' wife.

Question: When did the story of Yitro happen?

Answer: This is a controversial issue in the *Babylonian Talmud (Zvachim 116a)* and among the Torah commentators as well.

The discussion in the *Talmud (Zvachim 116a)* says Yitro comes prior to the receiving of the Ten Commandments but after the splitting of the sea and the war with Amalek. The other side of the controversy says that having heard that the Israelites had received the Ten Commandments, Yitro joined them.

Among the later commentators there is the *Ramban* who says that Yitro came before the giving of the commandments is proven in *Exodus 18:5,16*. The opposing view is held by the *Ibn Ezra*, who suggests that the Torah mentions Yitro as an example of goodness in the world as opposed to evil as exemplified by Amalek.

Question: What was Yitro's political position *(Exodus 18:1)*?

Answer: Yitro was a high ranking minister of Midyan, a country in the Middle East between Jordan and Saudi Arabia.

Question: How many commandments do we have in *parshat Yitro?*

Answer: The Torah gives seventeen commandments, of which three are positive while fourteen are negative.

Question: Why did Yitro befriend Moses and aid the Children of Israel?

Answer: According to the sages, there are two different explanations. One explanation is that Yitro came to the Jewish people with friendship and good intentions. A second explanation is that he sided with the nation that was presently "on top" and popular (i.e., the group that was now in God's favor) (*Talmud Sanhedrin 94a*).

Question: Yitro heard what God did for his son-in-law Moses and for the Children of Israel *(Exodus 18:1)*. What did Yitro hear?

Answer: Yitro heard of the unique miracles that occurred to the Hebrews, in particular the splitting of the sea. He looked up to and respected his son-in-law Moses. He was in awe of the fact that after years of enslavement in Egypt the Hebrews were suddenly set free. Yitro also was impressed that the Hebrews miraculously won the war against Amalek, who were known to be a strong group (*Babylonian Talmud, Zvachim 116b*).

Question: How many names does the Torah record for Yitro?

Answer: Yitro had seven names. Often in the Bible, individuals were given multiple names, which had important meanings. Yitro's were the following:

He is referred to as *Yeter;* in Hebrew it means "addition," because he added one extra portion to the Torah *(Exodus 18:21)*. This was his original name. Another is *Yitro.* When he converted, the sages added one letter to the end of his name *(Rashi, Exodus 18:1)*. *Hovav* in Hebrew means "to love." Thus according to the sages implies he loved the Torah *(Rashi, Numbers 10:29)*. He also was called *Reuel,* meaning "a friend to God" *(Exodus 2:18; Mechilta Exodus 18:1)*. He was referred as *Chever,* Hebrew for "a friend." He became a friend/close to God *(Book of Judges 4:11)*. *Kaynee,* another of his names in Hebrew, means "to buy." He bought himself a portion of the Torah. An alternate explanation of this word means "zealous." He was zealous for the sake of the Torah *(Samuel A 15:6;*

Mechilta Exodus 18:1). And finally *Putiel* the name that tells the world that he had given up his idol-worshipping (*Midrash*).

Question: What leadership advice did Yitro give to Moses?

Answer: Yitro would see people come to Moses from all over to receive prayers or blessings from him, ask him to resolve disputes, or have him explain or teach them laws. Yitro felt that Moses was dealing with too many routine matters for a man of his stature and was becoming worn out. Yitro spelled out the management plans that would empower Moses to stay more focused and help him better serve his people and God. Sometimes, people in powerful positions are unable to "give away" responsibility. He had the wisdom and humility to delegate and accept help from others and work cooperatively for the common good of his fellowman. Therefore, Yitro advised Moses to divide the work among the princes of the tribes so Moses could deal with matters that were beyond the ability of others.

Question: How did Moses choose his officers?

Answer: According to *Rashi*, Moses picked his officers with God's help. However, other commentators say that Moses chose his officers by himself.

Question: What were the qualifications and requirements needed to become one of Moses' key officers?

Answer: One must be God-fearing. A man who fears the Almighty will not fear man. He also is not the kind of person who would accept bribes because he believes God monitors all. Another trait would be the ability to make decisions and see the truth in conflicts. He should also be an accomplished man. A wealthy man would be able to resist the pressures of those who would attempt to influence his judgment (*Rashi*). A man who despised money would not be swayed by financial considerations.

Question: The Torah states: "The Hebrew people temporarily lodged there opposite the mountain" *(Exodus 19:2)*. What do the sages learn from this?

Answer: They learn that the Children of Israel camped opposite the mountain in unity, because only in unity would God give the Children of Israel the Ten Commandments.

Question: "You have seen the miracle which I made in Egypt and I took you on the wings of eagles to me" *(Exodus 19:4)*. What does this mean?

Answer: This shows the love God has for the Children of Israel. Just as an eagle carries its young on its back to protect them from shooting arrows, so did God protect the Children of Israel against the Egyptians at the Red Sea.

Question: The Torah describes how people, animals, mountains, and trees were filled with excitement when the Children of Israel received the Torah. What makes the Torah so special?

Answer: Many years ago, businessmen and tradesmen would board a ship together with their merchandise and travel to different ports to show their wares. Such was the case with a Jewish group of merchants who boarded a ship bound for Pakistan for a week-long business journey through the Arab countries. To amuse themselves during the trip, each businessman would take time to show the others his wares. One showed fine samples of his jewelry; the other had carefully woven carpet samples; still another had displays of material, and so on. Each described his merchandise with much pride. This provided an opportunity to pass the time on the ship and allowed them to become better acquainted with one another. Eventually, though, boredom set in. The men were looking for something with which to amuse themselves. Suddenly, the men focused on one lone man sitting by a window of the ship with a book quietly mumbling to himself. He looked like a religious Jew. They began to make fun of him. "Who are you, strange man? What are you mumbling over there?" they said. "I am a rabbi," he answered, "and I am learning the Mishnah. Perhaps I can encourage you to learn with me," he offered. The men, while completely bored, just continued to make fun and would not join the rabbi in study. As they continued to make fun of the rabbi, a storm suddenly broke out on the sea. Soon, the storm became worse, and the captain of the ship warned everyone to get into lifeboats as the large ship was about to sink. The people were saved, but they were stranded in a strange and unfamiliar land. The businessmen began scrambling for help. They did not know where to turn for food and shelter. The rabbi immediately tried to find a synagogue. He soon found one and saw a group of people sitting and learning Torah. They immediately realized that he was a scholar and asked him to stay with them and teach a lesson. They treated him with honor and gave him all that he needed. The businessmen, now poverty stricken, asked the rabbi for help. The people of the city helped the poor businessmen with food and hospitality on the merits of the rabbi. Subsequently, the rabbi remarked, "It is true that each one of you has fine merchandise to sell to make a living. However, the best business is not jewelry, carpets, or material goods. All of these can be made today and lost tomorrow. It is only the knowledge of Torah that can never be lost or taken from you. The study of the Torah can only lead you in the right direction of life. As it has been said: the best schorah, payment is Torah!" (*Mishlei 3:14; Ralbag; Midrash*).

Question: What is the meaning of each of the Ten Commandments?

Answer: To believe with complete faith that the Creator is One and unique. The meaning is quite literally that there is no other god.

The prohibition against idolatry has three facets: not to believe in idols; not to make idols, and not to worship idols in any way.

Do not utter an oath in vain means it is forbidden to use God's Name in a casual manner for any purpose.

To keep the holy the Sabbath means to remember the Sabbath and observe its laws, and keep it Holy.

Honor your parents refers to respecting one's parents; performing deeds that raise the status of parents; giving them food, drink, comfort, and happiness.

Do not murder. You shall not kill.

Do not commit adultery. Do not have relations with another man's wife.

Do not steal. Do not kidnap or force a victim to work for you or sell him into slavery.

Do not bear false witness. Do not give false testimony. Do not gossip.

Do not covet. One must control one's desires for a neighbor's possessions. Guard against jealousy of your fellowman's wife, ox, and donkey.

Question: The Ten Commandments were inscribed on two tablets, each tablet containing five commandments. What is the difference between the right tablet and the left tablet?

Answer: The five commandments on the right tablet are those between God and man, while the five commandments on the left tablet are between man and his fellowman. The commandments on the right tablet are positive commandments, while the commandments on the left tablet are negative commandments (*Kli Yakar*). The five commandments regarding the interaction between God and man contain the Almighty's Name, while the five on the left, dealing with man-to-man issues, do not contain His Name.

Question: The first of the Ten Commandments says, "I am the Lord, your God..." *(Exodus 20:2)*. Is this a positive or negative commandment?

Answer: *Rambam* calls this a positive and negative commandment. This means, if you believe with complete faith in God, you fulfill a positive commandment. However, if you don't believe in the existence of God, you violate a negative commandment. To show how important this commandment is, *Rambam* put this commandment first on the list of his positive commandments and first on the list of negative commandments in his book *Sefer Hamitzvot*.

Sefer Hachinuch, however, lists it as a positive commandment (*Mitzvah No. 25*), to believe with complete faith that there is but one God, the basic foundation of Judaism. *Ba'al Halachot Gedolot* suggests that the statement made here is just that, a statement. God says I am the Lord, your God. That acceptance of divine sovereignty is a given and stands apart from any other declaration in the Torah.

Ramban says this is two commandments. The first is to know that God exists; the second is to recognize that God is One. We fulfill this commandment in our daily life by reciting the *Shema* Yisrael, "Hear O Israel, the Lord our God, the Lord is One." Here we have two of God's Names as we have in the first of the Ten Commandments. One name is for compassion and mercy and the other name is for judgment, like a father who disciplines his child with a combination of judgment and mercy. Therefore, while we concentrate on the meaning of this prayer, we fulfill this commandment.

Rambam supports his own opinion with a passage from the *Talmud (Makot 23b)* "Moses commanded us the Torah" (on behalf of God) (*Deuteronomy 33:4*). The word Torah in *gematria* (biblical numerology) is 611. The number of biblical commandments is 613. These extra two commandments are the first two commandments in the Ten Commandments, which everyone heard directly from God, at the time of the revelation of the *Divine Presence* at Sinai. Therefore, it is counted as part of the 613 commandments (*See Mechilta; Exodus 20:2; Yad HaMelech; Abarbanel; Ramban; Ikarim 17:3*).

Question: The Torah states: "You shall not steal" (*Exodus 20:13*). What type of stealing is the Torah referring to?

Answer: Here the Torah is referring only to a kidnapper who steals people and sells them into slavery, not to one who steals money. The commandment not to steal money and the like is found in the *Book of Leviticus* where it states "You shall not steal,..." A money stealer (*Leviticus 13:11*) is obligated to pay his penalty in tithe (*Talmud Sanhedrin 86a*).

Question: The Torah states here in *Exodus 20:13*: "You shall not covet your friend's house, nor your friend's wife, ox, donkey..." While in *Deuteronomy 5:18*, it is written: "You shall not covet your friend's wife, nor desire your neighbor's house, ox, donkey." Are there any differences between the com-mandments as they are written in Exodus and as they are written in Deuteronomy?

Answer: The sages tell us that the Ten Commandments, as given in this *parsha*, Yitro, are direct quotes from God. The commandments tell us what one can and cannot do. When Moses repeated the Ten Commandments in the *Book of Deuteronomy*, he changed the emphasis. Moses knew his people. He saw how his people interacted. Based on that information Moses addresses the weaknesses of his people. He changes the order and the language to suit the nation. First, that you shall not covet a man's wife because that affects one's family. Moses understood that there are many ways that possessions can be returned, but when someone upsets another's family or someone else's wife, there really is no way to make this right again. The Torah also addresses even the subtle nuances of sin. For instance, a woman might sense a covetous thought from a man, and although nothing physical happens, her attitude toward her husband is subtly changed and some damage is done. Therefore, Moses put the wife first.

Here in this *parsha*, the commandment not to covet your friend's house is put first, while in Deuteronomy, the order is rearranged and the wife is placed first. Here in our *parsha*, "do not covet" is written for all the items listed. In Deuteronomy, the language changes. "Do not covet" is written concerning your neighbor's wife, but "do not desire" is written about your friend's house and other possessions.

Question: According to the explanation above, what is the difference between coveting and committing adultery with someone else's wife?

Answer: There is a concept expressed by the sages which is called the three steps: the first is desiring something mentally without taking action; the second is only talk; the third and final step is physically taking an impulsive action.

The prohibition of do not covet refers to one's thoughts. Only God knows what one is thinking. We believe with complete faith that we have the ability to control our will and desire.

Mishpatim
Chapters: 21:1 - 24:18

Synopsis:

The biblical religious and civil laws; the commandment of the Sabbath and holidays; Moses went for forty days and nights on Mount Sinai.

Question: In the *parsha* the first word is "And." What did the sages teach from this?

Answer: The sages teach that along with the Ten Commandments received by Moses at Sinai, he received the civil law (*M'chilta 21:1*).

Question: What is the purpose of *Parshat Mishpatim* in the Torah?

Answer: In the western world, there is a distinction between church and state. The Torah teaches that all areas of life are intertwined. There is no separation of laws. The laws in this portion deal with all aspects of daily life.

Question: Part of the civil law is penalty for inflicting bodily injury. *Exodus 21:22-28* says, "Eye for an eye, tooth for a tooth..." What does this mean?

Answer: This issue deals with a basic tenet of Judaism. According to the sages (*Babylonian Talmud, Bava Kama 83b,84a*), the concept "eye for an eye" is interpreted as financial restitution. One must be careful in viewing laws such as these, and look to the Oral Torah for their correct interpretation.

There is a law in the Torah (*Deuteronomy 25:11,12*) that states that if two men are fighting and the wife of one comes in the middle of them and punches him publicly in an embarrassing place, the Torah's rule is: "You cut her hand, do not have any compassion." The sages explain that the concept of measure for measure is to be fulfilled through monetary payment. Since she embarrassed with her hand, she should pay money back "with her hand." The *Rambam* says that although the perpetrator deserves physical punishment, the Jewish court does not have the authority to do more than estimate the damage of her actions and convert it to a monetary amount.

The statement of "an eye for an eye ... a tooth for a tooth,...etc." is a statement that needs explanation, as it is not to be taken literally. If a man takes out another man's eye, what good does it do for the man who lost an eye to take out the eye of the one who hurt him? After taking the eye, he would be no better off. Obviously, this is not the intention of the Torah; it is written this way to emphasize that in rectifying the damage, there must be total equality. To do justice in a case like this, one considers whether the injury was accidental or deliberate, whether the injured party contributed to cause of the injury, and many other factors.

At first glance, much of the meaning of Torah is not black and white. There is need for explanation and amplification. Both written and oral components are needed. Discussion of this concept is well beyond the scope of this book.

Question: What is the biblical law regarding the punishment for the owner of an animal that causes injury or death to a person?

Answer: There are two categories of animal damage: intentional damage and damage caused during the animal's normal routine.

A domestic animal going wild is an unexpected and unusual occurrence and therefore the owner's vigilance in this matter is not to be expected. However, if the reputation of an animal becomes known as dangerous, the owner's responsibilty grows. A man-killing animal is always put to death, but the treatment of the owner is another matter entirely, and will depend on whether the owner had been warned about the animal's behavior. The *Rambam* says the issue really revolves around the owner and his degree of carelessness in guarding potentially dangerous animals.

The question of payment also is an issue in this matter, and again involves the owner's sense of responsibility in guarding his animals. Restitution for damaged property depends once again upon the vigilance of the animal's owner. He may be fined half the value of damage done for the animal's first three offenses, and full damages once the animal has gained a reputation as reckless.

The author cautions the reader that the topic is one that needs extensive study. The *Talmud* devotes a a great deal of time to the various aspects of this body of law.

Question: Where do we learn the importance of clearly teaching civil law to people?

Answer: God said to Moses, "You must take the civil law and deliver it to the people in the clearest way possible" (*Babylonian Talmud, Eruvin 54b*). The sages give an allegory: "the same way that you prepare your table for guests, is the same way you must deliver the civil law."

Question: "If you buy a Hebrew servant…" *(Exodus 21:2)*. What is the Torah speaking about?

Answer: The Torah is speaking about a specific circumstance. If a Hebrew steals and cannot pay the fine that the religious court demands he repay his victim, he is sentenced to serve the victim until the debt is paid.

Question: The *Talmud* proclaims, "Whoever buys a Hebrew servant, buys himself a master." What does this mean?

Answer: According to the religious/civil law (*Exodus 21:3*), the buyer of the Hebrew servant is obligated to give the servant's wife and children full nourishment and has full responsibility for his physical and/or mental problems. The master is also obligated by law to make sure that the servant gets all the luxuries that he himself gets. The *Talmud* says if your servant does not have a pillow like yours then you must give it to the servant.

Question: "And then the servant shall serve his master forever" *(Exodus 21:6)*. How long is "forever"?

Answer: Forever means until the jubilee (a maximum of fifty years) (*Babylonian Talmud, Kiddushin 16a*).

Question: According to biblical law, in what manner can a male or female servant become free?

Answer: A Hebrew servant is released after six years of service. This applies to both male and female servants. At the onset of a Jubilee Year (50th), all servants are freed regardless of time served. If a servant pays the balance of his debt he is released.

Question: According to the biblical law, what is the punishment for a person who curses his father or mother?

Answer: The person who curses his father or mother is stoned to death (*Leviticus 20:9*). The reader is cautioned to again explore this issue in depth for proper understanding.

Question: What is the punishment for a person who hits his father or mother?

Answer: The person who hits his/her parent with no intention of killing them but causes them to bleed deserves strangulation (*Exodus 21:16,17; Babylonian Talmud, Sanhedrin 84b*). A child is exempt from the death penalty if blood was not drawn or a black and blue mark was not left (*Babylonian Talmud, Sanhedrin 84, Chulin 11*). These laws need careful study for fuller understanding.

Question: According to the biblical law, what is the punishment for a person who strikes another person, not his parent?

Answer: The person who strikes another person must pay the victim five different payments: damage according to the court appraisal (the decrease in the monetary worth of the victim); payment for the victim's pain and suffering; medical expenses; lost time and wages; embarrassment payment.

Question: According to the biblical law, how is a kidnapper punished?

Answer: Two witnesses to the crime must pass a rigid investigation and identify the kidnapper in court. Then, the kidnapper receives the punishment of strangulation (*Exodus 21:16; Babylonian Talmud, Sanhedrin 85b*).

Question: In biblical law, what are the four different death penalties?

Answer: The four types of death penalties are stoning, burning, by the sword, strangulation.

Question: The Torah states: "shall surely be put to death" *(Exodus 21:16)*. What does this phrase mean?

Answer: If the Torah does not specify the manner of execution, then death is by strangulation. The *Talmud* goes through much discussion concerning this issue.

Question: "If there are two people fighting with the intent to kill each other and a pregnant woman passes by and is punched in the stomach accidentally and has a miscarriage because of this, the person responsible must pay the husband compensation for the loss of the fetus" *(Exodus 21:22)*. What is the law if they kill the woman?

Answer: This is a very controversial issue among the sages *(Babylonian Talmud, Sanhedrin 79a)*. One side says the killer should receive the death penalty because the two men fighting had the intent to kill. The fact that the woman was killed instead of one of them is irrelevant. The issue remains the intent to kill. The other side says that the person responsible must pay to the woman's inheritors the monetary value of what the woman was worth.

Question: If a man digs a pit that is a danger to animals, but not deep enough to kill an animal if it fell in, and then another man came

199

and dug the pit deeper, so that it could then kill an animal if it fell in, who is held responsible if an animal should fall in and die?

Answer: The Talmud says the second person, even if he dug only a tiny bit more, is responsible for the death of the animal (*Babylonian Talmud, Bava Kama 51a*).

Question: What is the biblical decree if one steals livestock?

Answer: Instead of paying the value of the stolen animal, the thief must pay five times the value of a stolen ox and four times the value of a sheep only if he subseqently slaughtered or sold the stolen animal. Again this is an area that has engendered much discussion, that goes far beyond the scope of our book (*See Rashi Exodus 21:37 and Babylonian Talmud Bava Kama 67b*).

Question: According to the Torah, what is the difference between a thief and a robber?

Answer: Torah law differentiates between a thief and a robber. The thief is someone who steals without anyone seeing him. He sneaks and snatches covertly, afraid of being discovered. The robber is one who has no shame, no fear, who forces someone else to hand over his valuables publicly (*Babylonian Talmud Bava Kama 79a*).

Question: According to the Torah, why is a thief punished more than an armed robber?

Answer: *Rambam* explains that the religious court, in addition to forcing the robber to return what he stole, sometimes gives him a physical punishment in order to warn others not to imitate this action. However, because the robber committed his crime out in the open (which is considered to be less of a crime than that of a thief), the religious court will never obligate him to return more than he stole.

On the other hand, the thief took advantage of the weaknesses of the victim (i.e., the victim was sleeping, or trusted him), and this crime was easier to commit. Therefore, the biblical law says that it is not enough for him simply to return what was stolen. He is required to pay to the victim double the amount stolen.

The reason for this distinction is as follows: The Torah looks at the root of the person's action and the attitude that led to the commission of the crime.

The thief shows by his action only a fear of people; since he waited until he was absolutely sure that no one would see him, he demonstrated a lack of concern that the Creator is watching over him. The thief, it would appear, has more sinister plans and would not stop if he had to harm and even kill to accomplish his goal. The robber, however, committed his crime during the day. It seems that he is intending no physical harm. Therefore, according to the Torah, the robber's punishment is only because he took the possessions that belong to someone else.

The thief receives double punishment, for he actually commited two crimes. The first is obvious and the second is a demonstration of lack of faith in the Creator. The robber, however, merely took the possessions belonging to someone else, showing he has no fear of the people. *Rabbi Yochanan ben Zachai* explains why there is this difference between the thief and robber (*Babylonian Talmud, Bava Kama 27a*). "The robber acts as though he has the same respect for man and God (master and slave). The thief is more afraid of the servant than of the master. By so doing, the thief acts as though the Creator's eye does not see, and he has therefore demonstrated a lack of faith." The *Meiri* explains that the thief committed a sin not only against his fellowman but against God. The robber did not demonstrate a lack of faith, as he committed the crime either because of a true need of, or simply a lust for, money.

Question: According to Jewish law, what stolen item could never be returned?

Answer: The sages call *"sleep robbery"* something a robber could never return. If someone makes it impossible for a fellowman to sleep, he is stealing something very valuable to that person. According to some, disturbing a person's sleep is considered a big sin, because the person who loses sleep can never recover it. Moreover, if the person who loses sleep cannot function (i.e., in his job or studies, etc.), it is very difficult to appraise the amount of damage. Also, time wasted can't be returned to him. According to the sages, the sin of sleep robbery will be tried in the court of Heaven. Even though the person who deprived someone of sleep did not do it on purpose, he is still accountable for the harm. There are three steps in repenting for this sin: One must ask for forgiveness and receive full pardon; one must promise not to repeat it and be careful in the future; and lastly, study seriously the rule of *sleep robbery* (*Mictav M'Eliyahu; Rambam*).

Question: If a person asks a custodian to safeguard something of value and this item is somehow stolen, damaged, or lost while in the care of this custodian, what is the biblical law? Would the custodian be charged or exempt for the damage or loss of the item?

Answer: There are four different categories of custodian: unpaid custodian, paid custodian, borrower, and renter.

For the unpaid custodian if an object in his care is stolen or lost or something beyond his control happened, like a natural disaster the custodian is exempt. If, through the custodian's negligence, the object is lost, the custodian is held responsible. If the object is an animal and it dies, even by natural causes, the custodian is still responsible.

The paid custodian is responsible if the item is stolen, lost, damaged through negligence, or an animal died, even in normal work, the custodian is responsible. Only in the case of a natural disaster is he exempt.

For one who borrows an item responsibility derives in all instances except for an occurrence beyond his control.

For one who rents an object, opinions differ regarding responsibility in instances of theft, loss, and negligence. If the event resulting in loss was beyond the custodian's control, or the object died of natural causes, the custodian is exempt from payment.

Question: If the owner is with the custodian when the item is stolen or lost, is the custodian exempt or guilty?

Answer: All four custodians are exempt if the owner is with them. They are charged only if the owner is not with them (*Choshen Mishpat 291:28*).

Question: What procedure does the custodian have to go through to be exempt from paying?

Answer: In order to be exempt, the custodian has to come to the religious court and make three vows in front of the judges: the first, that he guarded the item with trustworthiness and was not negligent; second, he swears that the story that he described happened exactly as it was told; and last, that he never touched the item (*Babylonian Talmud, Bava Matziah 6a; Tosfot D'h Shevuah*).

Some sages say another vow must be added: that the item is not now in his possession (*Choshen Mishpat, Hilchot Shaelah Ufikadon 6a*).

Question: The regulations for the renter are controversial among the sages. What are the halachic rules concernng renters?

Answer: The renter is bound by the same rules and regulations as the paid custodian.

Question: The Torah states: "Don't tease an outsider or foreigner because you were once an outsider in the land of Egypt" *(Exodus 22:20)*. What is the connection between the beginning and the end of this phrase?

Answer: The Torah is exhorting us against practicing bigotry and oppression, since we have suffered the effects of both (*Babylonian Talmud, Bava Metziah 59b*).

Question: What is the special rule regarding the orphan, widow, and convert?

Answer: *Exodus 2:21-22* tells us we must be very kind to a child who does not have a father or a mother. The same verse includes the widow. The convert is likewise given special consideration (*Exodus 22:20*).

Question: What are the special rules and regulations concerning a moneylender *(Exodus 22:24)*?

Answer: It is a biblical prohibition for the lender to ask for the return of his money or to be bothersome if the lender is certain the borrower does not have the money. According to the commentator *Rashi*, there is a special prohibition against embarrassing the borrower (*Babylonian Talmud, Bava Metziah 75b*). There is a biblical prohibition not to charge interest to the borrower.

Question: What behavior does the Torah require of all judges?

Answer: It requires that every individual judge make his decision even if he feels it will not coincide with the majority of the other judges. A judge must examine the truth and base his decision on his full knowledge and experience of biblical and civil law. The judge should give his opinion even if it's not pleasant or "politically correct" to say it. We follow the decision made by the majority of the judges.

Question: What are the names of the festival of Passover *(Exodus 23:15)*?

Answer: It is called the passover, the festival of *matzah*, and referred to as the festival of spring.

Question: What are the names of the festival of *Shavuot (Exodus 2 3:17)*?

Answer: It is called the festival of receiving the Torah, the harvest festival, festival of the first fruits, and the festival of Weeks.

Question: What are the names of the festival of *Sukkot (Exodus 23:17)*?

Answer: It has been called the festival of reaping grains and the festival of joy. The holiday is also referred to as the Festival of Booths.

Question: Which commandment do we have for all three festivals?

Answer: There is the commandment to go to the Temple in Jerusalem during the festivals.

Question: What does the Torah intend when it says "You should not cook a kid in its mother's milk" *(Exodus 23:19)*?

Answer: This forms the basis for the prohibition against mixing milk and meat, one of the foundations of the kosher dietary laws.

Question: Why do Jews eat kosher food?

Answer: There are many reasons why people eat and drink. The biological-medical reason is to maintain growth and sustain the body. There are also social, psychological, and emotional reasons. All involve a person's relationship to society as well as individual and emotional components.

The less tangible reason is strictly spiritual. The kosher dietary laws spelled out in the Torah were prescribed by God. They were given to enable a person to achieve and remain in the highest spiritual dimension. The kosher diet helps to connect and strengthen the link between a person's body and soul; as everything in the world was created by God, God is aware of all the elements, formulas, ingredients, and variables of His Creation. If God tells man to follow the kosher dietary laws and other instructions in the Torah, then this must be in man's best interest. Man should comprehend the limits of his understanding. It is only God Who sees the full scope and ramifications of everything in the world just like an inventor who knows his product best.

If a person buys vitamins and ignores the recommended dosages and swallows twenty vitamins a day instead of the specified two, he may or may not feel the adverse effects right away, but one day it will catch up with him.

Even the brightest and most qualified nutritional specialist cannot second-guess the true meaning behind God's dietary laws. Man must understand that in this world, although many things are clearly definable and tangible, many are not. Knowing exactly which food is right or wrong for our total well-being is not as easily recognized. That is why we trust in God to guide us in our food choices.

Question: How many times is the prohibition of mixing milk with meat written in the Torah?

Answer: It is written in the Torah three times. The first time is *Exodus 23:19*, the second, *Exodus 34:26*, and the third time, *Deuteronomy 14:21*. All three times this prohibition is written in the same exact words.

Question: Why does the Torah repeat the same idea about the kosher dietary laws three times?

Answer: The sages explain (*Babylonian Talmud, Chulin 115b; Shulchan Aruch, Yorha Da'ah 87a*) that each time it is repeated, it has a different meaning: in *Exodus 23:19* it involves the prohibition of cooking milk and meat together; in *Exodus 34:26* it explains the prohibition of eating milk and meat together; and in *Deuteronomy 14:21* it refers to the prohibition against receiving any benefit from mixing milk and meat together.

Question: How do we explain the prohibition against eating milk and meat together?

Answer: At the beginning of Creation, it was forbidden to slaughter animals for food. Man ate vegetables, fruits, and herbs. Only after the Flood, when the vegetation was destroyed, did the Almighty permit humans to feed upon animals in order to prevent starvation. However, the act of slaughtering animals in itself is an act of cruelty. God placed limits on slaughter. The killing of an animal for sport is prohibited; it must be for sustenance. The Almighty further limited the species which are permissible for consumption. The slaughter must be accomplished in such a way that the animal experiences as little pain as possible (*shechitah*). Through these limitations God elevated eating to a spiritual level for mankind.

Meat represents the life of the animal, and milk represents the ability to reproduce and sustain life. This is an animal's function, to eat and reproduce. God created man with many more functions. Separating man and animals puts Godliness into all man's activities (*Rabbi Samson R. Hirsch*). Milk comes from an animal, so the mixing of milk and meat together is considered a double act of cruelty (*Oznayim Latorah*).

By creating man and animals, the Almighty has shown us that He is the Master of the Universe. He gave humans the power of control in certain things, but He also prescribed limits to these things. One of these limits is the mixing of milk and meat (*Rabbi Y. Breuer*). In fact, the simple act of mixing the two together with no intent to cook or consume the mixture is equally forbidden (*Shulchan Aruch, Yorha Da'ah 87a; Drisha 87a*).

Rambam (Moreh Nevuchim 3:48) explains that the biblical prohibition against mixing milk and meat exists because idol worshippers mixed milk and meat.

Question: The Torah says "kid" and "his mother's milk." Does this mean specifically a kid or only the kid's mother?

Answer: The sages tell us (*Shulchan Aruch, Yora Da'ah 87a; Drisha 87a; Chochmat Adam 40:1*) that the kid is not necessarily just a young goat; this also includes a cow, lamb, or ox. "His mother's milk" is not only from his own mother, but it is also milk from any kosher animal.

Question: What is the biblical rule of mixing milk and meat together?

Answer: The sages (*Babylonian Talmud, Avoda Zara 66b*) teach us that in the same way a vessel absorbs something, a vessel will excrete something. Therefore, an empty vessel that has been rendered non-kosher must be heated at a very high temperature so that whatever did not wash off will be burned to dust and the vessel will be kosher again. Any food prepared in that vessel before it is *kashered* (ritually cleaned) is unfit to be eaten by a Jew. Certain vessels cannot be *kashered* and therefore become unusable and should be destroyed to prevent inadvertant use.

Question: The Torah states: Moses took the Book of the Covenant and introduced it to the Children of Israel. They replied by saying, "...we will do and we will obey" (*Exodus 24:7*). What does this mean?

Answer: Moses showed the people the book in which the Covenant between them and the Almighty had been written. The *Talmud* says that God offered the Torah to every nation in the world. All refused to accept it because they found one law or another too difficult to observe. The Children of Israel however, because of the unique miracles that happened to them thrrough the hand of the Almighty, willingly and completely accepted all of God's laws.

Terumah

Chapters: 25:1 - 27:19

Synopsis:

God commanded Moses and the Children of Israel to build a Tabernacle; the contributions for the Tabernacle; the directions for constructing the Ark; the table, the menorah, the curtain, and the Altars.

Question: "They will make me a Sanctuary and I will dwell among them..." *(Exodus 25:8)*. What is the meaning of Sanctuary?

Answer: *Rashi* explains that the Sanctuary is the place where the Almighty's presence resided inside the Temple. Other commentators (*Rabbeinu Bachayei; Ibn Ezra*) explain that the Torah itself is called the House of God's Sanctuary, and this house will sanctify the Children of Israel. In the future, this house will be the main source of God's presence. *Sforno* explains that in the Sinai Desert, before the Children of Israel built the Golden Calf, they had a high level of spirituality because they were so sure of their faith of God. God's presence was upon each individual. But due to the Golden Calf, their level of spirituality fell. As a result they were in need of a place where the Almighty's presence might reside among them. The Sanctuary inside the Temple became that site.

Question: How many different contributions does an average person have to give to the Tabernacle?

Answer: The sages taught us (*Yerushalmi Talmud, Shkalim 4a; Babylonian Talmud, Megila 29b*) that there were three different types of contributions: each individual was responsible to give a beka (type of a coin) from which were made the sockets to hold the pillars that supported the ark cover. Whatever was left after the sockets were made went to pay for the hooks for the pillars. Each individual was obligated to give a beka to purchase the public, community offerings. The third donation was left to each individual to choose from the list of thirteen needs for the Tabernacle. The donation had to be made *n'div lev* (voluntarily).

Question: The Torah states: "They will make a Holy Place for Me and I will dwell with them" *(Exodus 25:8)*. What does dwell mean in this context?

Answer: The Sanctuary is a place whose sole purpose is for the worship of the Almighty. Even the most beautifully ornamented building is meaningless unless it is totally dedicated to God (*Rashi*). A person in the right frame of mind will receive the sanctity of the place, but if the person is not in the right frame of mind it can have a very serious adverse effect (*Ibn Ezra*).

The building of the Tabernacle was a symbolic action. The aim was to show the people that God is not only in the Heavens, but on Earth as well (*Abarbanel*). Although it was symbolic, a person needed to be conscious of the fact that he had to conduct himself as if he were in the presence of the Almighty.

Since electricity was invented, we have been able to perceive light in every place in the world, even in the darkness. Similarly, the Tabernacle was the ray of light of all Creation. The Tabernacle reaffirmed the spiritual power latent in all Creation, just as the invention of electricity proved the existence of light in the remotest of locations. However, just as it is only by the actions of man that light is brought to the physical world through electricity (or fire), so too, it is up to man to bring light to the spiritual world. With both kinds of light, mankind must be careful to use them well, or they will be lost (*Rabbi Simcha Zeesl from Kelm*).

There is an enduring commandment to build the Temple, in order to be weaned from worshipping idols (*Rambam; Yad Hachazaka, Hilchot Beit Habechira 1:2*).

Question: What did the Ark represent?

Answer: The main feature of the Tabernacle was the Ark, which held the Ten Commandments. The cover of the Ark was made of solid gold symbolizing the glimmering soul of man, created in the image of God.

Question: What was the function of the table in the Sanctuary (*Exodus 25:23-30*)?

Answer: The table was made of pure gold. Placed on this table were always twelve loaves or *showbreads* placed in two columns of six loaves each. These loaves of bread were baked fresh every Friday and placed on the Golden Altar on the Sabbath. Four priests would bring the *showbreads* to the golden table, which stood inside the sanctuary. Four other priests would remove the breads of the previous week and distribute them to all of the priests (*Babylonian Talmud, Sukkot 5b, Menachot 96b*). The miracle of these breads was that they remained warm and fresh the entire week they were in the sanctuary.

Question: What was the design of the *menorah* in the Tabernacle *(Exodus 25:31-40)*?

Answer: The *Menorah* or candelabra was one of the most beautiful of the sacred vessels. Its creation was a complicated process. The *menorah* was fashioned from a single piece of solid gold as the Torah states, "And you shall make a *menorah* of pure gold; of one piece shall you make the *menorah*...its tongs and scoops shall also be made out of pure gold" (*Exodus 25:38*). Its height reached eighteen handbreadths (approximately 180 centimeters). If a *menorah* of gold could not be made, then one of ordinary metal could be used and would be kosher to kindle in the Temple.

In fact, this is how the Hashmonaim, during the original Chanukah episode, were able to kindle a simple menorah, which they fashioned out of seven metal rods. Later, when they regained some of their wealth, they made a *menorah* out of silver, and later still, they finally created it from gold once again (*Babylonian Talmud, Menachot 28*).

The *Menorah* had seven lamps and a three-legged base. Each lamp was supported by a stack designed (from the bottom up) with a decorative cup, knob, and flower into which a lamp was inserted (*Babylonian Talmud, Sukkah 50b, Yuma 52a, Menachot 28b,88b; Akaida Sha'ar A*).

Question: What was the meaning of the *Menorah*?

Answer: There is a famous biblical phrase, "God's candle is a human soul." The candle symbolizes the soul of mankind. The soul of mankind aspires to be pure and lighter. Whenever the priest lights a candle on the menorah, he gives a ray of light for all mankind.

Question: How was the Tabernacle covered?

Answer: The Tabernacle had three covers: two were made of cloth, and one was made from animal hide. The three covers were draped over the top of the walls in order of size, with the smallest cover being first, and the largest cover on top, draping down the side of the walls up to the silver sockets.

Question: How many altars were in the sanctuary?

Answer: There were two altars: one was the inner gold altar, also referred to as the incense altar, and the other was the copper altar in the courtyard of the Sanctuary.

Question: How was the courtyard made *(Exodus 27:9-19)*?

Answer: The courtyard was made of curtains suspended from rods connected to poles anchored in copper sockets. The dimension of the courtyard was 50 x 100 cubits. The front of the yard had an entrance with its own set of curtains that could be entered from either side.

Question: Why do we read the Torah portion of *Zachor* *(Deuteronomy 25:17-19)* in addition to the portion of the week?

Answer: We read *Parshat Zachor* from a second Torah on the Sabbath before the festival of Purim in order to remember what the evil nation of Amalek did to the Children of Israel after they left Egypt. Amalek brutally attacked the Israelites without provocation, even after the whole world had witnessed the great miracles that God did for the Israelites. Since that time, our history has contained a series of enemies like Amalek.

Purim

Synopsis:

The festival of Purim falls in the time period that Parshat Tetzaveh.

Question: What is the festival of Purim?

Answer: This festival occurs on the fourteenth day of the Hebrew month of Adar, corresponding to the month of March. The story is related that King Achashvarosh ruled over 127 countries. Haman, his minister, was anti-Semitic and plotted to annihilate all the Jewish men, women, and children. Haman pushed King Achashvarosh to threaten and terrorize the Jewish people. Ultimately all of Haman's schemes failed. He, along with his ten sons, were hung in public and their deaths were witnessed and recorded in the history books. The name Purim comes from the Hebrew word for the lottery that was used to choose the date of the intended annihilation the Jews by Haman.

Two heroes emerged out of this event. One was an honest and beautiful orphan, Esther, who became Queen; the other was her uncle Mordechai. Mordechai would be rewarded and promoted to a high post within the Persian government by the king for his truthfulness, loyalty, and profound intelligence. Consequently, the rabbinical Supreme Court (*Sanhedrin*) established the festival of Purim as a holiday to publicize the miracle of the deliverance of the Jewish people from the tyranny of Haman (*Babylonian Talmud, Magillah 2b, Yerushalmi Talmud Magillah; Rambam, Hilchot Magillah 1:5*).

Question: What is the meaning of the word *magillah?*

Answer: *Magillah* means "tractate" or "scroll." This word comes from the Hebrew root *gll*, which means "to roll," because very old books were written on parchment scrolls and rolled up.

Question: During the year, how many *magillot* do we read?

Answer: During the year we read five *magillot: Song of Songs. Ruth, Lamentations, Ecclesiastes,* and *Esther.*

Question: Which of the *magillot* are we obligated to read?

Answer: We are only obligated to read *Magillat Esther.* The reading of the others is based on custom (*Masey Rav 175*). There is an opinion held by Rabbi Alyhu from Vilna requiring us to read all five, but only if a *minyan* (group of ten men over the age of thirteen) is present.

Question: Does the word "obligated" above mean the same as commanded?

Answer: Yes. It is a positive commandment. It is *mitzvah* created by the Rabbis (*Talmud, Magilah 5a, 7a; Peulat Sachir; Harah; Tury-Aven*).

Question: What do we do during the festival of Purim?

Answer: The festival of Purim encompasses a few days. On the thirteenth of Adar, we fast. This is the last of the three days that Esther fasted prior to her meeting with King Achashvarosh. The fast ends the evening of the fourteenth of Adar. We hear *Magilat Esther* read that evening and the following morning. It is mandatory that one hear the magillah once in the evening and once the following day. We are commanded as part of the holiday to give charity to the poor, and to give gifts of food. These foods must be of two different food types and be ready to eat (*Mishloach Manot*). There is much celebration on this day.

Question: Where do the above rules come from?

Answer: *Magillat Esther.*

Question: What are the customs during the reading of the *Magillat Esther?*

Answer: Every time the reader says the word Haman, we drown it out with lots of noise as a symbol of our desire to drive out the evil forces against the Jewish people, such as Haman. We dress in different types of costumes to have fun and merriment.

Question: What are some of the rules governing the person reading the *magillah?*

Answer: The one who reads the *magillah* has to say blessings before and after the reading. He must read the *magillah* from an original handwritten parchment scroll. He unrolls the entire *magillah* and folds it like in ancient times in a fanfold, not rolled up. He reads the *magillah* with different tunes. Some sections are read with a happy tune (major) and some with a sad tune (minor). He has to repeat a few words that are written and pronounced differently. It is preferable that he stand up and that two people hold the *magillah* from both ends. He has to say the entire list of Haman's ten sons in one breath.

Question: The Day of Atonement in Hebrew is called *Yom Hakipurim.* Why is the name Purim contained in the name despite the apparent contrast of the two holidays?

Answer: The sages saw an important relationship between the two. For both holidays we pray, and there is a fast connected to each. In the Purim story, we learned that there was a decree to destroy the Jewish people, not merely to kill the male children as Pharaoh decreed, but to eradicate the entire Jewish people as the Nazis tried. In the Purim story, the Jews fasted and prayed and ultimately God "reversed" the situation. The expected total destruction of the Jews by the Persians turned into a great triumph for the Jews over their enemies. The Jews are to celebrate the miracle of Purim with simcha. During *Yom Kippur*, we pray and fast in order to reverse any bad decree which may affect us. We must adopt the attitude of respect and concern for our fellowman that is typified by *Mishloach Manot.* We must give charity and feel for those who are less fortunate. This is the message that Purim brings.

Tetzaveh

Chapters: 27:20 - 30:10

Synopsis:

The priests received directions about lighting the menorah, making the priestly garments, to construct and use the Golden Altar.

Question: God commanded Moses to make holy garments for Aaron for beauty and glory and to be used by him and future generations of priests. Why did God command Moses to make such garments?

Answer: The *kohen* could only perform his task in these garments. The *kohen* was responsible to care to dress and conduct himself with dignity and respect for the One before Whom he stands. Also the garments worn by the *kohen* had to be purchased and made with materials owned by the nation (*Yoma 35b*).

The beauty of the garments that the priests wore had a spiritual impact on who came into the *Mishkan*. The *Sefer Hachinuch* says the garments gave the *kohanim* who wore them the ability to concentrate on what they had to do. The way that person approaches a task influences how well he will perform it.

The meaning of the garment had little to do with external appearance. The garment was symbolic of an internal glory; the external look was only a hint to the pure hand and pure heart of the *kohen* (*Ha'akeidah*).

The priest was part of the glory of Heaven. Therefore, the garment represented the glory of the Lord (*Ibn Ezra*).

God told Moses to pay attention to the priests' character as well as their external behavior and dress. The garments must be worthy of the priest who wears them. He should have self confidence and everybody would respect him (*Haktav v'haKabbalah*).

The priests were the teachers and educators of the entire nation. Therefore, as the people who represent the religion, they had to appear in beautiful garments, thus giving more honor to the position (*Sforno*).

The high priest had two connections, one to the spiritual world and one to the material world. Therefore, his dress needed to represent this combination by being both spiritual and yet worldly (*Ramav*). There were special enhancements to the garments worn by the *Kohen Gadol* which were comprised of some very holy items.

The priest had two aspects, external and internal. The external one is the priest's dignity, resulting from being chosen as God's messenger to the people (*Malbim*).

The position of high priest, was in the same category as a king. The high priest had to dress with the same dignity as a king. The high priest wore a woolen tunic and a crown similar to those worn by royalty (*Ramban*).

One of the requirements for the high priest was to purify himself and be isolated from all the people. This condition would exist only if he was respected by his people such that they recognized the fact that he was on a much higher spiritual plane than they (*Ha'amek Davar*).

Question: Why did God command Moses to transfer the high priest position to Aaron?

Answer: The sages said that Moses got punished because he refused to be God's messenger in Egypt. As the Torah quotes, "The wrath of God burned against Moses and God said Aaron your brother the Levite..." (*Exodus 4:14*). *Rabbi Shimon ben Yochai* said: God tells Moses that Aaron is a *Levite* and you are a priest. "From now on, he will be the priest, and you will be the Levite" (*Babylonian Talmud, Zevachim*).

Other sages say that it was not a transfer of position nor a punishment. Moses served as a priest the first seven days, and then Aaron was appointed (*Midrash Rabba, Shmot B*).

Moses was on such a high spiritual level that he became far removed from the daily life of the average person. The job of a priest was to deal daily with the common folk, to teach them and show them the proper way to do God's commandments. So, on one hand, Moses chose to be the middleman between God and the people, which meant that Moses was on a level much higher than the average person was. On the other hand, this highest level of spirituality prevented Moses from dealing directly with the people's daily lives. Consequently, Aaron had to do it (*The Dubna Magid*).

Moses was commanded by God to proclaim that Aaron was chosen to be the priest; otherwise, the people would not accept Aaron's authority. Therefore, Moses indoctrinated Aaron for seven days, and afterwards Aaron took over as high priest (*Abarbanal*).

Moses was responsible for teaching all of the rules and regulations of the Torah to all of the Children of Israel so he could not function as a priest in the Temple. Furthermore, the priest (*kohen*) and his descendants had to come from holy lineage. Moses' children came from Yitro's daughter, which meant his son had no lineage. Therefore, the Torah describes Aaron's lineage in great detail (*Ibn Ezra*).

Question: How many categories of *kohanim* (priest) do we have?

Answer: Two, the high priest and the regular priest.

Question: How many vestments did the kohanim wear?

Answer: The high priest wore eight vestments, sometimes referred to as the *Golden Vestments* because there was some gold in their design. During the *Yom Kippur* services, he only wore four, which were made out of wool and were white. The ordinary priest only wore four vestments.

Question: What is the *ephod*?

Answer: The *ephod* was worn over the tunic and robe. It was similar to a woman's apron. It extended from below the rib cage to the ground. It had two shoulder straps. On top of the straps were two gold settings which contained precious gems with the names of the tribes inscribed on them. Attached to the two shoulder straps was *choshon*, held in place by means of rings, gold chains, and woolen cords.

Question: What is the breastplate (*choshon*)?

Answer: The breastplate measured 1 x 1.5 cubits in size worn on the chest. It is refered to as the Breast Plate of Judgment for two reasons: one, it atoned for the erroneous judgements made by judicial courts, and second, when consulted it provided clear answers for the nations.

Question: What kind of head plate did the high priest have and why?

Answer: This head plate is called the *tzitz*. It was placed on the forehead and tied behind the head. The head plate was two finger widths wide and had the words "holy to Me" written on it. The words were there so God would accept the type of offerings that may only be offered by a high priest.

Question: Which procedure was used to inaugurate the priests?

Answer: This inaugural event lasted eight days, beginning on the twenty-third of Adar and ending on the first day of Nisan. It was performed by Moses who up until this time was *Kohen Gadol*. It was this service that would place Aaron and his sons in the role of *kohanim*. The event demanded more than just offerings which were insufficient to consecrate the Tabernacle and the *kohanim*. The words of Moses were also necessary. There also needed to be two bulls of atonement for Aaron and two for his sons. Accompanying these would be thirty loaves of unleavened breads of three types. There was need of oils which Moses would use to anoint his brother and his nephews.

Ki Tesa

Chapters: 30:11 - 34:35

Synopsis:

*The procedure for the census of the Israelites; the contri-
butions for building the Mishkan (Tabernacle); the commandment of keeping the Sabbath; the Israelites miscounted the days Moses was up on Mount Sinai; the people built the Golden Galf and worshipped it; Moses broke
the tablets; Moses begged God for forgiveness; 3,000
Israelites died as punishment; Moses brought down the
second tablets; the thirteen attributes; the commandment
of the festivals; Moses saw God face to face.*

Question: We read about the sin of the Golden Calf and the resulting punishment. When Moses came back down the mountain, at the entrance to the camp, Moses yelled: "Whoever is on God's side come with me." The Levite tribe came over to him. Moses told them, "This is what the God of Israel said: each one take his sword from his scabbard and kill each of the idol worshippers even if it be his brother, his or any relative" *(Exodus 32:26,27)*. Only the tribe of Levi had the faith in God to fulfill Moses' request and about 3,000 people died on that day *(Exodus 32:28)*. Was Moses a killer or did he fulfill God's mission?

Answer: To better answer our question let us consider the following story. Dr. Daniel Horowitz is a distinguished surgeon with a wife and three children. Dr. Debra Shapiro was his longtime childhood friend, and later, they were medical colleagues. Dr. Shapiro married Chaim Sofer when she was 29 years old. Dr. Horowitz was one of the important guests at her wedding. Over the years, Dr. Horowitz and Dr. Shapiro-Sofer met on social occasions. As close friends, Dr. Horowitz felt heartbroken that his close friend and colleague was childless for seventeen years. Fertility procedures and many other efforts did not help.

Dr. Horowitz became ecstatic when he heard that his friend had become pregnant. Everyone was overwhelmed with joy when she gave birth. She named the baby Naomi. She was very pretty and sweet. Everybody loved her. A few years passed and baby Naomi started crying nonstop every night. The parents took her to doctor after doctor but nothing was found to indicate a serious problem. Shortly thereafter Naomi began sleeping almost twenty-four hours a day. Her parents took her to a specialist, who found extensive lesions in her right knee. X-rays showed the need for emergency surgery. Her parents were told that they had to immediately amputate from the knee down to remove the growth, or the lesions would continue to spread widely and rapidly. Two other specialists were consulted on this case. These two doctors also agreed on the immediate need for surgery. The expert surgeon recommended to perform the emergency operation was Dr. Daniel Horowitz, the lifelong friend of Dr. Debra Shapiro-Sofer.

Can you imagine the pain that Dr. Horowitz must have felt when he discovered who his patient would be? Here he is preparing to amputate the leg of his friend's two-year-old baby. He performed the operation and saved Naomi's life. The surgery left Dr. Horowitz traumatized. Despite the agony of performing this procedure, Dr. Horowitz took the right action.

The biblical commentators explain that Moses was forced to save all of the Children of Israel from extinction. There needed to be an "amputation" within the people of Israel. The Torah described how God told Moses, "let Me annihilate this nation, and I will make you (Moses) a great nation" (*Exodus 32:10*). However, Moses said "no." He begged, pleaded, and prayed for compassion and mercy for his people. By the same token, Moses realized that he could not allow this situation to continue. He knew the people must repent immediately. Otherwise, all would risk mortal punishment from God. Therefore, Moses took action despite his pain, and "proclaimed whoever is for God come to me"(*Exodus 32:26*). Moses tried to give the sinners one last chance to repent. Tragically, the conclusion was that 3,000 people died.

If we carefully read the Torah and Jewish history, we see that sometimes our leaders, in order to save the nation, needed to react physically. The sword is a dramatic last resort.

Question: What was the procedure for this census?

Answer: This census was taken because God wanted to know how many people left Egypt. But, the Torah teaches us that it is forbidden to directly count people. Therefore, to accomplish this task, God requested that everyone contribute a certain amount of money, in a certain coin. This coin represented a person and was counted instead of counting the individuals. The money was then used to build the Tabernacle. We learn from this that when someone does a task or contributes to a holy cause, he himself is lifted up to a higher spiritual level (*Talmud, Bava Batra 10b*).

Question: What amount of money were the Children of Israel commanded to give for the purpose of the census?

Answer: Each person was obligated to give a half shekel. In those days, this was considered a lot of money for poor people and a modest amount for the rich.

Question: Was it possible for someone to give more toward the building of the Tabernacle if they wanted?

Answer: No, God wanted to make everyone's contribution equal. "The rich shall not increase and the poor shall not decrease" (*Rashi, Exodus 30:15*).

Another explanation was to avoid conceit on the part of person who may opt to say, "I have more of a share in the Temple than you" (*Da'at Z'kanim; Miba'elei Hatosfot*). Thus, all the people were equal investors in this grand project (*Sefer Hachinuch 105*).

Question: Beginning with what age did one have to give to this charity?

Answer: From the age of twenty years and older, because age twenty is when men are chosen to serve in the army (*Rashi, Exodus 30:14*).

Question: According to biblical law, are we allowed to count the Children of Israel?

Answer: The Torah prohibited the counting the Children of Israel directly unless it was absolutely necessary, not even for atonement. This prevented the evil eye from affecting them. Thus, instead of directly counting people, the half shekel was used to do so. Therefore, according to the Jewish law, if we have to count a *minyan* (ten people for daily prayer) we do so by reciting a biblical sentence composed of ten words. Even Moses, when he had to count to collect the atonement money, used money to do so.

Question: Knowing the biblical prohibition against count-ing the Children of Israel, why did King David count people after the war? Was he punished for doing so?

Answer: King David thought, incorrectly, that the prohibition to count the Children of Israel only existed in the time of Moses. Consequently, he was punished (*Ramban; Rashi*).

King David was punished not only because he counted the peo-ple but also because he began counting individuals from the age of thirteen. The Torah explicitly prohibited including in a census individuals from under twenty years of age (*Levush Orah*).

King David was punished because he counted the Children of Israel when it wasn't necessary (*Babylonian Talmud, Yuma 22a*).

Question: From what material was the *Kiyyor*, the cup used to pour water over one's hands and feet, made?

Answer: It was made of copper (*Exodus 30:18*).

Question: For what purpose was the *Kiyyor* made?

Answer: Although the *Kiyyor* was for washing the hands and feet, it implied a need for sanctity as well (*Ramban*). For *Rashi* (*Exodus 30:20*) tells us that if the *kohen* did not wash before entering the Tabernacle he would die.

Question: In which place was the *Kiyyor* put?

Answer: The *Kiyyor* was placed between the altar and the meeting tent (*Exodus 30:18*).

Question: How was the "oil of sacred anointing" prepared?

Answer: We do not know. We do know that it was made from a combination of oil and spices, and the exact formula was only given to Moses (*Ohr Hachayim*). According to Jewish tradition, it will be discovered at the end of our present days when the Messiah comes (*Rabbi Samson R. Hirsch*).

Question: What was done with the "oil of sacred anointing"?

Answer: All the tabernacle tools, Aaron, and his sons were anointed (*Exodus 30:26-29*).

Question: How many different ingredients made up the incense that was kept in the Tabernacle?

Answer: Eleven ingredients made up the incense that was kept in the Tabernacle (*Babylonian Talmud, Kritot 6a; Yerushalmi Talmud, Yuma 4:5*).

Question: How many times a day was incense offered?

Answer: The incense was offered twice a day, once in the morning and then again in the afternoon.

Question: Where was the incense kept?

Answer: The incense was kept inside the Tabernacle on the altar of gold.

Question: Were the smells of all eleven ingredients pleasant, and why?

Answer: All of the ingredients smelled pleasant except one galvona, which had a terribly foul aroma. This comes to teach us that even sinners of Israel are to be acknowledged; that they are not too insignificant to be included in our prayers (*Rashi, Exodus 30:34*).

Question: Today, is there any evidence or proof of the temple incense?

Answer: In December of 1995, I was taken to a mountain cave located between the Dead Sea and Jerusalem by a group of expert American-Israeli archaeologists who proclaimed to have found some of the Temple's incense. I tasted the incense powder found there. It looked like two different light brown soils. It had a uniquely sweet and aromatic taste and was different from anything I had ever tasted before. This is no proof that these substances were related to the Temple service.

Question: Who is Bezalel *(Exodus 31:3)*?

Answer: Bezalel was one of two who were appointed to oversee the construction of the Tabernacle. He was also a nephew of Moses. He was endowed with a Godly spirit. *Rashi* says that he was personally called by God to oversee the construction. Our sages say Bezalel knew the secret of the holy letters and words that were used by God to create Heaven and Earth. He maintained a degree of universal wisdom (*Babylonian Talmud, Brachot 55a*).

Question: How old was Bezalel when he received his position?

Answer: Bezalel was commissioned by Moses, on behalf of God, to build the Tabernacle when he was thirteen years old (*Babylonian Talmud, Sanhedrin 69b*). Some commentators say that the Almighty called on Bezalel personally to supervise the construction.

Question: What is the significance of the Sabbath day?

Answer: It is a sign between God and His people that in six days the Lord made the Heavens and the Earth and that on the seventh day He rested. "Be mindful of the Sabbath, to make it holy. You should labor for six days and do all your work, but the seventh day is the Sabbath for the Lord your God. You may not do any manner of work, neither you nor your son, nor your daughter, nor your male or female worker, nor your cattle, nor the stranger who dwells among you. Because it was in six days that the Lord made the Heavens and the Earth, the sea, and all that they contain, and He rested on the seventh day. That is why the Almighty blessed the Sabbath and made it holy" (*Exodus 31*). This is one of the tenets of Judaism. This fact is highlighted every Friday evening, at the beginning of the Sabbath when one makes *Kiddush* (a thanksgiving blessing recited over a raised cup of wine), saying: The Children of Israel should keep the Sabbath, observing the Sabbath, throughout the generations, as an everlasting covenant (*Rambam*).

Question: What prompted the Children of Israel to build the Golden Calf?

Answer: The *Golden Calf* was made by the Children of Israel to replace Moses. The rabble rousers thought Moses was dead or had abandoned the people so they incited the people to make an image. The people needed a leader, an intermediary between themselves and God. And when they believed Moses to be dead they were seduced by the whim of the rabble. They called upon Aaron to fashion an image which they could look to and through which they could then talk to God. Substituting for Moses, Aaron knew that the Golden Calf was not an idol of God, which is why he helped them. He also felt it was still too soon to wean them away from idolatry, having just left Egypt, a land filled with idolatry. He thought that it would take time to fashion such a statue. But he fell victim also because what emerged from the flames after he had tossed in the metal was a finished image of a Golden Calf.

Question: How could the Children of Israel, who witnessed so many miracles in Egypt and in the wilderness, try to transfer the glory of God to the Golden Calf?

Answer: It would seem apparent that even the greatest signs and miracles cannot change the behavior of a human being overnight. A person needs constantly to educate himself before his spirit can be transformed completely (*Hagut*).

The Israelites expected Moses to bring from heaven something tangible on which they could focus and direct their worship. They thought the calf would achieve this goal. Only a minority of the people who assimilated (3,000 people) thought about worshipping idols. Nonetheless, everyone was held responsible because each member of Israel is responsible for the next (*Kuzari; Abarbanel*).

The Children of Israel sinned due to their impatience. They miscounted forty days and thought that Moses had left them or had died and would never return.

Question: What did Aaron do to delay the Children of Israel in making the Golden Calf?

Answer: Aaron told the men to bring the earrings of gold from their wives and children because he was certain that they would refuse to give them, and that the time would be wasted by the men trying to get their families' cooperation.

Aaron had the Children of Israel build an altar with him, and he told them that "the God festival would be tomorrow." He had counted the days correctly and believed that the next day Moses would return (*Rashi, Exodus 34:4-5*).

Question: How was the Golden Calf made?

Answer: Aaron bound up the gold and threw it into the fire. He had hoped a molten mass would emerge, requiring additional time to beat and fashion into a calf. Instead, the Egyptian sorcerers, who had intermarried with the Hebrews in order to leave Egypt, activated their sorcery, and a Golden Calf emerged.

Question: How did the Almighty react to the building of the Golden Calf?

Answer: The Almighty wanted to destroy all of the Children of Israel immediately.

Question: How did Moses convince God not to destroy them?

Answer: Moses used the special merit of the forefathers to soften God's heart and save the Israelites. Moses reminded God about Abraham, who devoted himself in God's ways, even placing himself in harm's way with Nimrod who threw him into the fire in Ur Kasdim, and who was willing to sacrifice his son, Isaac, on the altar. Moses also reminded God of Jacob, who went into exile in Charan (*Rashi, Exodus 32:13; Pirkei Avot 5:4*).

Moses mentioned to God that the creation of the calf was not as bad as Egypt's sin. Thus, God's mercy on Israel should be equal to His judgment of Egypt. Since He did not totally destroy Egypt, He should not destroy the Children of Israel (*Ibn Ezra*).

Moses pointed out to God that the Children of Israel are His people, and that their destruction would reflect upon Him. It would not look good in the eyes of the world that He would liberate a group of people, take them out to the desert, and then destroy them! Moses also mentioned to God the merits of the forefathers Abraham, Isaac, and Jacob, thereby fulfilling Pharaoh's prophecy (*Ohr Hachayim*).

Question: How were the Tablets written?

Answer: The Tablets were written by the "finger of God" so that they could be read from either side, the front or the back (*Exodus 32:15, Rashi; Ohr Hachayim; Babylonian Talmud, Sabbath 104a*).

Question: How were the Tablets broken?

Answer: Moses threw the Tablets at the base of the mountain (*Exodus 32:20*).

Question: What did Moses do to the Golden Calf?

Answer: Moses melted the Golden Calf. He ground the gold to dust, mixed it with water, then gave it to the Children of Israel to drink (*Exodus 32:20*).

Question: Why was the tribe of Levi chosen to serve in the Temple?

Answer: When Moses returned from receiving the Tablets and had seen the actions of the Children of Israel with the Golden Calf he called "whoever is on God's side come with me" (*Exodus 32:26*). The tribe of Levy accompanied him. For this they were rewarded by being chosen as Temple servants (*Babylonian Talmud, Yuma 66b; Bechor Shor*).

Question: What personal price did Moses pay for the sin of the Golden Calf?

Answer: The sages explain that when Moses prayed and begged God to save the Children of Israel, he was so distraught that he gave God a condition: "If you do not forgive them, I'll erase my name from Your book that You have written." Therefore, he was erased from one biblical portion. Throughout *Parshat Tetzaveh* God spoke to Moses but not by name, refering to him as "You."

Question: How did Moses become very wealthy?

Answer: The Almighty allowed Moses to take the sapphire from the first tablet. The sages say God gave it to Moses because he was the only one who did not touch the possessions of the Egyptians who died in the Red Sea (*Babylonian Talmud, Sabbath 87a*).

Question: How did God speak to Moses?

Answer: God spoke to Moses face to face, like a man speaks to his fellowman (*Exodus 33:11*).

Question: The *Midrash* says: "Before Moses died, he came to Heaven. God asked him, 'Who do you think will be the next leader after you?' Moses replied, 'Atmeel ben Kanaz.' Moses had numerous disciples but Atmeel was the best scholar. God replied, 'You're wrong. Joshua will be the next one.'" Why was Joshua chosen?

Answer: Moses' servant, Joshua, would never leave the tent (*Exodus 33:11*). God appointed Moses as a leader when he was a shepherd, not a scholar. Likewise, Joshua was appointed by God because he was always first at the holy tent and the last one to leave. Joshua was a very humble caretaker: he helped with everything that was needed for the people and always was very loyal to God and Moses. For this he was rewarded to transmit the Torah from Moses to the Elders (*Pirkei Avot 1:1*).

Question: When did Moses go to Mount Sinai to get the second Tablets?

Answer: Moses went to Mount Sinai to get the second tablets on the twenty-ninth of the month of Av. This usually corresponds to the summer period of the English calendar.

Question: When did Moses receive the second Tablets?

Answer: Moses received the second Tablets on *Yom Kippur,* the "Day of Atonement."

Question: What is the connection between the parsha and the haftorah?

Answer: Both the *parsha* and *haftorah* deal with a nation in doubt. Just as the *parsha* dealt with the doubt raised when the nation miscalculated Moses' return, so here in the *haftorah* the nation once again is in doubt. While under the rule of king Achav and his non-Jewish idol worshipping wife Jezebel, the nation was torn in two. As the parsha told the story of the Golden Calf, the haftorah tells a story concerning King Achav and the Prophet Elijah. King Achav's wife, Jezebel, killed most of the prophets of the Almighty. Obadiah managed to hide 100 of them from her. God sent Elijah to confront Achav. Elijah encountered Obadiah and told him to tell his king that Elijah was ready to meet him. The result was the meeting on Mount Carmel when Elijah challenged the prophets of Jezebel to a test. The result was a victory for the Almighty. The entire nation declared "Hashem–He is the God." These words are recited in the *Yom Kippur* service.

Vayachel

Chapters: 35:1 - 38:20

Synopsis:

The Commandment to keep the Sabbath; collecting contributions for the Tabernacle; the building of the Tabernacle; the construction of the Altar, table, menorah, sink, screen, and courtyard for the Tabernacle.

Question: When did Moses assemble the Children of Israel and give them the command to construct the Tabernacle?

Answer: It was the day after *Yom Kippur* (Day of Atonement), when he came down from receiving the Torah for the second time. He had just spent eighty days and nights learning Torah with the Almighty. Moses also learned that God forgave the Israelites for the incident with the Golden Calf. When Moses came down from Mount Sinai, he brought with him the second set of tablets. Now, the Children of Israel were deserving and ready to fulfill God's commandment to build the Tabernacle.

Question: The Children of Israel were commanded to build the Tabernacle immediately. Was it permissible for them to build on the Sabbath?

Answer: It is prohibited to violate the Sabbath even to build the Tabernacle to the Almighty (*Mechilta 35:2*).

Question: Why did the women play a more important role than the men in the building of the Tabernacle *(Exodus 35:22)?*

Answer: The women played the more important role because upon hearing that precious metals were needed to build the Tabernacle, they immediately contributed all their jewelry. The majority of women also did not participate in the creation of the Golden Calf. The women refused to hand over their jewelry for that purpose (*Ohr Hachayim; Ramban*).

Question: How do we know that God did not like the fact that the princes of the Children of Israel were the last to contribute materials for the building of the Tabernacle?

Answer: The princes felt they should let every person contribute what they wanted. At the end, the princes agreed to contribute whatever was missing. They thought that there would be a substantial amount lacking, and their contributions would be the greatest. To the contrary, all the individual contributions were so great that there was no need for the leaders to contribute. According to *Rashi*, the Torah's description of this event has the Hebrew word for "leaders" spelled with two missing letters. This was their punishment, which indicated God's displeasure to the leaders, who were so late and misguided in their contributions (*Rashi*).

Question: How do we know that the leaders learned from their mistake of hesitating to contribute to the building of the Tabernacle *(Exodus 35:27)*?

Answer: When they built the Altar, the leaders were the first to bring their offerings (*Rashi, Exodus 35:27*).

Question: What is the family relationship between Moses and Bezalel?

Answer: Bezalel was the son of Uri, son of Hur. This means that Bezalel was the son of Miriam. Moses was his uncle (*Rashi, Exodus 35:30; Babylonian Talmud, Sotah 11b*).

Question: How do we know that there was equality among the people who worked together on the construction of the Tabernacle?

Answer: The sages teach us that "and the nobleman is not recognized ahead of the pauper" (*Tanchuma 13*). God chose two wise men to manage the construction of the Tabernacle, Bezalel and Oholiav. Bezalel came from the tribe of Judah, recognized as the most aristocratic of the tribes. Oholiav came from the tribe of Dan, a less prestigious tribe. He was the son of a maidservant. God put them together as equals in the construction of the Tabernacle (*Rashi, Exodus 35:34*).

Question: What kind of wood was used in the planks of the Tabernacle?

Answer: Acacia wood was used to build the Tabernacle.

Question: In what material were the planks coated?

Answer: The planks were coated in gold.

Question: In this parsha the Torah describes how the Ark was constructed. Why was Bezalel's name the only one mentioned among the builders?

Answer: Bezalel devoted himself totally, more than the other workers, that is why his name was the only one mentioned (*Rashi, Exodus 37:1*).

Question: There were large basins, used only by the priests (*kohanim*) before performing the service in the Tabernacle. What was their source?

Answer: The Israelite women had mirrors when they were still slaves in Egypt. They used these mirrors in order to adorn themselves and make themselves attractive to their husbands. Making themselves attractive to their husbands would foster intimacy bringing about more Jewish children (*Exodus 38:8*). God rewarded these women who devoted themselves to creating future generations under difficult circumstances by exclusively using these mirrors in the making of the basin (*Rashi, Tanchuma; Unkeles; Ibn Ezra*)

Pekudei
Chapters: 38:21 - 40:38

Synopsis:

The census of the nation; contributions for the construction of the Tabernacle; the commandment of the half shekel; the high priest's vestments; the completion of the temporary Tabernacle; Moses blessed the Children of Israel; the Glory of God appeared in the Tabernacle.

Question: Why is the Tabernacle called the place of testimony?

Answer: After the sin of the Golden Calf, the Almighty was furious with the Children of Israel, but God forgave them. As a sign of God's forgiveness, He had them build the Tabernacle to clarify the relationship and interaction between God and the Children of Israel. The Tabernacle was called "the place of testimony" because it was a confirmation that God forgave them. It was to be a "resting place" for God so that the Children of Israel would feel His Holy Spirit upon them (*Rashi*).

Question: What was the job of *Itamar*, the son of Aaron?

Answer: He was responsible for assigning, to each family in the tribe of Levi, the different tasks that needed to be done in the building of the Tabernacle (*Rashi*).

Question: What part did Moses take in the construction of the Tabernacle?

Answer: *Rashi* tells us in *Exodus 39:33* that Moses did not do any work in the actual construction of the *Mishkan* (Tabernacle). But the people brought the Tabernacle to Moses (*Exodus 39:33*), meaning they brought to Moses the completed walls, which were lying down. Moses lifted the walls of the Tabernacle himself, which was miraculous because they were very heavy. The Almighty left the erecting (the standing up) of the Mishkan, to Moses himself (*Rashi; Midrash Tanchuma*).

Question: In the building of the Tabernacle, how many times is the phrase "that God commands," written and what is the significance of this number?

Answer: It is written eighteen times, parallel to the eighteen blessings found in the *Amidah* prayer (*Yerushalmi Talmud*). The *Amidah* prayer is the silent prayer said during each of the three prayer services held daily.

Question: "Moses saw the excellent work done on the Tabernacle, so he blessed them" *(Exodus 39:43)*. What blessing did Moses give them?

Answer: Moses blessed the nation for the work that they had done in building the Tabernacle. He called upon the Almighty to rest in the work that they had just completed. He called upon the pleasantness of the Almighty to be with the people for all time *(Rashi)*.

Question: How was the work split between Moses, Aaron, and Aaron's sons on the eighth day of service?

Answer: On the eighth day of the inauguration of the Tabernacle, Moses, Aaron, and Aaron's sons where all equal for the priesthood *(Rashi)*.

Moses prepared the *showbreads*;	Aaron and his sons offered the daily sacrifice.
Moses kindled the *Menorah*;	Aaron and his sons offered the calf.
Moses offered the incense;	Aaron and his sons offered the deer.
Moses offered public sacrifice;	the Aaron and his sons offered the sheep and ox.

Question: During the forty years of wandering the desert, how did the Children of Israel know in which direction to travel and when to make camp?

Answer: God gave the Children of Israel the *Pillar of Clouds* and the *Pillar of Fire* to lead and protect them in the desert. They followed the direction of the pillars and set up camp where the pillars stopped *(Exodus 13:21; 40:38)*.

Question: What is the meaning of the phrase, "Be strong, be strong, and may we be strengthened," which is said at the end of each of the books of Moses?

Answer: The sages teach us that the study of Torah needs encouragement. They draw upon the example set by Moses when he handed the leadership of Israel to Joshua. He told the Children of Israel and Joshua on three different occasions to be strong: *Deuteronomy 3:28, Deuteronomy 31:6,* and *Deuteronomy 31:23.* After the leadership was handed over, God said to Joshua three times, "Be strong": in *Joshua 1:6, Joshua 1:9,* and *Joshua 1:18.* So to commemorate and encourage one another to continue the study of Torah as we complete one of the *Five Books of Moses* (The Bible), we stand up and say to one another: "Be strong, be strong, and may we be strengthened" (*Abudraham; Bereishit Rabba Joshua 1:8; Ta'amei Dinim Uminhagim, Aarech Siyum page 157*).

It is a worldwide custom that when the Torah reader finishes the last sentence of each one of the five books of Moses, the entire congregation stands and encourages one another
with the following proclamation:

"CHAZAK CHAZAK V' NITCHAZEK!"

(STRENGTH...STRENGTH...AND BECOME STRONG)

III

The Book of Leviticus

Vayikra

Chapters: 1 - 5

Synopsis:

General guidelines for presenting offerings in the Tabernacle; specific details on the different kinds of offerings; specific procedures for offering sacrifices.

Question: Why do we sacrifice innocent animals to atone for our sins?

Answer: It is necessary to keep in mind that the Torah comes directly from God. Many of the laws that were given to us through Moses from God may at times appear to be beyond simple understanding, but with some study they become clearer. Here are the views of some of our sages on the subject:

When one commits a sin and watches an animal being slaughtered he ponders the idea that this animal is a substitute for himself in atoning for that sin. With the animal's blood pouring out and its innards gutted one is to think, "Maybe that was meant for me!" This gives one a real chance to repent for his transgressions (*Ramban*).

There are many examples throughout history of civilizations that worshipped animals. For example, the Egyptians worshipped sheep, the Kasdim of Iraq worshipped goats (*Genesis 11:28; Ramban*). We are commanded to destroy these idols and worship only God (*Rambam, Morah Nevuchim, Sec. 3*). The Israelites, on the other hand, were permitted by the Almighty to use specific animals as *korbanot* (sacrifices) to atone for their sins or to bring as offerings of thanks.

The *Zohar* discusses the subject of *Gilgulei Neshamot*, "reincarnated souls." It is written that sometimes the soul returns to the physical world to correct past sins that were committed in its past life. The kabbalistic sages explain that some animals are the reincarnated souls of persons who have returned to this world to repair the damage that they did to their own soul while they resided in human form. Sometimes they returned as sacrificial offerings in the Temple. They return to the Almighty pure and satisfied once they are offered as sacrifices on the altar in the Temple (*Kitvey Ha'ari; Kitvey Hasulam*).

God gives man a chance to clear his conscience and his soul (*Maharal of Prague*). God allows sacrifices as a way for man to deal with the psychological exigencies that arise when he unintentionally commits a sin, but feels guilty and wishes to repent. *Korban* comes from the word *karov*, meaning to come close. This *korban* was the man's chance to come close to the Almighty with a pure spirit.

God is the Creator of all things, inclusive of man and animal. Only the Almighty can give man permission to offer animals. These sacrifices are to be dedicated to the Almighty alone. He gives permission to use only particular animals as a final cleansing of man's mind and soul (*Ba'al Ha'akaidah*).

The sacrificial act in the Temple reminds us of when God commanded our forefather Abraham to sacrifice his son Isaac on the altar (*Genesis 22*). At the last minute, the angel told Abraham not to kill his son. The Bible states that "Abraham found a ram and offered it as a sacrifice instead of his son Isaac." That place later became the site of the Temple. Abraham was willing to sacrifice his son for the sake of fulfilling God's will. Abraham, by taking this action, proved himself as the founder of the Israelites, the guiding light for every generation. The fact that the angel of the Almighty prevented Abraham from sacrificing his son shows the significance and sanctity of human life (*Rabbeinu Bechayei*). Abraham demonstrated that we must be willing to sacrifice ourselves to fulfill God's will. Since the Temple is not in existence today, fasting is considered a form of sacrificing ourselves as a substitute for a sacrificial offering on the altar.

This is a law of God, and therefore is to be accepted (*Rambam, Hilchot Meilah, chapter 1*).

Question: Since there is no Temple in existence today, by what means can a person bring an offering to the Almighty?

Answer: The ultimate offering to the Almighty is one's prayers. In the morning prayer service we say, "Master of the Universe, You commanded us to sacrifice an offering on a daily basis. As a result of our iniquities, the Temple in Jerusalem was destroyed. Consequently, all Temple offerings were suspended, with the exception of prayer. But You, said 'Let our lips substitute for the sacrificial offering' (*Hosea 14:3*). Therefore, may it be Your will our Lord and God of our ancestors that our prayer that comes from the depths of our heart toward our lips be acceptable before You as an equivalent of the offerings given in the past."

It is our fervent hope that the Almighty accepts our prayers and sees them as a substitute for the offerings we would be obligated to bring if the Temple were in existence today.

Question: Why does the Almighty require man to offer a daily sacrifice?

Answer: People attend to their personal hygiene on a daily basis, and clean their clothing and homes with regularity. In a similar fashion, we must tend on a daily basis to our spiritual and mental health.

Question: What is the Tabernacle?

Answer: The Almighty commanded Moses to build the Tabernacle. Moses then commissioned Bezalel to oversee the construction of the entire process. The Tabernacle can be likened to a portable, prefabricated religious building that was a temporary central site of worship. Its complete design and structure are detailed in the Torah. Constructed of gold, silver, copper, and fine woods, it consisted of many rooms, partitions, and curtains. Like a house each room was designed with a specific purpose in mind.

Question: Why was the Tabernacle built *(Leviticus 1:1)*?

Answer: The Tabernacle was built as a resting place for God's Divine Presence, *Shechinah,* and as the place for Moses and the Children of Israel to offer service to God. The most important function of the Tabernacle was to provide a place where the Children of Israel could pray and communicate directly with God (*Rambam; Ramav*).

Question: Why does the first word in the book of Leviticus (*Vayikra,* "he called") end with a small א, alef?

Answer: This parsha talks about the offerings in the Temple. The small **א** symbolizes that all donations, contributions, or offerings, of whatever size, were acceptable.

Question: If someone wanted to repent and brought an offering or contribution to the Temple, but it was not 100 percent "pure," was the contribution or offering acceptable (*Leviticus 1:2*)?

Answer: The Torah uses the word "pure" to suggest that one who is bringing a sacrifice is doing so with an absolutely clean conscience (*Mishnah Tamurah 1:1*). In the phrase, "If a man brings an offering," the word *adam* means man. The sages state that the first man, Adam, was the first one to bring a pure offering to God. He brought a variety of fruits that grew in the Garden of Eden (*Ramav*). Adam never took from anyone. God provided all for him, therefore Adam's offering was acceptable. The sages teach us that any contribution or offering brought to the Temple that does not honestly belong to the repenter is unacceptable (*Noam Elimelech; Vayikra Rabba 2:7; Rambam*).

Question: Was it possible for two people to give an offering together?

Answer: Yes. The sages tell us that an offering from more than one person was acceptable. The Torah uses the plural *takrivu*, "bring an offering," which means that a group of people could join together to bring a single offering (*Rashi, Leviticus 1:2; Torat Kohanim 3:1*). From a psychological point of view, one does not like to admit publicly that he has committed a sin and is obligated to bring an offering. If one brought a sacrifice together with others, he felt more comfortable. Offerings were acceptable as long as they were not stolen.

Question: What does the Torah say about a person who promises a contribution, yet does not fulfill his obligation?

Answer: The Torah considers him to be a sinner and gives the religious court full authority to force the person to give the promised contribution (*Rashi, Leviticus 1:3*).

Question: What is the biblical attitude toward someone being called up for an aliyah (special honor accorded to someone taking part in the reading of the Bible) and promising a contribution, then later refusing to fulfill his obligation?

Answer: In *Deuteronomy 23:24* it is stated, "Whatever comes out of your mouth, you must fulfill"; in *Numbers 30:3*, it says "Whatever comes from his mouth, he must fulfill." Not keeping one's word is one of the worst possible sins because this promise is made in front of at least ten people, and in front of an open Torah scroll. The Torah is considered "witness" to this promise; reneging on one's promise is considered an insult to the Torah.

Question: We know that the high priest, the *Kohan Gadol,* wears special garments. Was it acceptable for the high priest to wear a garment that belonged to a regular priest?

Answer: *Rashi* to this verse explains the language, "the sons of Aaron the *kohen.*" He emphasizes the fact that when Aaron, the *Kohen Gadol,* is in his state of *kehuna* he is entering a unique state of being. If he wears the garments of a regular *kohen* at that time his service is invalid. By the same token a regular *kohen* invalidates his service if he wears any but his own garments (*Rashi, Leviticus 1:7,8; Torat Kohanim 9*).

Question: If the offering had a blemish, was deformed, or was missing a limb, was it acceptable?

Answer: Our sages teach us that defective animals were unacceptable as *korbanot* (scarifices to the Almighty). However, if a bird had a defect, it was acceptable, as long as the fowl was not missing an entire limb (*Rashi, Leviticus 1:14*).

Question: When are turtledoves and other doves acceptable *(Leviticus 1:14)*?

Answer: For both it was the sheen of the neck feathers that determined acceptability. The turtledove was acceptable when its neck feathers developed a sheen, while other doves were acceptable only when young and before their neck feathers developed a sheen. During the time their neck feathers were changing, neither was acceptable.

Question: What do the sages teach us from the phrase, "pleasing aroma to God" *(Leviticus 1:17)*?

Answer: This phrase is found a few times in the Torah. Our sages teach us (*Talmud Menachot 110a*) that despite the amount given all offerings are accepted equally. The term 'aroma' indicates the Almighty's pleasure in the offerings of His people.

Question: The Bible tells us that when the priest took the bird offering, he had to remove the bird's crop with its feathers. Why did the priest do this, instead of using the entire fowl?

Answer: A bird's diet is not controlled; birds eat whatever they find. Thus, the contents of the bird's digestive tract were considered stolen. This is not a consideration with animal offerings (*Rashi, Leviticus 1:16; Vayikra Rabba 3:4*). From this, we learn that even though we bought a fowl with our own money with good intentions, since the bird's food was considered "stolen" the bird's crop was considered unacceptable as an offering. One was forbidden to bring anything stolen as an offering on the altar.

It is found in several places in the Torah that our ancestors were very careful to keep their animals from grazing in other people's fields (*Genesis 24:10*). The Torah emphasized this to require us to follow in the path of our ancestors. It is almost impossible to control what a bird eats.

Question: Why does the Torah use the word "soul" in reference to the meal offering *(Leviticus 2:1)?*

Answer: Since a poor person usually brought the meal offering, and went through great sacrifice to bring it, the Almighty considers it as if he is donating his own soul.

Parshat Parah Adumah
Chapters: 19:1 - 22

Synopsis:

Rules and regulations regarding the Red Heifer; discussion of contamination and purification process.

In addition to the regular weekly Torah reading, this portion is read at the Maftir aliya. This section can be found at the very beginning of Parshat Chukas.

Question: Why do we read this particular biblical portion, called *Parah Adumah*, in addition to the regular portion of the week just prior to the festival of Passover?

Answer: We read this additional portion of the Torah, called *Parah Adumah (Numbers 19:1-22)*, to commemorate the days when the Israelites offered sacrifices in the Temple in Jerusalem. They were required to purify themselves before coming to Jerusalem on the festival of Passover. Consequently, we read this prior to the Passover season.

Question: What is the commandment of the *Red Heifer*, the *Parah Adumah?*

Answer: The commandment of the *Parah Adumah*, the *Red Heifer*, defies human understanding. The *red heifer* had to meet very specific and rigorous standards. It had to be perfect, without blemish. Its hair had to be completely straight, and the animal must never have performed labor of any sort. The *kohen* slaughtered this heifer and sprinkled its blood on the altar. The heifer was then burned and its ashes collected and placed in an urn and used in the purification process.

A person or object that had become spiritually contaminated by coming in contact with a deceased person was not permitted to have contact with the general population until they had gone through a purification process. For their status to change, the ashes of the *red heifer* had to be sprinkled on that person or object. The contaminated person stood opposite the *kohen*, and the *kohen* threw some of the ashes on him. This act resulted in the purification of the individual, who was then able to reenter the camp and the Tabernacle. The *kohen* who had performed the ceremony became contaminated. After nightfall, the *kohen* purified himself by immersing himself in water.

Question: Why does the *kohen* become impure after he finished these services?

Answer: The Torah determined that the *kohen*, who sprinkled the ashes of the *Red Heifer*, became impure to show that an individual, no matter what his position might be, does not control events. Man is not the ultimate source of the best things in life. We must always think of how dependent we are on the Almighty, the source of all blessing.

Tzav

Chapters: 6 - 8

Synopsis:

Detailed procedures for the various offerings in the Tabernacle: the sin offering, the meal offering, the elevation offering, and the guilt offering; a guide to the rules of dress for the kohanim and the consecration of the kohanim.

Question: What does *Parshat Tzav* deal with?

Answer: This *parsha* relates many of the laws and instructions handed down by Moses to the Israelites. Some of these instructions specifically target the *kohanim*, relating to their daily sacrifices in the Tabernacle and the purification of people who have become impure through contact with the dead.

Question: Why is animal sacrifice not practiced today?

Answer: The Torah requires sacrifices to be made only in the Temple. Since the Temple does not exist today, animal sacrifice cannot be brought.

Question: Can we satisfy God's requirement for offerings today even though animal sacrifice is not permitted?

Answer: The prophet Hosea (*Hosea 14:3*) said: "Let the offerings of our lips and tongue replace the animal sacrifices of the Temple." Our sages say that when the Temple is rebuilt, with God's help, then and only then will animal sacrifice once again be permitted.

Question: How is this Torah portion, which deals with Temple sacrifice, connected to our daily life?

Answer: God blessed man with five senses: sight, sound, smell, touch, and taste. The Temple offerings made use of all five senses. Today, we can only simulate the sense of sound with our voices lifted in prayer and the blowing of the shofar; the sense of sight with the Torah and its decorations; the sense of smell with the *havdalah* spices (the post-Sabbath spices); the sense of taste with the matzah and bitter herbs of Passover; and finally the sense of touch with the *lulav* of the festival of *Sukkot*. In this way, our offerings are much more than a dry, silent reading of the prayer book. Most importantly, we must pray with concentration and strong intent to make our prayers truly an offering to the Almighty. The sacrifices of old required direct action by the people, not merely passive participation. Judaism requires of us more than just the moving of our lips. We must actively perform good deeds to complete our offerings to God. The sacrifice itself was not the final goal: the goal was to sensitize people and bring them closer to God, through repentance of their sins.

Question: According to the prophet Isaiah *(Isaiah 1:11)*, God says, "Why do I need your numerous sacrifices...I am satiated with offerings...I do not desire them..." So why do we make offerings?

Answer: The offerings were not the end, but the means to the end. The prophets did not want people to feel that after a sacrifice they were forgiven and could return to sinning. Isaiah goes on to quote God: "Remove the evil of your doing...desist from doing evil. Learn to do good, seek justice, take up the cause of the widow and orphan...[then] your sins will whiten like snow...." The sacrifice is to "arouse" man's heart and bring him closer to God. We are to understand that when we finish praying, everything is still not settled. Prayer is but the beginning of the process of self-improvement.

Question: Why can we not eat blood, but are commanded to put blood on the altar for atonement?

Answer: In the Torah, blood is seen as the "essence of life." Aside from the medical consideration that ingesting blood is unhealthy, it is seen as a heathen practice. Many primitive sects have blood-drinking rituals bordering on idolatry and therefore, the practice is forbidden on that basis (*Rambam, Moreh Nevuchim*). Furthermore, since blood is used in the atonement process, it is contradictory to use it as a source of nourishment. As part of the separation of the spiritual from the material, this prohibition serves to differentiate man from animals who drink blood. The holiness of the blood is demonstrated by putting it on the altar as something only for God, not for humans (*Ramban; Rabbeinu Bachayei; Abarbanel*).

Question: How can we see from this *parsha* that the Torah is not in chronological order?

Answer: We see in the book of Exodus, *Parshat Pekudei*, that Aaron and his sons were consecrated as the *kohanim*. Some of the laws pertaining to Aaron's consecration are given here in *Parshat Tzav (Leviticus 8:2)*.

Shmeni

Chapters: 9 - 11

Synopsis:

God appointed Aaron as Kohen Gadol (high priest); the priestly duties; the death of Aaron's sons, Nadav and Avihu; the prohibition against drinking in the Temple; rules of mourning for kohanim; rules and regulations pertaining to Kashrut; lists of animals, birds, and fish permitted and forbidden to be eaten.

Question: What were the events leading up to the death of two of Aaron's sons?

Answer: Moses served as High Priest for eight days. On the first day of Nisan, Moses called Aaron and his sons and the elders of Israel and conferred upon Aaron the position of *Kohen Gadol.* Aaron presented his offering to God and blessed all of the Children of Israel. It was a very happy occasion and considered a good sign when a fire descended from the Almighty and consumed the calf that Aaron offered on the altar. Then, two of Aaron's sons, Nadav and Avihu, without being commanded, offered an "alien fire" to God. Because of this unsolicited offering, two streams of fire came down from the Almighty, entered the nostrils of Nadav and Avihu ,and completely incinerated them.

Here we see that just as "the Almighty blew in Adam's nostrils the soul of life" (*Genesis 2:7*), the Almighty can take away life (the soul) in a similar fashion (*Zohar*).

Question: Why did Aaron's sons deserve to die?

Answer: Our sages give many possible reasons:
They did something they were not asked to do; therefore, they were disobedient (*Ritva, Talmud Yoma 53a*). They may have brought the fire offering in order to appear overly righteous (*Ramban*). Or they entered the Holy Place in the Tabernacle where only the high priest may enter and then only on *Yom Kippur* (*Sifra*). They entered the Temple in an intoxicated state, wearing inappropriate clothing (*Rashi*). They chose to use fire from a different source, without first getting permission from Moses (*Rashi*). For reasons of sanctity, Moses wanted to kindle the first incense with heavenly fire. However, Aaron's sons took it upon themselves to decide which fire to use (*Rashbam*). They arrogantly fought with and insulted their other two brothers in front of people. This degraded the priesthood (*Ramav*). They remained unmarried because they felt no one had the lineage to marry them. This arrogant attitude raised anger in the

Almighty, which eventually led to them to pay with their lives (*Yalkut*). They did not fully believe that the fire of the incense came from Heaven and wanted to perform a "test" (*Ba'al Hakaidah*). Their death was a punishment for Aaron, because of the sin of the Golden Calf (*Ramav; see Shemot 32:35, 34:7; Rashi, Leviticus 9:2*).

Question: Was their punishment too severe for their transgression?

Answer: In effect, the transgression of Aaron's two sons violated a biblical ruling. The fact that this punishment was justified is shown by the Torah text, which says, "... the fire consumed them and they were dead." The repetition is for emphasis (*Ba'al Haturim; Bechor Shor; Taz*).

Question: Why does the Torah refer to their offering as an "alien fire"?

Answer: Since the service that Aaron's sons were attempting was contrary to God's commandment, it was seen as "alien." The fire that came to destroy them was also an "alien fire" (*Da'at Z'kanim; Shut Harosh end of rule 13; Rashbam*). The decision about which priest was to bring the incense was to have been made by lottery. Nadav and Avihu disobeyed and brought incense on their own accord. As usurpers, their fire was unacceptable, "alien" to God (*Abarbanel*).

Question: What is the reason for Kashrut *(Leviticus 11)*?

Answer: The main purpose of *kashrut* is to separate holy from unholy. If one is allowed to indiscriminately eat any form of food, one will eventually lose the ability to discriminate between what is clean and what is dirty, between things that are fit to eat and things that are not. It is only through self-control and selection of the most suitable forms of sustenance that we distinguish ourselves from animals, eat anything. Lack of discipline in eating may not cause physical harm, but it does prevent our soul from reaching its highest level of spirituality (*Sefer HaChinuch*).

Question: Are there valid health reasons for the kosher diet?

Answer: Sages, the *Rambam* and *Ramban*, say that there are definite health advantages to following the rules of kashrut. However, *Abarbanel* says that the Torah is not a book on health practices. Gentiles who do not follow kashrut are no less healthy. He does say that not following kashrut is related to "alien practices," and therefore is an abomination, similar to the worship of idols. He also points out that the Torah alludes to health benefits.

Question: Why are some animals considered kosher and others not?

Answer: Some sages contend that forbidden animals have intrinsic characteristics that render them unfit. Regardless of their status, the Torah requires that all animals be treated with kindness. All the sages agree that, whatever the reasons, we are obligated to follow the laws of kashrut (*Ha'Gaon from Rogatchov*).

Tazria

Chapters: 12 - 13

Synopsis:

Laws regarding impurity and purification; diagnosis and treatment of leprosy.

Question: What is the meaning of tazria?

Answer: The simple meaning of the word is "seed". This *parsha* recounts the laws of purification that were given to the Israelites during their wandering in the desert. They included the diagnosis and treatment of the dreaded disease, leprosy. The *kohen* was charged with the responsibility for deciding whether to isolate or purify the leper, depending on his condition.

Question: What is the connection between the *parsha* and the *haftorah?*

Answer: The *haftorah* tells the story of Na'aman, a famous Syrian general, a most powerful and honored man, who lived in the time of Elijah, the great prophet. Na'aman came to Elijah because he had leprosy and wanted to be cured. The great prophet told him that he should bathe in the Jordan River seven times and that God would cure him. Na'aman had expected Elijah to work magic and bring about an immediate cure. Na'aman reacted angrily and with great arrogance. He felt that Elijah had not shown the proper respect for his position. He could not understand that Elijah was showing him that all things, including a cure, come only from God, not from man, even one as great as Elijah. Ultimately, Na'aman followed Elijah's instructions and was healed completely. To Na'aman's credit and true greatness, he returned to Elijah to thank him and give full praise to the Almighty for the cure.

Na'aman implored Elijah to accept gifts for helping to cure his leprosy. Elijah steadfastly refused. There is an important lesson for us to learn and apply to our everyday lives. In the face of trial or tribulation, we must place our faith in God, even though it is apparent that an individual is aiding us (i.e., a doctor).

Metzora

Chapters: 14 - 15

Synopsis:

Isolation for and contamination by leprosy; hygienic considerations and sacrifices related to leprosy.

Question: Why does the Torah devote so much attention to leprosy?

Answer: The great scholar and teacher, Rabbi Moshe ben Maimon (*Rambam*), says that leprosy is a disease sent by God to warn those who speak *loshon hora* ("evil speech"). Rambam revealed that there is a strong connection between leprosy and a person's evil speech. God blessed us by giving us the power to speak. We must learn, therefore, to appreciate this gift. We must remember that speech is a privilege. Once something is said there is no way to retrieve it. This is why it is imperative to think and choose our words carefully before we speak (*Rambam, Hilchot Tuma'at Tzara'at; Chafetz Chayim, Shmirat Halashon 1:5*).

Question: When is *loshon hora* permitted or required?

Answer: *Loshon hora,* derogatory or damaging statements, is permitted in a situation where it is required to speak evil of a person in order to protect another person from potential harm. For example, if a *shidduch* "potential marriage" is planned, and one party has a serious illness or defect they are trying to hide, a third person who knows the facts is required to warn the inquiring party that he or she is being misled. It would be the same for any potential relationship, be it personal or business, in which a person might come to harm. The *Talmud* tells a the story that took place when Rabbi Yehuda was a boy. A fruit vendor came to Yehuda's father and complained that his son had destroyed his business by taking a case of tomatoes and turning it over in the street. Because Yehuda was a quiet, well-behaved boy, the father was surprised at this report. He questioned his son and found out that the merchant had been fooling his customers by filling the case with rotten tomatoes and placing a layer of better ones on top. When a customer bought the tomatoes, the dishonest merchant placed the rotted ones from the bottom of the case into the customer's bag. Yehuda saw this and turned over the case in order to show the people that they should not trust this merchant. This action was permitted, in order to prevent additional misdeeds by the merchant.

Question: What might happen to a person who speaks evil?

Answer: Rambam says that the first result of an evil act might be trouble with one's house (*Rambam, Hilchot Tumaat Tzara'at 16:10*). John recently went with a real estate broker to see an apartment. He liked it and wanted to buy it. The broker told John that another person named Bill was interested in the property as well. Upon hearing this, John immediately began to tell the broker that Bill was an untrustworthy cheat. The broker made his decision to sell the apartment to John based on this information. From the day he moved in, John experienced an unending series of mishaps: the plumbing failed, electricity would not work, and even the walls of the house started to crumble. There was no end to the repairs he was forced to make. John concluded that he was being punished for his disparaging remarks about Bill.

Question: In *Leviticus 15* the Torah tells us to "immerse in water." What is this in reference to?

Answer: Our sages explain that to immerse as the Torah describes is to place one's entire body, without any blockage between the body and the water, into a body of water. The water must be pure rain water, and a certain quantity must be present. We refer to this type of structure as a "*mikvah*" (ritual bath). The specifications of how the water got to this vessel, its size and shape are detailed at great length, in the Torah and in the *Talmud (Tractate Nidah)*.

Question: Why does the Almighty command His people to utilize this mikvah, this ritual bath?

Answer: *Leviticus 20:7* states, "You shall sanctify yourselves and you will be holy, for I am the Almighty your God." The Almighty commands us to keep our bodies in a state of spiritual purity.

The Torah states in *Leviticus 20:18* that "If a man lies with a menstruating woman they both shall be cut off from among their people." The understanding of this verse is that the relationship between husband and wife is held in high regard by the Torah. While the woman is menstruating and for a period after, the husband and wife must separate from each other in a sexual manner. After this separation the woman immerses in a mikvah, to purify herself, thereby permitting her husband to resume sexual contact with her. There are many fine books that explain the subject in greater detail than we are able to do here. Ask your rabbi and he will give you the names of these books. It is a subject worth the exploration.

Question: How does one reverse a decree of being "cut-off" from among the people"?

Answer: Examples of how one may become "cut-off" are when a man may unintentionally discharge semen as he sleeps, or a married couple will mistakenly relate with one another sexually while the woman is in an "impure" state due to menstruation and has yet to go to the *mikvah*. The Almighty provided a unique opportunity to express regret and a means by which one can reintroduce oneself back into the community. This is accomplished by immersing one's self in the mikvah. The instructions for doing so are discussed in this parsha. Furthermore, the prophet Isaiah (1), rebuked the people and instructed them to follow the path the Almighty had laid out. He told the people that the Almighty had punished them as a direct result of their impure lifestyles, of being lack in their interpersonal relationships. Isaiah tells the people to utilize the ritual baths (*mikvaot*) as the vehicle by which to cleanse themselves and to draw closer to the Almighty.

Question: God commanded His people to uplift their marital relationships. How might one accomplish this?

Answer: Because it is extremely important to maintain strong and loving relationships within the home, the Torah directs couples to become role models for their children, and also for each other. This relationship the Torah says will perpetuate holiness for into future generations. There are discussions within the *Talmud* as to why the Almighty required such guidelines. One of the reasons offered is that the Creator knows the character traits of his creations and those that might lead one to acts not becoming a wholesome person. Therefore the Almighty commanded us to abstain and then to physically reunite at the requiste times following immersion in the *mikvah.*

Question: What is the connection between the *parsha* and its *haftorah?*

Answer: Both the *parsha* and the *haftorah* discuss leprosy. The *haftorah* tells of the siege by the Arameans of a Jewish city in which the inhabitants were about to die of starvation. There happened to be four lepers outside the city. In need of food, they felt they had little to lose by approaching the Aramean camp. When they got to the camp, they found it deserted. The lepers were able to eat. They then notified the city dwellers that the Arameans had fled, thus saving the city. The parsha on the other hand provides the procedure by which a person who had become afflicted with this disease is to be purified once the *kohen* has declared him to be free from leprosy.

Acharei Mot

Chapters: 16 - 18

Synopsis:

The requirements for the Yom Kippur service confession, the lottery to Azazel, incense, fasting, atonement; service auxiliary to the Tabernacle; the prohibition of eating blood; the prohibition against marriages with one's immediate family; incest, sodomy, bestiality, and homosexuality.

Question: How does this *parsha* begin?

Answer: This *parsha* begins with the death of Aaron's two sons, Naḍav and Avihu. The sons had attained a high level of religious authority and spirituality because their father was the high priest. In spite of the awesome nature of their position and responsibility, they drank too much wine and felt they could do no wrong. They approached the holy altar in an improper manner and were killed immediately. This severe punishment was the result of their arrogance: they abused their position in pursuit of self-aggrandizement (*Rashi; Ramban*).

Question: What types of prohibited behavior are listed in this *parsha?*

Answer: The *parsha* has a highly detailed list of actions that are prohibited. These behaviors range from incest to unfaithfulness to homosexuality to bestiality to the eating of prohibited foods; all these actions are abominations before God. There is also the prohibition against unrestrained behavior and self-indulgence, which results from disregarding the moral consequences of one's actions.

Question: What sexual relationships does the Torah prohibit?

Answer: Sexual relations that involve close relatives: parents, children, siblings, step-siblings, aunts, uncles, and the like, are prohibited. Sexual relations are prohibited between individuals related by marriage and not by blood, to avoid the jealous feelings that would be aroused. The prohibition against these types of relationships is partially based on genetic protection, as well as protection of family harmony (*Talmud*).

Question: What is the Torah's attitude toward homosexuality?

Answer: Despite all the modern notions about homosexuality, the Torah considers it unnatural, and therefore an abomination. It is forbidden without exception. The relationships stated in the previous answer are thought of as undesirable and could never be condoned. They are prohibited but are not abominations, because they consist of a normal activity involving unsuitable partners. An abomination however, is a totally unnatural activity with unacceptable partners and the Torah treats it as something that God hates (*Ramav*).

Kedoshim
Chapters: 19 - 20

Synopsis:

Requirements for observing Sabbath; honoring one's parents; giving to the poor; honesty in business; justice; love for one's fellow man.

Note: *This parsha is one of the richest in the Torah because of the number of important principles of proper human behavior that it contains. Almost all aspects of human relations that are accepted in civilized societies have their roots in this parsha.*

Question: What do the sages teach us from the decree: "A man shall fear his mother and father"?

Answer: It is forbidden to sit in a parent's place, to interrupt a parent who is speaking, or to contradict what a parent says. All these are signs of disrespect of one's parents.

Question: When are we allowed to refuse to obey a parent's instructions?

Answer: It is permitted only when a parent tells a child to do something against the Torah. A parent cannot command a child to kill, to steal, or to bow to an idol. The Torah in cases such as these allows the disobedience (*Talmud*).

Question: What are the obligations of a judge?

Answer: When sitting in judgment, a judge must give equal and full opportunity to each side to state its case. He must not favor one party over the other. A rich and powerful man is not entitled to any advantage before the law, nor is a judge allowed to bend over backwards to help the poorer or weaker side.

Question: What is included in the prohibition: "Thou shalt not steal" (*Leviticus 19:11*)?

Answer: All stealing is prohibited, including taking something with the idea of returning it or taking something to irritate or aggravate someone. Even taking something as a joke is not allowed.

Question: Why is "...Thou shalt not steal" written twice in the Torah?

Answer: *Shemot 20:13* with the mentioning of the Ten Commandments, the phrase, "thou shalt not steal" is written in Hebrew in the singular form; in this *parsha*, *Leviticus 19:11* it is written in the plural. The sages explain that use of the singular form means that the commandment refers to kidnapping whereas the plural refers to stealing money or objects.

Question: What does the phrase: "...the wages of your worker shall not abide with you until morning" mean *(Leviticus 19:13)*?

Answer: A worker's wage must be paid to him without delay. However, the sages add a very rich interpretation. Both parties prior to the beginning of the work must clearly understand the terms of employment and payment. The person doing the hiring is responsible for assuring that there is no misunderstanding. Above all, payment must be prompt; it is unacceptable to delay such payment. It is considered a form of stealing if the worker does not receive his wage at the appropriate time.

Question: What is the significance of the following commandment: "you shall not place a stumbling block before the blind" *(Leviticus 19:14)*?

Answer: Our sages explain that this verse does not only apply to those who are literally blind. The concept is extended to those who are "blind" to the implications of their actions. We are forbidden to take advantage of another person's ignorance or naiveté. For example, a doctor advises a patient to take a series of treatments that will not benefit him but will earn a great deal of money for the doctor. Jewish law forbids such a person from taking advantage of another's ignorance.

Question: What is meant by "...do not seek revenge or bear a grudge..." *(Leviticus 19:18)*?

Answer: Revenge is an attempt to harm someone or deny someone something because of a real or imagined act done by this person. The Torah forbids this. Sometimes the aggrieved person will decide to refrain from a vengeful act, but will do so in such a way as to embarrass the other person. The Torah also forbids this. For example, Dan asks Jack to borrow his truck. Jack refuses; Dan buys his own truck. Later, Jack's truck breaks down and asks Dan if he may borrow his. Dan says "Of course you can! I am not like you." The Torah is very specific in its dictate that one is not permitted to seek revenge or bear a grudge (*Rashi*).

Question: Is it allowed by the Torah to consult with a fortuneteller?

Answer: The Torah says, "You shall not indulge in sorcery or believe in lucky times" (*Leviticus 19:26*). The Torah also writes, "do not turn to sorcery" (*ibid 19:30*). It is forbidden by the Torah to make decisions based upon superstitious notions. This prohibition forbids all manners of seances, fortunetelling, and any other fakery that purports to predict the future. The Torah calls these things abominations, and says that God hates them.

Question: A woman left money with a man for safekeeping. She died. Her grandson came for the money, even though he had no papers or proof of deposit. The man denied the deposit and was taken to court. Based on his oath that there was no deposit, the court let him go for lack of evidence. According to this parsha, what serious sins did the man commit?

Answer: He stole; he lied and he committed blasphemy of God's name.

Question: What is meant by the command in this parsha: "Love thy neighbor as thyself" (*Leviticus 19:18*)?

Answer: In the *Jerusalem Talmud (Nedarim 9:4)* we learn that this commandment is the essence of the entire Torah. Our sages tell us that the biblical word for love implies that we must close our eyes and place ourselves in our fellowman's shoes; it is only then that we can feel the way he feels or understand the things he does. This in all likelihood will lead us to a more positive perspective and understanding of our fellowman.

The sages continue by relating a story of a man who inquired about learning Torah. He happened upon one of the sages, but requested to learn while standing on one leg. He was immediately dismissed. The man then went to Hillel, another one of our sages, with the same request. Hillel answered him "What is hateful to you, do not do to your fellowman. This is the entire Torah. The rest is all commentary. Go and study it" (*Babylonian Talmud, Shabbat 31a*). We must deal fairly with our fellowman in all respects and details. In our relationships with our fellowman, we are not allowed to fool or mislead in any way, or to any degree. Everyone knows how he or she feels when fooled or defrauded. We must keep those feelings in mind when interacting with others.

Emor

Chapters: 21 - 24

Synopsis:

Regulations pertaining to priests (kohanim) and high priests; requirements for disqualifying animals for sacrifice; the commandments surrounding the festivals of Passover, Shavuot, and Sukkot; the counting of the Omer; order of days of Rosh Hashanah and Yom Kippur; use of the menorah; punishment of the blasphemer.

Note: This parsha, together with the previous one, Acharei Mot, form the fundamental basis for Judaism in the Torah. Parshat Emor contains sixty-three different commandments, of which twenty-four are positive and thirty-nine are negative.

Question: According to our sages, which type of *mitvah* is considered to be one of the most important type of *mitzvot* and why?

Answer: One of the most important type of mitzvot is the one for which one receives no reward or thanks. This type of *mitzvah* is referred to as a *Chesed shel Emet.* For example, escorting the deceased to its resting place is a pure way of expressing human kindness and showing respect for the holiness of life. We know that the dead can never thank or reward us in any way for our kindness. The sages say that all that is done in consideration of the dead should be sincere and unselfish.

Question: What is the obligation of the *kohen* (priest)?

Answer: The *kohen* must remain at a very high level of purity. He is forbidden to engage in any activity that might contaminate him (i.e., contact with a dead body, except under certain conditions). He is also forbidden to marry a divorced woman or the widow of another priest (*Leviticus 21:1-9*).

Question: Under what conditions is a *kohen* allowed contact with the dead?

Answer: With few exceptions, any contact with the dead is strictly forbidden. The *kohen* is required to tend to the dead if the deceased is a member of his immediate family; or if there is no one else to perform the required duties for the dead. In performing these duties, the *kohen* is placed in a temporary state of spiritual impurity, unable to perform any of his priestly duties.

Question: Which relatives belong to the category of immediate family?

Answer: In the case of the *kohen* tending to the dead, biblical law limits immediate family to one of the following relations: mother, father, wife, son, daughter, brother, and virgin sister (never married, no children).

Question: If a *kohen* adopted a child, is this child considered a member of the *kohen's* immediate family?

Answer: The subject of adoption is debated by the sages. Because the child is not biologically related, the status of the child within the family unit is in question. The essence of the sages' conclusions is as follows: Rabbi Tzvi Waldenberg (*Tzitz Eliezer, vol. 6, ch. 21*) says that if the adoption occurred at a very early age, and the relationship between both sides is as a parent with a child, then the child is considered to be part of the family. Therefore, for instance, in the case of marriage or divorce, and so forth, we use the adopted parent's name and we add, in parentheses, *hamegadlo*, which means, "who raised him." However, Rabbi Waldenberg, may he rest in peace, although recognizing an adopted child as being part of the family unit, states that in the case of a dead body, if the father is a *kohen* he is not allowed to touch the body, or be closer than four cubits to it. Rabbi Moshe Feinstein (*Igrot Moshe*), may he rest in peace, said that even though there are very important emotional and psychological elements involved in an adoption, the biological element still exists and is relevant; therefore, the child is not to be considered as immediate family. Again, this is just the tip of the iceberg relating to adoption matters (*See Mevaser Tov, Even Haezer 124; Shevet Halevi 5:205; Levush, Even Haezer ch. 22; Chatam Sofer, Ohr Chayim 140*).

Question: What is *Met Mitzvah?*

Answer: *Met Mitzvah* is the tending to the needs of the deceased who has no relative to do so (i.e., the preparations prior to burial, eulogizing, burial, and care of the gravesite). In general, it is forbidden for Jews to come in contact with a corpse, even though care for a dead body is absolutely essential. There usually are designated individuals in a community who perform these duties, such as the *Chevrah Kedishah* (Sacred Society), undertakers, and so forth. These individuals are allowed to tend to the dead because they are professionals who are dedicated to and prepared for these tasks. However, if these specialized individuals are not available, it then becomes necessary for others to see to the needs of the deceased.

Question: According to the Torah, which is the first month of the year?

Answer: According to the Torah, there are two types of years, both of which have legal and religious ramifications associated with them. There is the year that begins with Tishrei, coinciding with the fall months in the English calendar, and is used for counting years and starts from the time that God finished the Creation. The other year, which begins with the month of Nisan, the onset of spring in the English calendar, sets in motion the cycle for the festivals.

Question: What is the *Omer*?

Answer: Literally, *omer* is a measurement of grain; it is also the name given to the offering that was brought every day for a period of forty-nine days, counting from the second day of Passover to the day just prior to the festival of Shavuot. One was not permitted to partake of his new grain until he had brought a requisite amount of barley to the Temple as an offering for his fields. Newly harvested grains could not be used in any offering in the Temple until the fiftieth day after the first day of Passover, which is the festival of Shavuot, the celebration of the giving of the Torah to Moses.

Question: From when to when do we count the *Omer*, and why?

Answer: We count the forty-nine days of the *Omer* from the morning of the first day of *Pesach*, Passover, until the festival of *Shavuot*. We literally "count the days" until the giving of the Torah, as a child counts the days to his birthday. The days are counted in anticipation of a joyful event.

Question: What time of day do we count the *Omer*, and what if a person forgets to count once?

Answer: *Genesis 1:5*, in the Torah states "there was night and there was morning,...." For the Israelite the twenty-four hour *day* begins with the beginning of nightfall and ends when the following daylight ends. Therefore, the *Omer* is counted in the evening with a bracha, a blessing. If, however, one forgets to count in the evening one counts during the following day(light) without a bracha. If one forgets to count for the entire twenty-four-hour period (night then day), one continues to count the remaining days of the *Omer* without a *bracha* (blessing). The daily counting of the *Omer* enables an individual to build his feelings of excitement to the ultimate joy of receiving the Torah.

Question: How do we know that we have to light a candle every Friday night?

Answer: "On the *Shabbat* (Sabbath) on the *Shabbat* the priest must light the menorah..." (*Leviticus 24:8*). The sages teach that the phrase "on the *Shabbat*" is repeated to emphasize that we must light candles every Friday night.

Behar
Chapters: 25 - 26:2

Synopsis:

Sabbatical year (the seventh year of a seven-year cycle), Jubilee year (the concluding year of a fifty-year cycle); sequence regarding the use of land and its produce; prohibition against selling the Holy Land in perpetuity; Levites' eternal right of redemption of their own property; the commandment of helping another in a time of need.

Question: What is the meaning of the word *shmittah?*

Answer: The literal meaning of the word is "release." The Almighty requires that we release the land; let the land (the Land of Israel) rest for one year out of every seven. This is because the land really belongs to God, and we cannot do with it entirely as we wish. This is also the case with all that we like to think of as our belongings. We are given use of "things" during our lifetime, but ultimately everything belongs to God. The purpose of *shmittah* is to remind us that we do not have total possession or control over anything in this world.

Question: Why do the laws of *Shmittah* exist only in the Holy Land?

Answer: The Almighty refers to the Holy Land (Israel) as "My Land" (*Leviticus 25:23*). A similar concept is applied here with reference to the Land as was applied to the Creation of the universe: the Almighty rested on the seventh day; in likeness, then, the Almighty wants His land also to rest. The Almighty therefore commands Moses to inform the Israelites that once they have entered into the Land they must rest the Holy Land in the sabbatical year or *shmittah* (*Ramav*). Other commentators say that it is also done for the regeneration of the soil, as modern ecologists have proven.

Question: Do the laws of *shmittah* apply today?

Answer: Our sages tell us that the commandment as it was written and understood is applied when two conditions are met. The first of these conditions is the existence of the Temple in Jerusalem. The second is that the majority of the Jewish people live within the borders of the Holy Land. As long as these two major criteria are not met then the law is not applied in its absolute sense. However, the sages decreed that the laws of *shmittah* should be observed nonetheless. This observance is a law issued from the earlier rabbis, and is to be followed.

Question: What is the meaning of a "bad buy" *(mekach ta'ut)*?

Answer: There are two aspects to this term. When you buy something you may return the object if a defect or misrepresentation becomes apparent. However, if you damage the item or become dissatisfied with it in some way and return it under false pretenses, this is wrong. Even though there might be no proof of your deception, God would know, and the sin is very great.

Question: Must a real estate broker reveal defects in a property that he or she is trying to sell to a client, even though he or she would be risking a commission in doing so?

Answer: Yes. This *parsha* (*Leviticus 25:14*) states: "When you make a sale to your fellow or make a purchase from your fellow, do not aggrieve one another." This tells us clearly that in all aspects of business, it is wrong to take advantage of one's fellowman. It is wrong to knowingly sell something, without fully disclosing all one knows about it.

Question: A businessman receives payment from a customer. On checking his books, he finds that the customer has, in fact, unknowingly paid twice. The customer dies. What is the businessman to do?

Answer: The businessman is required to search for any of the customer's heirs and return the money to them. The source of this commandment is found in this *parsha Leviticus 25:23*, which says, "…you should fear your God."

Question: During many years in business, the owner made a great deal of money, not all of it in a totally honest way. Later in life, the man does teshuvah, "repentance," and becomes scrupulously honest. He is greatly bothered by his ill-gotten gains, but he no longer has enough money to repay all that he took. How does Jewish law deal with this situation?

Answer: Here we deal with the question of people who feel that they have been too sinful in the past to be able to achieve a full return to God. For example, one who stole a large amount of money and now feels unable to return it. When he desires to make amends for this past sin, the sages are faced with a dilemma. On the one hand, we want people to return to God. On the other hand, the problem exists of fulfilling the requirement to return the money. Therefore, one must consult rabbinical authorities (his rabbi or judge) to determine the sum of money that will be large enough so that the man will feel distress paying it, but small enough to allow him to continue to provide for his needs. This formula, devised by the sages, is called *takanat hashavim,* "decree of repentance" (*Talmud; Tur; Rambam*).

Question: Is there any other way for God to teach besides punishment?

Answer: It is written in the book of *Isaiah 45:7,* "The Lord said, I am the One Who created light and darkness, makes peace and creates evil; I am the Lord Who created all of these." Let us begin by stating that God did not create punishment. Punishment, just like reward, is a consequence of an action. Unlike today's understanding that if one commits a crime one is sent away to jail, it is looked upon as rehabilitation, a learning experience. If that happens all the better, but the reality is, these are the consequences that one must accept for doing an action. It is man's evil deeds and actions that create the misery and punishment that he must deal with. God created a paradise of blessing, free of all suffering.

Question: How does the Torah describe charity in this *parsha?*

Answer: There are many forms and ways by which one can perform the commandment to give charity. In this *parsha* the Torah concerns itself with the issue of poverty, and the responsibility to correct that situation. *Rambam* says that the highest form of "charity," *tzedaka,* is to do something that prevents your fellowman from falling into hardship or poverty. We are commanded to take immediate action if we see our fellowman in a desperate situation. It is an act of charity to give food to a poor, starving man, but it is better to help him achieve the means of earning his own living. Paying to train an unemployed person in a trade that will support him is much more beneficial to the recipient than merely giving him money to buy food. Some commentators explain that the series of admonitions contained in the next *parsha, Bechukotei,* are the consequences that result from ignoring your fellowman who is in trouble.

Question: What is the most important principle of *Parshat Behar?*

Answer: Trust between people is the principle of greatest importance dealt with in this *parsha.* If a person trusts you, you must be honest with that person regardless of personal self-interest.

Bechukotei

Chapters: 26:3 - 27

Synopsis:

Blessing and cursing; punishment and reward for deeds done; value of gifts to the Temple; sacrificial offerings in the Temple.

Question: By what other name is this *parsha* known, and why?

Answer: *Parsha Tochachah,* "admonition," is the other name for this *parsha.* The first part of the *parsha* tells of the rewards to be derived if we live by the laws of the Torah; the second part informs us of the consequences if we do not.

Question: Why does the *ba'al koreh,* the "Torah reader," read a major part of this *parsha (Leviticus 26:14-26:46)* in a soft voice?

Answer: We read this part of the Torah portion in a soft voice because it tells of the consequences that will befall Israel if she does not follow the path of the Torah. This custom evolved in order to avoid causing sadness on the Sabbath.

Question: The first three phrases of the *parsha* seem to be repetitious. What is the Torah's intention by this?

Answer: The *parsha* opens with the verse, "If you will follow My decrees and observe My commandments and perform them..." The meaning of which is that one is obligated to study the law, learn the law, and perform the requirements of the *mitzvot.*

Question: What is a major difference between the study of Torah and the study of any other subject (i.e., science, math, etc.)?

Answer: With any secular subject, the learning is most often but a means to an end. Torah study, on the other hand, is in and of itself a reward. Studying Torah, even without mastering it, is a worthy and desirable goal.

Question: What is the significance of the series of admonitions in this *parsha?*

Answer: The admonitions are written in the form of a series of wrongs. It starts with not learning Torah, which leads to being against the learning of Torah, to condemning learned people, and finally to being against the Torah itself. This clearly mirrors human experience (*Rashi*). How often does a person start out with a small misdeed or untruth and is led astray to commit a more serious sin?

Question: What is the purpose of these admonitions?

Answer: The purpose of the *Tochachah* is to make us aware of the spiritual and physical costs of violating the Almighty's covenant with Israel.

It is a worldwide custom that when the Torah reader finishes the last sentence of each one of the five books of Moses, the entire congregation stands and encourages one another with the following proclamation:

"CHAZAK CHAZAK V' NITCHAZEK!"

(STRENGTH...STRENGTH...AND BECOME STRONG)

The Festival of Shavuot

Synopsis:

The festival of Shavuot falls at the time when we start to read from the Book of Numbers.

Question: How many candles do we light for *Shavuot,* and when do we light them?

Answer: We light at least two candles in honor of the festival. We must light these each of the two evenings of the holiday. Lighting on the first night occurs at sundown. Lighting on the second night takes places no earlier than one hour after sundown. It is laudable to light a candle in memory of one's deceased loved ones. Lighting of any candles on the second night must be done by transferring a flame from an already existing light source.

Question: What is the source of the custom of decorating the Ark with flowers and greenery on *Shavuot?*

Answer: God chose a mountain from which to give us the Torah. Mount Sinai was one of the lowest mountains and it was also the most modest, so God selected it for those reasons. This teaches us the importance of modesty. Because Mount Sinai was covered in greenery, we decorate the ark with flora. *Shavuot* does not have the tangible symbols of other holidays, like *matzoh* or the *sukkah.* The idea surrounding *Shavuot* is more abstract. So we use flowers and greens to show special respect and honor to the Torah and the ark on this holiday.

Question: What is the reason for the widespread custom of eating dairy products on *Shavuot?*

Answer: The Torah mentions the phrase "milk and honey" several times, and depicts the Land of Israel as a land flowing with milk and honey. On the three days before we were to receive the Torah God commanded that we refrain from many things in order to prepare ourselves for accepting the Torah. One of the restrictions was to refrain from eating meat in any form. To commemorate that, we eat dairy products on *Shavuot.*

Another reason for this custom is to commemorate a heroic deed of Yael, a matriarch of Israel. On *Shavuot* we read from the *Book of Judges*. The portion read tells of a wicked general who attacked the camp of the Israelites. When he entered the tent of Yael, he was smitten by her beauty. Pretending to welcome him, she offered him milk to drink and cheeses to eat; the food ultimately made him sleepy, whereupon she slew him as he slept. When his army discovered that he had been murdered they retreated in fear.

Question: Why is the festival called *Shavuot?*

Answer: From the first day of Passover to *Shavuot* we count forty-nine days. Forty-nine days is exactly seven weeks, and the word *shavuot* means "weeks."

Question: Why is the festival of *Shavuot* called, the holiday of *Matan Torah?*

Answer: *Matan Torah* means "giving of the Torah." After counting the forty-nine days of the Omer, we reach the fiftieth day, which is the first day of the festival of *Shavuot.* This is the day Moses transmitted the Torah from God to the Israelites.

Question: What other names are used for *Shavuot* and why?

Answer: *Chag Hakatzir* is another name; meaning "holiday of the harvest." *Shavuot* is also known as *Chag Habikurim,* "holiday of the first fruits." The Israelites were commanded to bring the first fruits of their harvest to the Temple. The priests used ten percent, and all the rest was for the poor. This is to emphasize the fact that everything belongs to God, and we are only allowed to use the goodness of the earth temporarily. So we bring our first produce to God.

Question: Why do we read the *Book of Ruth* on *Shavuot?*

Answer: Ruth took upon herself the Torah and *mitzvot*. She also demonstrated the desire to convert to Judaism at whatever cost to her personal wellbeing. Her life is a paradigm of chesed "kindness" and modesty. The book begins and ends with acts of kindness. The *Talmud* calls Ruth the "mother of royalty," listing among her descendants King David, King Solomon, and *Messiah*.

Question: Why do we read *Akdamot* responsively before the Torah reading on *Shavuot?*

Answer: The purpose of the *Akdamot* is to describe for us the tremendous love relationship between God and Israel. It also tells of the Almighty's greatness, along with the abiding faith and obedience to God and to His Torah on the part of the Jewish people. It is read in the responsive form to demonstrate the reciprocal nature of this relationship that exists between God and Israel.

Book of Ruth

Synopsis:

The ancestry of King David; description of moral integrity; incite into the difficulties surrounding conversion to the Jewish faith; a look at the laws of yibum.

Question: How do the sages characterize Naomi?

Answer: Naomi is seen as a righteous, but weak, woman. Her husband forced her and her children to leave Israel and settle in Moab. By leaving Israel she left her heritage and her roots. When her husband died, she did not have the courage to leave her sons in Moab and return to Israel by herself. It was only by force of circumstance, after the death of her sons, that she returned to the Holy Land.

Question: What is the story of the *Book of Ruth?*

Answer: Elimelech was one of the wealthiest men of his day. For a time, he gave charity and responded to the hardships of others. He eventually left the Land of Israel to escape the increasing demands of the poor and the famine. His wife, Naomi, and their two sons had to follow him to the land of Moab, Israel's enemy. As the sages say, "One sin leads to another." Elimelech turned his back on his brothers in Israel when they needed him. For this God punished him by causing him to lose all of his wealth. He did not learn a lesson from this, and stubbornly remained in Moab. As a result, he died, leaving his widow and two orphaned sons in a strange and hostile land. His sons also did not learn from their father's experience. Instead of returning to Israel, they decided to stay in Moab and marry Moabite women. Both married women of wealth. One of them was Ruth, daughter of the king of Moab. They lived in Moab ten years, during which time the brothers lost their fortunes and finally their lives. Naomi had heard that the famine in the Holy Land was over, and she decided to return. Naomi's two daughters-in-law wanted to go with her to the Holy Land. She tried to convince them to remain in Moab among their own people. "I have no children, no money, and even no friends in Israel. I am too old to have children, so there certainly is no reason for you to follow me." At first, both daughters-in-law insisted on going with her. When Naomi told them of the problems they would encounter in Israel, one of them, Urpah, decided to remain in Moab. Ruth, however, was undeterred by all of her mother-in-law's arguments and insisted on going with her, becoming Jewish, and accepting all of the hardships of Naomi's life.

297

Question: What do we learn about conversion from the *Book of Ruth?*

Answer: "How do we determine the sincerity of a person who wants to convert?" ask our sages in the *Talmud.* They look to the *Book of Ruth* to learn how strong and pure the intentions of a convert must be. Naomi questioned Ruth three times. All three times Ruth showed that she had only absolutely pure motives, so Naomi accepted her conversion. From this book we also see how great are the difficulties of being a Jew. We must relate to a convert the harsh realities facing the Jewish people. If, after all this, a person still wants to be part of the Jewish destiny, and do the requisite study, and accept upon themselves the yoke of the Torah, they then are accepted. Once converted, they are to be accepted wholeheartedly and without reservation as Jews.

Question: The story of Ruth talks about heredity. Our sages glean from this book laws regarding yibum. What is this law of *yibum?*

Answer: According to Torah law, if a man dies childless and has a brother, the sibling is obligated to marry the widow. This is to ensure progeny. If the sibling refuses to marry his sister-in-law through the practice of *yibum*, he is required by the Torah to perform *chalitza* (she removes a sandal from his foot), which is the way of divorcing her and thereby rejecting his duty to marry her. These laws are discussed in detail in the *Book of Ruth.* The *Talmud* and *Rambam* in his *Mishnah Torah, Hilchot Yibum* discuss the actual laws as they relate to us today.

Question: Who wrote the *Book of Ruth?*

Answer: The prophet Samuel wrote the *Book of Ruth* (*Babylonian Talmud, Bava Batra, 74a*).

IV

The Book of Numbers

Bamidbar
Chapters: 1 - 4:20

Synopsis:

*Moses led the Israelites in Midbar Sinai; God appoint-
ed leaders of the nation from the twelve tribes; tribes were
situated within the camp; the Israelites carried the
Tabernacle to each place of encampment; Aaron's sons
offered "alien fire," which caused their death; God sanctified firstborn sons; the family tree of the tribe of Levi
was described; the law of redemption of firstborn sons
and the rules of the work in the Holy Tent of Meeting
were given.*

Question: What does the word *midbar* mean?

Answer: The word *midbar* has been traditionally translated as "wilderness" or "desert." The implication of the term would be a lack of natural resources or shelter. The lack of these necessities forced the Israelites to learn to depend on God.

Question: How were the Israelites organized in the *Midbar*?

Answer: Each tribe had their own flag and they were divided as follows: on the east were the tribes of Judah, Issachar, and Z'vulun. To the south were the tribes Reuven, Simeon, and Gad. On the west were the tribes of Ephraim, Menashah, and Benjamin. In the north were the tribes of Dan, Asher, and Naftali. In the center was the tribe of Levi whose responsibility was carrying the Ark (*Ha'amek-Davar, Abarbanel*).

North
Dan, Asher and Naftali

West	Center	East
Ephraim, Menasha, and Benjamin	Levi with the Ark	Judah, Issachar, and Z'vulun

South
Reuven, Shimon, and Gad

They each had a flag with a unique symbol representing the name of the tribe. They also each had a flag representing their physical location: north, south, east, or west (*Ramban*).

Question: In this *parsha*, the Israelites are formally organized into the twelve tribes and a census is taken. How many people were counted?

Answer: They counted 603,550 people, comprised of 186,400 people in the east; to the south 151,450; to the west 108,100 and in the north 157,600 (*Sifri*).

Question: One man from each tribe was chosen to act as its leader. Who were these twelve men, and why were they chosen?

Answer: When the Children of Israel left Egypt with the Egyptians in full pursuit, they stopped at the edge of the Red Sea, where there was a raging storm. Moses called out to God to help them, and God answered, "Move forward; I will protect you" (*Exodus 14*). Moses told the people to continue, but they hesitated out of fear of the dangerous waters. The Egyptians were closing in from the rear. The sea was roiling in front of them. The Israelites stood around not knowing what to do. This was a moment of crisis that cried for strong leadership. Suddenly, an individual named Nachshon ben Aminadav jumped into the raging waters. He possessed full faith in God and believed that if it was God's will for him to go forward, God certainly would protect him from harm. Almost immediately, eleven other men seized upon Nachshon's example and jumped into the raging water.

The twelve men sank until the water reached their chins. Just then, God parted the sea and the rest of the Israelites were able to follow the twelve men across the dry bed of the Red Sea to safety. These twelve individuals had complete faith and trust in God, and were not afraid to act on their faith, even at the risk of their very lives. As a result of their totally selfless act these men were chosen to lead the twelve tribes in the desert. They had demonstrated a faith and leadership of the highest level.

Naso

Chapters: 4:21 - 7

Synopsis:

The descendants of the tribe of Levi: Gershon, Kehat, and Merari; sons of Gershon; sons of Merari; purification of the Camp; atonement for sins; reminders of iniquity; inscription of curses; elevation offerings; the command to Aaron and his sons to bless the congregation; the offerings brought to the Tabernacle; Moses' instructions to the Israelites regarding appropriate use of the Tabernacle.

Question: Why does the *kohen* have to recite the blessing in the exact way that it is written in the Torah?

Answer: This *parsha* contains God's instructions to the *kohanim*. They are told, in detail, how to bless the Israelites in the Temple. These well-known blessings begin with the phrase, "May God bless you and keep you." The *kohanim* are considered to be "holy vessels." They are the conduits of the blessings from God to the people. The *kohanim* do not initiate the blessings nor are they the source of the blessings. All blessings are from God. The Kohanim only transmit God's blessings.

Question: God said: "Let the *kohanim* put My Name on the Children of Israel and I will bless them" *(Numbers 6:27)*. If God said that He would do the blessing, why does the Almighty need the *kohanim* to function as intermediaries?

Answer: God wanted the *kohanim* to be examples of holiness to the entire nation. Their role was one of dedication to serving God. The tribe of *Levi (levites and kohanim)* did not receive a portion of the Land, as did the rest of the tribes. They were to rely on the rest of the nation for their sustenance. In this way, the priestly class was relieved of ordinary, mundane chores to fully focus on their service to God.

God wanted His people to be unique, to fervently and completely believe in a God that they could not see or hear. Belief in God for the Israelite is entirely a matter of faith. One serves what appears to be a "hidden" God. The *kohanim* were necessary to act as the intermediary for the nation in its daily contact with God, offering up for the nation those sacrifices deemed necessary.

Question: What is the meaning of the word *duchan*?

Answer: In the Temple there was a stage where the *kohanim* sat, which was fifteen steps (some say three steps) high. From this stage the *kohanim* blessed the people. We commemorate this act in our synagogues today by the steps that we walk up to the Ark (where the Torah scrolls are stored) and from there the priests bless the entire congregation. This stage and the ritual performance are called by the sages, *Duchan* (*Rashi; see Ezekiel 42:12; Babylonian Talmud Sanhedrin 42a*).

Question: Do *kohanim* have the authority to modify the Torah or the prayer service?

Answer: No. The *kohanim* must follow the prescription mandated in the Torah. No one, even the *kohen*, has the authority to change one single word or letter of the Torah. God uses the *kohen* to transmit His requirements to the people. That is why a *kohen*, when he gives the priestly blessing *duchan*, is required to repeat the lines exactly as they are called out by the representative, *shaliach tsibur*, of the entire congregation during the prayer service.

Question: What is our responsibility if a *kohen* refuses to perform his priestly duties?

Answer: We must try our best to persuade the *kohen* to perform his duties, reminding him that he was born into this role. According to Jewish law, if a *kohen* stubbornly refuses, he must leave the sanctuary, while the rest of the *kohanim* perform their duties. He also can be deprived of receiving an *aliyah* (being called up for a portion of the Torah reading) to the Torah on that day (*Shulchan Aruch 128*).

Question: During the *kohen's* ritual performance he has to raise his arms straight out in front with his palms facing the floor and his fingers spread with the little and ring fingers touching and the middle finger and index fingers touching. What is the reason for this?

Answer: The *Zohar* explains that this comes from the book *Song of Songs 2:9*, "...the *Divine Presence* is watching us through the lattice."

The five spaces between the fingers represent the spaces that are described in this sentence. This means that even if there is a wall between man and God, He is still watching us. During the time the *kohanim* bless, they transmit a ray of light from the *Divine Presence.* The *Zohar* explains that when we become better people then we will receive more rays of light (*Shulchan Aruch, Magen Avraham 128; Zohar*).

Question: How do we explain the apparent contradiction between the command that the *kohen* must bless the people "with love" and the understanding that giving the blessing is fulfilling a duty?

Answer: The *Zohar* states: "The *kohen* who comes to *duchan* and does not have a full heart for everyone in the congregation risks strong punishment." It is forbidden for the *kohen* to dislike any person in the sanctuary (*Shulchan Aruch*). Because the blessing is not coming from his heart, it is not a sincere blessing.

Although the *kohen* stands before the entire congregation and simultaneously blesses the entire congregation, the text of the blessing is written in the singular. This is because, no matter how many people are present, the blessing is individual. It is intended for each and every person present. For this reason, the word for "with love" is written in the singular.

Question: How many parts are there to the priestly blessing, and what is the meaning of each?

Answer: There are three parts to the priestly blessing. The first is the blessing for sustenance, material comfort, and protection. The second is for a "ray of light" from God for understanding the wisdom of the Torah. The third is that God should bestow peace on Israel in all aspects of life.

Question: Why is the congregation not allowed to look at the *kohanim* during this blessing?

Answer: During the Temple Era, the *Divine Presence* rested on the *kohanim* as they recited the blessing. It was announced, prior to the blessing, that anyone who looked upon the hands of the *kohen* as he blessed the congregation might suffer damage to his eyesight. As a continuation of this practice it is common in synagogues today not to look at the *kohen* as he *duchans*. Furthermore, *kohanim* should in no way be distracted from their holy task, as they might be if everyone was looking at them. Likewise, members of the congregation should be concentrating on the blessing and its meaning with closed eyes.

Beha'alotcha
Chapters: 8 - 12

Synopsis:

The menorah; the Levites' work shifts in the Temple; the second Passover offering in the desert; the Cloud that led the Israelites through the desert by day; the playing of the trumpets; Moses' invitation to his father-in-law, Yitro, to accompany the nation on its journey; the carrying of the Ark; Moses' special prayers; the complainers; Moses' frustration and petition to God for help; God's reply via the creation of the Sanhedrin; the prophecies of the new prophets; Miriam's leprosy and her isolation from the community; the return of Miriam to the community; the Israelites' continued movement through the wilderness.

Question: Why do Jewish courts require a long and arduous procedure when someone wishes to convert to Judaism?

Answer: Our answer is partially based upon this *parsha*. At the time of the Exodus, some non-Jews joined the Israelites in order to get out of Egypt. They had no real intention to be part of the Jewish nation. In the wilderness they complained bitterly about every discomfort and fomented unrest. The Torah refers to them as the "rabble" and even says that they were "bad in the eyes of Moses." For this reason, the rabbis today must make sure that the potential convert is pure and sincere in his or her intention to become Jewish. For example, when a couple comes to a rabbi and says that the non-Jewish partner wishes to convert because of love for the other person. This is not sufficient. A couple married after one partner's "quick" conversion. They had two children. Today, they are separated and the children now attend synagogue on Saturday and church on Sunday. The rabbi's responsibility is quite clear. This type of situation is to be prevented. It is incumbent upon the rabbinate to thoroughly investigate the intentions of a potential convert, to avoid regrets and problems later. The convert must study all of Jewish history and laws in order to understand what it means to be part of the Jewish people. The case of Ruth, mentioned at the end of the previous section, is the example to which potential converts are directed. Once accepted, the convert is to be made to feel comfortable and at home with his or her Jewishness.

Question: The trip from Egypt to the land of Canaan should have taken only three days. Why are the Israelites forced instead to wander the *Midbar* for forty years *(Numbers 10:29-34)*?

Answer: The long travel time was the heavy price paid by the Children of Israel as a result of the actions of the rabble. They "poisoned the atmosphere," and Israel was not strong enough in their faith and dedication to resist these few. Not only did the journey take forty years, but the entire generation that left Egypt died out and only their descendants were allowed to enter the Holy Land (*Numbers*

14:23). Some commentators say that the people suffered from a slave mentality, and did not have a strong concept of the value of the Holy Land. They were not yet ready to fight for the Holy Land.

Question: Who are these rabble? What did they do that merited the Israelites such a punishment?

Answer: The rabble were those people who took advantage of the exodus of the Israelites from Egypt. They attached themselves to the Israelites because they believed it would benefit them. There was no commitment to share the spiritual or communal responsibilities required of the Israelite nation. These "converts" agitated for rebellion against Moses and Aaron and spread rumors and lies about the "good old days" in Egypt. The result of their corrupting influence was the forty years of wandering in the desert.

Question: Was there any truth to the complaints of the rabble?

Answer: In most instances, the statements made by the rabble were untrue. Regardless of the nature of the complaint, the manner by which they presented their complaints was the problem. There is a difference between constructive attempts to resolve a situation and simply attempting to destroy the structure of the community. They claimed that they were given good food for free in Egypt and that in the wilderness they had to struggle and eat manna. The truth is that in Egypt they paid for their food with cruel slavery. In the desert, the food (*manna*) was free, like the rain from Heaven (*Numbers 11:5-10*).

Question: What is the significance of the *menorah* as described in this *parsha*?

Answer: The *menorah* contained seven candles, The burning candles symbolize the spiritual bond between God and man. This idea has been adopted by all other major religions. The lighting and maintenance of the *menorah* were to be the gift to and responsibility of the *kohanim*.

Question: Is seven a significant number in the Torah, since there are seven candles?

Answer: Yes. There are seven days of Creation, culminating with the Sabbath–the seventh day; the bride circles the groom during the wedding ceremony seven times (a Jewish tradition that came from the Bible); mourners sit *shiva* for seven days; the festivals *Sukkot* and Passover are seven days long; there are seven weeks between Passover and *Shavuot*, before Joshua conquered the Holy Land, he circled the city of Jericho seven times; the Sabbatical Year in the Holy Land is the seventh year; the Jubilee (fiftieth) year is the culmination of seven sabbatical years; and the new year on the Jewish calendar (*Rosh Hashanah*) is the seventh month from the redemption of Egypt. This is part of a long list suggesting the deep meaning of the number seven.

Question: What is the significance of the *menorah* and candles for us today?

Answer: We try to recreate the feeling of the Temple in our synagogues and in our lives. We light candles both at times of great joy and sadness. Thus, we light candles on the Sabbath, holiday evenings, and during *shiva* (times of mourning) and *yahrzeits* (anniversary of the death of a loved one).

Lighting candles is a tradition passed down from our matriarchs Sarah, Rebecca, Rachel, and Leah. It serves as a boundary between the weekday and the Sabbath. This tradition is illustrated by the *menorah* in this *parsha.*

Question: Why is it that *Numbers 10:35-36* begins and ends with a backward nun (‫נ‬)?

Answer: There are a few explanations. One is that they separate these verses from the negative feelings that come before and after (*Talmud, Shabbat 115*), in which the Israelites behaved badly, complained, acted fearful, and were weak in their faith in God.

Furthermore, the original plan was for the Israelites to travel a direct route to *Eretz Yisrael* in three short journeys, with two stops. However, because they sinned and angered God, they were "turned around" and made to wander the desert for a full forty years. The letter nun that separates the verses about the journey of the Ark are also "turned around" (*Pa'anayach Raza l'Rabbi Yitzchak Halevi*). Some commentaries (*Noda b'Yehudah 74, Drush V'Kabbalah*) suggest that they are a reminder of the destruction of the two Temples.

Question: Why is the letter *Nun* (נ) used?

Answer: In the Torah, there are fifty paragraphs from the beginning of the book of *Bamidbar* to these special verses. The letter *Nun* has a numerical value of fifty (*Rabbeinu Bechayei; Babylonian Talmud Sabbath 121, Maharsha*).

Question: When we remove the Torah from the ark during the synagogue services we recite the verse, "When the Ark travels..." *(Numbers 10:35).* What is the reason for this?

Answer: In the wilderness, after receiving the Torah, the Israelites had more responsibilities placed on their shoulders. They had to bear the burden of carrying the heavy ark through the wilderness. In return, they received God's protection against the enemies of the Torah. This is borne out by the following verse: "Your enemies will be scattered and those who hate you will flee before you" (*Numbers 10:35*). Throughout history there have been enemies of Torah in every generation. Therefore, as we open the ark, we proclaim our adherence to the Torah and ask God's assistance in removing obstacles from in front of us.

Question: What is the reason for reciting the verse, "When it rested he would say, reside calmly, O God, among the many thousands of Israel" *(Numbers 10:35)* when we return the Torah to the ark?

Answer: In biblical times the connection between God and Israel was more tangible and direct than it is today. It is our prayer today that we merit a return to this intimate relationship with God.

Question: God said to Miriam and Aaron, "Listen to Me. If there is any prophet among you, I will appear to him only in a vision or a dream. Only with Moses, My servant, will I speak mouth to mouth" *(Numbers 12:5-9)*. Do we have prophets today?

Answer: *Rambam* says that today there are no prophets. However, the *Talmud* refers to the phenomenon of dreams with deep meaning. If a dream recurs three times or if a dream traumatizes a person, we have to ask rabbinical authorities whether it requires a fast. On the other hand, King Solomon said that all dreams are meaningless. The controversy remains unsettled.

This question is illustrated by a story that took place in Mexico City. A man named Roberto lived in the same wealthy neighborhood as did an elderly woman named Juanita. Roberto would visit Juanita occasionally. However, they had not met for three months. One day, out of curiosity, he knocked on her door, but nobody answered. He looked in all of the windows. He saw, from outside the window, that the house was in shambles. Roberto called the police immediately. They found that Juanita's safe, where she kept all of her money, was empty, and that the house looked as if someone had broken in. Juanita was missing. The investigators found evidence that led them to believe that she had been murdered. They sent out a document with her picture, to be printed in all of the newspapers and magazines and broadcast on all news programs.

Meanwhile, in southern Mexico, a young boy had a recurring dream: at a house two blocks from a river a thief climbed over a fence into a window, robbed the house, and fought with an elderly woman, killing her. He then took her body into his wagon and buried her near the entrance of a forest. This boy described all of the details of the dream to his parents. They thought it was important to report this to their neighborhood police. At first, the police did not take them seriously. However, the family kept coming to the police again and again, so they finally wrote down all of the details.

One of the officers who heard about the dream had seen the broadcast about Juanita. He asked his friends if it was possible that the dream had any connection to Juanita's disappearance. The boy showed the investigators the exact car, house, and place of burial. They found Juanita's body. Because of details from the dream, the police also identified the criminal.

Clearly this story is not a tale of coincidence, but is it an example of prophecy?

Question: Where in the parsha do we find that God's reward for good deeds may occur even after a great deal of time has passed?

Answer: At the end of this parsha we read of Miriam, who, as a young girl, watched over Moses from the time he was placed in a basket in the river until he was safely retrieved by Pharaoh's daughter. Eighty-one years later, Miriam was stricken with leprosy for gossiping (*loshon hora*) as the Israelites were preparing to leave an encampment in the desert. Just as she had waited to ensure Moses' safety, she was rewarded then, by God, Who required the Israelites to wait for her to heal before traveling onward (*Rashi, Numbers 12:15*).

Shelach

Chapters: 13 - 15

Synopsis:

Moses sent spies into the Holy Land; the spies reported; controversy occurred among the spies; the Israelites reacted with fear; Joshua and Caleb attempted to calm the people; the people wanted to remove Joshua and Caleb; Moses prayed to God for forgiveness; God relented but decreed that the Israelites must wander in the wilderness for forty years; God punished the spies and the Israelites; the people who violated the Sabbath in the desert are punished; the commandment of tzitzit was given

Question: What is the story of the twelve spies?

Answer: The *parsha* tells of God's permission to allow the people of Israel to send twelve "spies," who were twelve tribal leaders, to scout out the land of Canaan. It also tells of how Moses instructs them in how they are to view the land and its people. The Israelites were concerned about whether they could successfully invade the land and if the land would be able to support and sustain them. When the spies returned, they all reported back that the land was good, flowing with milk and honey. However, ten of the twelve spies were afraid, because they felt it would be impossible to defeat the Canaanites in a war.

These ten distorted their report to make it seem as though the Canaanites were giants, stronger than they actually were, and they convinced many of the Israelites that conquering Canaan would be impossible. Punishment for this lack of faith was that the Israelites were forced to wander in the desert for thirty-eight more years, causing an entirely new generation to enter Canaan. That is, all those who believed the ten spies would no longer be living at the time of entrance to the Promised Land. Joshua and Caleb, the two honest spies, were the exception. Both demonstrated complete faith and trust in God. They would enter the Promised Land.

Question: What is the significance of the spies?

Answer: God created a world in which people have free choice. Despite God's miracles and protection when leaving Egypt and subsequent wandering in the wilderness, the Israelites were still afraid and unwilling to trust Him. They had the choice of going ahead with faith in God's will, or questioning God's instructions. They chose the latter, thereby creating their own punishment. That is why the entire nation was punished, not just the spies.

Consider what might have happened had the nation of Israel not been swayed by the report of the ten spies.

Question: Why does the Torah go to such lengths to describe the fruits of this land *(Numbers 13:23)*?

Answer: Moses instructed the spies to bring back samples of the produce of the land. The grapes and figs were of such size that it took four men to carry one bunch *(Rashi)*. The spies tried to frighten the people with stories about giants who lived in Canaan, to go with the extra-large fruit *(Babylonian Talmud, Sotah 34a)*. The Israeli government today utilizes symbolism of the large fruit derived from this *parsha* to generate tourism.

Question: Why were the Israelites denied entrance to the Holy Land even after they had repented *(Numbers 14:39-45)*?

Answer: The Israelites were denied entrance into the Holy Land because of a lack of sufficient faith in God. Had they had faith and trust in Him they would never have responded to the corrupting influence of the rabble, nor would they have hesitated due to the spies' report. Instead of appreciating the value and greatness of what God had done for them, they placed physical and material risk above spiritual well-being.

Our sages tell the story of a matchmaker who wanted to make a match for the daughter of a wealthy man. He offered the rich father two choices. One was the very scholarly son of a rabbi; the other, the son of a rich man. The girl's father wanted the scholarly son of the rabbi, but only on the condition that the rabbi give his daughter some very expensive presents. When the rabbi heard this, he said under no circumstance would he allow his son to marry this man's daughter. The rabbi explained that the girl's father had no appreciation of the value of being part of a scholarly house. The rich man demonstrated materialistic priorities. In the same way, the Israelites showed no appreciation of the value of the Holy Land and were therefore denied entrance to it.

Question: "God, slow to anger, full of kindness, forgiver of willful sin, and Who purifies, but not completely, recalling the

sins of parents upon children to the third and fourth generations" *(Numbers 14:18)*. "Fathers shall not be put to death for
their children...and children should not be put to death for
their fathers; a man should be put to death for his own sin"
(Deuteronomy 24:16). Why do children have to suffer for the sins
of their parents? Why does one place in the Torah contradict
the other?

Answer: Literally, *Deuteronomy 24:16* states that parents may not be
killed or punished for the sins of their children and vice versa
(Rashbam). It was common that tyrants would punish or quell rebel-
lions by wiping out the families of those who were involved. Jewish
kings, however, are forbidden to do so *(Sforno)*. Even though God
speaks of visiting the sins of the father upon the son *(Exodus 20:5)*,
that applies only to offspring who approve of the sins of the past, and
seek to perpetuate them *(Ibn Ezra)*.

Question: What is the meaning of the commandment of
tzitzit?

Answer: We wear *tzitzit* or fringes as a constant reminder of our
obligations to God and our strong relationship with Him. We must
always be aware of our allegiance to God and Torah and demonstrate
total faith in the importance of fulfilling God's commandments. The
numerical value of the Hebrew word for *tzitzit* is 600. When we add
the five knots plus eight threads, we get the sum of 613, the exact
number of biblical commandments.

Question: Part of the commandment of *tzitzit* is to incorporate a
blue dyed thread. What is the source of this blue dye? Is it in use today?

Answer: The sages say that this dye comes from the *chilazon* (fish).
The *Talmud* describes the *chilazon* as a rare fish with bluish-green
blood that surfaces once every seventy years and thus cannot be har-
vested easily *(Babylonian Talmud, Menachot 44a)*.
Approximately 120 years ago a group of chassidim from the
Polish city of Rodzin announced that they had discovered the *chila-*

zon in a river in Italy. It is referred to as *Deyonon Harochim,* which is not actually a fish but a slug-type crustacean (*shabluliah*). The process of harvesting the dye is similar to "milking" venom from a snake. To this day the Rodzin chassidim incorporate this dye into their *tzitzit.*

Sixty years ago, the Chief Rabbi of Israel, Rabbi Y. Herzog, proclaimed that the chilazon discovered off the coast of South America is the biblical chilazon.

At the present time there is a company in Israel that claims to have the source for this dye and manufactures *tzitzit* with a blue thread.

One may ask, if this dye exists and is apparently readily available, why is it not universally accepted and incorporated in today's *tzitzitot?* The answer is that the *Talmud* states that one must hunt this rare crustacean and the modern process utilizes a crustacean that is readily available and gathered easily along the shoreline. Not all rabbinical authorities accept this process.

Question: The *haftorah* for this parsha comes from the second chapter of the *Book of Joshua.* What is the connection of the *haftorah* to the *parsha?*

Answer: Both the *parsha* and the *haftorah* speak about spies.

Joshua is the leader of the new generation. Learning a lesson from the past, Joshua sent two spies instead of twelve, as Moses had done. They investigated the land before they began the process of conquering it. The spies encountered a woman named Rachav. She was a clever woman who lived in a house on the border. The king of Jericho came to her, knowing that the spies had been there. He wanted her help in capturing them. Rachav had a difficult choice to make. She could choose to be loyal to the king, or she could help the spies. She had heard that the Israelites had won many wars against bigger nations. Understanding she had a better chance of survival with the Israelites, she chose not to betray the spies. She hid them on her roof, and made a deal with the them. She gave them the information that they needed, in exchange for her safety. She put a sign up in her window so that when the Israelites came, they would not harm her.

Korach

Chapters: 16 - 18

Synopsis:

Korach rebelled against Moses and Aaron; Korach summoned Datan, and Aviram, Eliab's sons and Reuven's grandsons; the earth swallowed Aviram, Datan and all their households and belongings, along with Korach; the 250 followers were consumed by heavenly fire; the Israelites complained against Moses and Aaron which brought on the plague that killed 14,700 people; the nation atoned; Aaron, the High Priest, brought a special offering to God, that brought an end to the plague; tithe for the levi.

319

Question: Who was Korach?

Answer: Korach was first cousin to Moses and Aaron, and one of the richest and most honored individuals of his time. Despite his wealth and position, Korach was jealous of the leadership roles God had bestowed upon Moses and Aaron. Korach used his position and wealth to undermine their leadership, and succeeded in creating an opposition group of 250 men, all of whom were prominent figures.

Question: What is the story of Korach?

Answer: The *Mishnah* says, "Jealousy, envy, and seeking recognition places a person apart from the world" (*Avot 4:28*). This wise phrase of the sages helps us understand Korach's mental state. The sages ask, "Why did a respected and honorable man such as Korach rebel and behave so disgracefully?" Korach was already very wealthy and the head of the tribe of Levi, but was unable to control his ambition (*Rambam, Sefer Hamada, Hilchot Daot, Chapters 2-3*). His jealousy and lust for power led him to instigate a rebellion against Moses. Some of Korach's 250 supporters had been Moses' and Aaron's most trusted advisors. One had even been the head of the religious court.

Korach's campaign attracted troublemakers and bitter people, such as Datan and Aviram. In Egypt, these two men had informed against Moses to Pharaoh, telling him that Moses had killed an Egyptian (who was about to kill an Israelite). Korach also convinced Onn, the son of Pellet of the tribe of Reuven, to join with him. The tribe of Reuven was upset, frustrated, and angry when God replaced it with the tribe of Levi. They were outraged, and went to Moses and publicly spoke against Moses. Moses was accused of nepotism for choosing Aaron to be *Kohen Gadol* (High Priest). Moses and Aaron were called charlatans, who were seeking to be higher in rank than anyone else. Moses reacted humbly and tried to convince them, twice, not to rebel. He tried to explain that God was the One Who chose them. Moses told the people that if God would create a phenomenon and the earth would open its mouth and swallow Korach and his followers alive, then they would know that it was God, and not

Moses who had been provoked. Another consequence was a heavenly fire that came forth and consumed the 250 supporters of Korach, who were burning incense in an attempt to usurp the role of the *kohanim*.

Question: What happened to Datan and Aviram *(Numbers 16:24-35)?*

Answer: The first time that they complained publicly, Moses sent a messenger to them, attempting to persuade them to talk to him and resolve their problem. Unfortunately, they reacted disgracefully. Datan and Aviram refused to come to Moses, but instead publicly replied, "You, Moses, took us out from a land of milk and honey (Egypt) and your only purpose is to dominate the people." This phrase demonstrates how much they perverted the truth. Unable to resolve the situation, Moses turned to God, saying, "Please Lord, do not accept their offering. When I uprooted my family to follow Your command to redeem the Children of Israel from Egypt, I, as a leader, was entitled to get a donkey to ride, but I did not take the donkey. I never used my authority to get anything that belonged to the public, even though I was entitled to. The people often were very difficult, yet I never embarrassed or insulted anyone." Moses, the great leader, was one of the most humble individuals who ever lived. He was willing to approach Datan and Aviram, two of his fiercest enemies, to implore them to recognize the peril in which they were placing themselves and to repent. They stubbornly refused. When he heard their reply, Moses became frustrated, and called loudly to God, "Master of the Universe, You know that whatever I did came directly from You and nothing came from my heart. If these people die a natural death, the people will not think that You, the Lord, sent me here. However, if the earth opens its mouth and swallows them with all of their families and wealth, then everyone will know that I was sent on behalf of the Almighty. Whatever I did was on Your behalf." When Moses finished talking, the wealth and households of Datan and Aviram were consumed, exactly as Moses had petitioned (*Numbers 16:13-34*).

Question: What phenomena happened in this *parsha?*

Answer: One phenomenon was that the earth opened its mouth and swallowed Datan, Aviram, and Korach, along with their families and all their wealth. The other was that a fire came from Heaven to destroy Korach's followers. These two punishments occurred one right after the other, and in different places.

Question: What is an example of Korach's attempt to undermine Moses' leadership?

Answer: Korach tried to embarrass Moses in public by posing what he thought would be trick questions. For example, "The Torah states that a four-cornered garment (*tallit*) is obligated to have *tzitzit* on its corners. (One of the threads of the *tzitzit* is dyed blue and should be placed in each corner.) Korach's question to Moses was, "If I make a *tallit* entirely from blue threads, must I still put a blue thread in each corner?" The intention of the question is not only an attempt to make a mockery of Moses and the laws of the Torah; it also implies that each member of the community ("the threads") is equally important, and no one should be singled out, as Moses was.

Question: Why did Moses take Korach's sin to heart?

Answer: Korach and Moses were first cousins. Moses was very troubled by this as he had expected that his own blood relative would be one in whom he could trust. It is easier to see who our true friends will be in times of trouble than in times of success. Also very troubling to Moses was that even with all the signs and miracles performed by God for the nation, still 250 leaders of the Israelites lacked faith and trust in God, and revolted against His commands.

Question: What is the difference between the sin of the Golden Calf and the sin of Korach and his followers?

Answer: The Israelites miscalculated time and assumed that Moses had died since he had not returned from the mountain. They created this idol, the Golden Calf, in which they could invest their belief for salvation and leadership. When the people discovered that they had erred, many attempted to correct their ways and Moses interceded with the Almighty to save the nation from destruction.

In the incident of Korach, there is again the issue of leadership, but this time it was an active participation to change the structure as the people had known it. Moses in this instance petitioned the Almighty to remove the enemies because they were overtly and purposely seeking to corrupt the nation for their own ends.

One should note that the Almighty granted these two petitions by Moses.

Question: Why did Korach even think that he could and should succeed in his rebellion?

Answer: In those days both people and religion were on a much higher level. People had strong instincts about the future, and often predicted correctly. Korach felt that there would be great leaders among his descendants. In fact, he was not wrong. The prophet Samuel was a descendant of Korach. Korach thought that with all the greatness and power that would come from his future generations, he should acquire some greatness and power for himself as well. The Torah (*Numbers 26:11*) says that Korach's children were not consumed. The *haftorah* for this *parsha* is taken from the book of Samuel.

Question: What did Moses and Aaron hope to achieve by their use of incense?

Answer: Moses and Aaron wanted to demonstrate that incense was a holy thing. When Korach's followers used the incense for their own purpose they were desecrating something holy and therefore received the death penalty. Moses and Aaron wanted to show that the incense was not what killed Korach's followers, but that the sin they committed did.

Question: Moses said to the rebels, "Here you know that everything comes on behalf of God and not on behalf of my heart... if these people die a natural death, God did not send me. However, if God will create a special phenomenon to occur, and the earth suddenly opens its mouth and swallows them, then you know that these people provoked God" *(Numbers 17:28-30)*. Why did Moses take a chance by describing the punishment so specifically with no advance communication with God?

Answer: Without such a phenomenon, they would have said that it was just the natural course of events and not something that was caused by their actions.

Measure for measure...Moses wanted the punishment to occur in the same way as the sin. Just as they opened their mouths against God, the earth should open its mouth and swallow them *(Rambam)*.

Moses wanted a phenomenon that affected all of the Children of Israel. All the Israelites heard the yelling and screaming as the earth swallowed the people. This phenomenon left the nation traumatized and forced them to come to terms with the consequences of the rebels' misdeeds (*Ha'amak Davar*).

Moses had such a high level of faith that he felt he could trust the Almighty to support his leadership in this time of crisis for the Jewish people.

Question: What lesson can we apply from this *parsha* to our lives?

Answer: There are many lessons that we can take from this *parsha*.

If you fight against someone out of personal jealousy, the probability exists that you might eventually become self-destructive (as Korach did).

We see the power of speech. The earth opened its mouth and swallowed them as a result of their mouths (*Numbers 16:31-33*). People can inflict great injury upon themselves or others via the spoken word.

God is just, and punishes or rewards *measure for measure.*

The world belongs only to God. Therefore, God, and only God, gives and takes honor, wealth, and so forth, as seen in *Numbers 16:32*, "The earth opened its mouth and swallowed them...and all their wealth."

You cannot be punished before you are warned (*Numbers 16:5, 12, 21, 26*).

You know your real friends when you are in trouble. The 250 men who joined Korach were leaders of Israel, and were expected to be loyal to Moses. However, they betrayed him. Moses was left with only his brother, Aaron, and very few elders (*Numbers 16:2*).

We have freedom of choice. Korach always had the opportunity to change his mind and return to God.

Question: What is the connection between the *parsha* and its *haftorah?*

Answer: In the *haftorah* (*Samuel 1:11*), Korach's grandson, the prophet Samuel, rebuked the Children of Israel for forcing him to leave his job as judge and proclaim a king (Saul). The way that Samuel rebuked the people was similar in many ways to Moses' rebuke of the generation of the desert (*Numbers 16:15*). "Testify about me by the Name of God. From whom did I take an ox or donkey or whom have I robbed? Did I take a penny from anyone, or did I refuse to do something for anyone?" (*Samuel 1:12:3*.

Chukat

Chapters: 19 - 22:1

Synopsis:

Rules and regulations about using the Red Heifer were given; Miriam died; the people demanded water; Moses struck the rock to get water; God punished Moses and Aaron by denying them entry to the Holy Land; Moses sent a delegation to the king of Edom, who refused to permit the Israelites to cross his land; Aaron died; war with the Canaanites; the people complained about food; God sent scorpions and serpents as a punishment, causing the death of many; the Israelites battled with the Amorites.

Question: What is the meaning of *Red Heifer (Numbers 19:1-22)?*

Answer: Certain requirements are necessary for the *Red Heifer.* The heifer must be totally red in color and it cannot have two black hairs in close proximity. The heifer must never have been used for any type of work. The *Red Heifer* is used for atonement or purification, such as from contact with a corpse. The kohen takes the ashes of the heifer and mixes them with water; they are then sprinkled on a contaminated individual or object. The sages see the *Red Heifer* as a mystery of the Bible. It is a law of God, beyond human understanding. The underlying theme of this *parsha, Chukat,* is beyond human comprehension. The word *chukah* literally means "law" or "decree," but the term applies to those laws or decrees whose reasons are presently beyond human understanding.

Question: What explanations are offered by the sages for the law of the *Red Heifer?*

Answer: The *Red Heifer* is atonement for the Golden Calf. Aaron produced the Golden Calf by melting gold. The *Red Heifer* must be burned to produce ashes for purification. Red is the color that symbolizes sin (*Isaiah 1:18*), and the *Red Heifer* must be one that never wore a yoke, symbolizing the sinner who casts off God's yoke (*Rashi, Numbers 19:22*).

Question: What is the famous contradiction that exists in biblical law regarding the *Red Heifer?*

Answer: A *kohen,* who is pure, is the only one who can perform the purification of others using the *Red Heifer.* After purifying someone, the purifier himself becomes contaminated. According to the sages, the reason for this is a mystery of the Torah that must be accepted on faith. This is yet another demonstration that only God may decide what is or is not pure (*Job 14:4*).

Question: How does a *kohen* become pure again?

Answer: He waits until the evening and then immerses himself in a pool of pure rain water (*mikvah*).

Question: Why are we obligated to follow laws that we cannot understand?

Answer: There are times when parents or teachers recquire things of children for reasons that are incomprehensible to the children at the time. Children must nevertheless comply. The reason may or may not become clear to the child as he matures. The relationship of man to God is parallel to that of child to parent. This relationship should contain the elements of faith (*emuna*) and trust (*b'tachon*). These two elements are essential for our acceptance of *chukim*.

Question: What is the story of the "waters in the desert," *Mei Meriva (Numbers 20:2-14)*?

Answer: Because of the righteousness of Miriam, as long as she lived there was a well of water available to the Israelites (*Song of Songs; Rabba 5*). When Miriam died, the Israelites did not mourn her adequately, so the water source disappeared (*Alsheich*). As the water supply dwindled, the Israelites began to complain bitterly. They felt despair, and talked of rebelling against Moses and Aaron. God spoke to Moses, telling him to take his staff, gather the people around a large rock, and speak to the rock. In front of all the people, God would let Moses bring forth water for the people to drink.

Question: In this *parsha (Numbers 20:12)*, God said to Moses and Aaron, "... you will not bring the congregation of Israel to the Holy Land." Why did Moses and Aaron deserve such a harsh punishment?

Answer: *Ramban* says, "This matter is one of the great mysteries of the Torah. There doesn't seem to be an acceptable explanation for this."

Nevertheless, many explanations have been offered by other biblical commentators:

Rashi: The sin was striking the rock, rather than speaking to it as they had been commanded.

Abarbanel: In addition to the sin mentioned by Rashi, God also took into account the following. Aaron had committed a sin in helping to make the Golden Calf, and Moses had to take responsibility for the spies that he sent to survey the Land of Israel, who returned with false, evil reports.

Rambam: Moses showed his anger toward the people when he said to them, "Listen now, O rebels..." The people felt that Moses was a reflection of God and therefore God must be angry with them.

Ibn Ezra: Moses and Aaron fell from their high level of righteousness and spirituality. The way they behaved in anger, "Listen O rebels ...," is the reaction of normal human beings, not high spiritual leaders. Instead of immediately fulfilling God's command to speak to the rock and bring forth water, Moses and Aaron changed God's order by starting to rebuke the Israelites. God did not order them to rebuke the Israelites, but they did so anyway. God told them to speak to the rock, but instead they hit the rock. The first time, no water came forth from it. Moses and Aaron had to learn a lesson that they had done something wrong. However, Moses took it upon himself to hit the rock a second time. All of this contributed to the punishment of Moses and Aaron.

Rabbeinu Chananel: Just before bringing forth the water, Moses said, "Shall we bring forth water for you from the rock?" This implied that Moses and Aaron had the power and were the source of the miracle. Clearly, Moses should have said to the people, "God shall bring forth water for you." This view is easiest to understand and accept, because the Torah states, "Because you did not believe in Me to sanctify Me in the eyes of the Children of Israel." At the end of the Torah, just before Moses' death, the Torah repeats this sentence.

Ba'al Ha'ikarim: Moses was punished because he waited until the people protested to attend to their need for water. As a leader, he should have anticipated a need and reacted accordingly. This was the one time that the Israelites complained bitterly to Moses and Aaron, and were not punished for complaining. Perhaps God was showing that He felt that their complaint was justified.

Chidushei Harim: God's instruction to Moses was that he should speak to the rock "before the eyes" of the people. The purpose was for Moses to make sure that the people understood that God alone was miraculously providing the water, not Moses. Moses merely struck the rock without educating the people as to what was really happening.

Ramav: God punished the Israelites because of their complaints, not Moses and Aaron. The Children of Israel lost their greatest leaders at this time. No future prophet or leader would ever compare to or achieve the same level of leadership and prophecy as Moses and Aaron. God's decision was that Moses and Aaron would not lead the Israelites into the Holy Land. The Israelites received more punishment than Moses and Aaron did. The next leader was clearly not of the same caliber of spirituality and prophecy as Moses and Aaron. For example, only Moses spoke to God "face to face" (*Numbers 12:8*).

Ba'al Haklomar: The punishment was very harsh. In *Exodus 17:5-6* Moses is commanded by God to strike the rock with his staff in order to get water. In Numbers we have a similar situation to the one in Exodus, where God tells Moses to take the staff and talk to the rock. Moses did the same thing both times, rather than literally following God's command. We might wonder whether one of the reasons that Moses made the mistake was ego.

Question: What is meant by the "Kiss of Death," *Metat Neshika,* of Aaron *(Numbers 20:26-29)?*

Answer: The Torah recounts Aaron's death this way: Moses dressed Aaron's son in Aaron's own garments, then Aaron died on Mount Hor.

After Aaron saw his son elevated to this high position, he lay down, totally free of pain, suffering, or fear. With God's "Kiss of Death," Aaron's soul was reunited with God. His death was easy, and his soul left his body easily, like "a hair is removed from a pan of milk." This is to be compared with the more common manner, when people's souls leave their bodies like "a thorn being removed from sheep's wool" (*Yalkut Shimoni*).

Question: According to *Midrashim (Tanchuma and Yalkut Vaetchanan)*, what was the exact sequence of Aaron's death?

Answer: When it was time for Aaron to leave this world, God said to Moses, "Go and prepare Aaron for his death."

Moses woke early in the morning and went to Aaron. He called to him from outside, "Aaron, my brother, come here!"

Aaron said, "My brother, why did you come here so early today?"

Moses replied: "All night I was thinking about the Torah and something bothered me very much because I have no answer. I couldn't wait to see you, and ask you."

Aaron said, "What is it?"

Moses said, "Bring me the *Book of Genesis*." They read together and they stopped at the sixth day of Creation, when God created Adam.

Moses said, "What happened to Adam, who brought death to the world? And I (Moses) who spoke to the angels and you (Aaron) who stopped death (*Numbers 17:13*), how many years do we have to live?"

Aaron said, "Not too much. Maybe a few years."

Moses said, "Much less."

Aaron replied, "So, maybe a few months."

Moses answered regretfully, "I am sorry, my dear brother, but it is much less."

Aaron stood up and trembled. He looked at Moses' face, eye to eye, and said, "You came here because of me?"

Moses started to cry and said, "Yes."

Aaron said, "I am afraid. I am so afraid of God's judgment."

Moses said, "My dear Aaron, do you accept God's judgment?"

Aaron looked to the heavens and said, "Absolutely. Blessed are You, Master of the Universe, Who judges with truth."

Moses said, "Are you sure, my brother?"

Aaron replied, "The Lord gave and the Lord took. May His Name be Blessed."

Moses said, "Please take your son, Elazar, and let us go to the top of the mountain."

The Children of Israel watched Moses, Aaron, and his son, Elazar, go to the top of the mountain. It is clear that if the Israelites knew that their beloved Aaron was going to his death, they would have begged for God's compassion. Because they did not hear the conversation between the brothers, they thought only that God had called them.

When Moses, Aaron, and Elazar reached the top of the mountain, they saw an open cave. They went in and found a lit candle on a table, and a bed. Moses said to Aaron, "My beloved brother, take off your priest's garment and give it to your son, Elazar."

Aaron did as instructed, and he put the garment on his son.

Moses said to Aaron, "You know, my dear brother, when our sister Miriam died, you and I took care of her. Now you will die and your son, Elazar, and I are taking care of you. But if I die, who will take care of me?"

The voice came from Heaven and said, "Do not worry Moses, the Lord will take care of you."

Moses said to Aaron, "Please, my dear brother, lie down on the bed."

Aaron immediately lay down on the bed.

Moses said, "Put your hands at your side."

Aaron did so.

Moses said with tears, "Close your eyes."

Aaron closed his eyes.

Moses said, "Close your mouth."

Aaron closed his mouth.

The *Divine Presence* came down with a cloud of fog and a Heavenly Voice and kissed Aaron, and took back his soul through his nose. Moses kissed Aaron on one cheek and Elazar kissed his father on the other. The Voice came through and said, "Moses and Elazar, please leave the cave." Moses and Elazar left, and the cave immediately closed.

Moses and Elazar returned down the mountain, where all of the Israelites were anticipating the return of the three men. The Israelites started to talk among themselves. They were wondering where their beloved Aaron was, because he loved the people and they loved him. Because three went up and only two came down, some Israelites turned against Moses and Elazar. The Israelites split into three opinions. One group said that Moses killed Aaron because he was jealous of him. The second one said that Elazar killed his father because he wanted to be the high priest and wanted to inherit the priesthood. The third group said that Heaven caused Aaron's death. A few people were outraged and angrily held Moses and Elazar by their arms and looked at them and asked where Aaron was. Moses replied, "The Almighty took him to the world to come." Some said, "We don't believe you, Moses. He may have said something you did not like, and you may have cursed him to death." They wanted to stone Moses and Elazar.

God ordered the angels to open the cave. They brought out the bier of Aaron, and it was suspended in the air. The angels were around the body. All of Israel saw this. As the Torah says, "Then the entire assembly saw that Aaron had been called to God" (*Numbers 20:28*). The angels proclaimed loudly, "The Lord gave and the Lord took. May His Name be Blessed" (*Yalkut Shimoni*).

Question: "The entire House of Israel wept for Aaron's death for thirty days" (*Numbers 20:29*). "The Children of Israel wept for Moses for thirty days" (Numbers 34:8). Why does the text say the entire House mourned for Aaron, and for Moses it says only the Children of Israel?

Answer: The *Midrash* says that Moses was a judge, and in that role he had to rebuke people. As for Aaron, he never told anyone that they acted inappropriately and always looked for and pursued peace. For example, two people got into a fight. Aaron went and sat by one and said, "Look my son, your friend was so depressed and broken-hearted and I heard him say, 'Why did I do such a terrible thing to my friend?'" Aaron sat by this man until the jealousy and envy had dissipated. Then Aaron went to the other man. He sat next to him, and said the same thing. As a result, when they met one another again, the two hugged and kissed each other. Aaron was considered the ultimate peacemaker. This is the reason why the Torah states that the entire House wept for Aaron (*Avot Derabbi Natan 12*).

Question: What were the cause and effect of the war between the Canaanites and the Israelites (*Numbers 21:1-3*)?

Answer: The king of Canaan had heard about the victories of the Israelites, and he felt that soon he would be forced to relinquish title to the Holy Land to them. Every general knows, "The best defense is a good offense." Therefore he went out and attacked the Israelites first.

The Israelites made a special vow to God, promising that if they won they would dedicate all the spoils of the war to the House of the Lord. God heard and accepted the word of Israel. The Canaanites lost the war and the Israelites fulfilled their commitments.

Question: What do we learn from the victory of the Israelites over Canaan?

Answer: Despite having an adversary of superior strength and numbers, the Israelites were victorious. This demonstrates the power of prayer of the sincere and full-hearted. The power of the Israelites came from the power of prayer (*See Genesis 27:22; Numbers 21:3; Babylonian Talmud, Gittin 57b*).

Question: During their time wandering in the desert the Israelites spoke out against God and the leadership of Moses (*Numbers 21:4-9*). Why did this happen?

Answer: The Israelites felt that they had circled around the desert for too long, and that they were fighting a neverending battle. They were upset with eating the same thing day in and day out.

334

Question: How did God punish the Israelites for speaking against the leadership of Moses?

Answer: God sent among them fiery copper snakes, which bit the complainers, many of whom died. They admitted they were sinners, and begged Moses to ask God to rid them of the snakes. In order to heal the people, God revealed to Moses a secret way by which to fashion heated copper into the form of a snake. By gazing upon the set of "snakes" fashioned by Moses, whoever had been bitten by the copper snakes was healed.

Question: What lesson do we learn from the story with the fiery snakes?

Answer: We learn the lesson of 'Measure for measure.' The snakes taught the Israelites a good lesson by biting them. The Israelites used their mouths in an evil way, and the snakes bit them because of their 'poison' mouths. Snakes as a rule instill fear and revulsion in people. Therefore even those not bitten by the snakes experienced some form of punishment.

They are called fiery because they were created for only this particular time and purpose. The way that the snakes killed was the same way that the snakes healed. From this we learn that the snake did not kill or heal, but that it was only the human deeds that caused such consequences. When the Israelites prayed to God and they repented, He healed them.

Question: Who was Og and why is he mentioned *(Numbers 21:33)*?

Answer: Og was the King of Bashan. He fought against Israel and lost. Although Og was more than nine feet tall, when he physically fought against Moses, he lost *(Babylonian Talmud Niddah 24b; Yalkut Shimoni)*. This demonstrates that physical superiority is not necessarily a guarantee of victory.

Question: What is the connection between the *parsha* and its *haftorah?*

Answer: In the *Haftorah, Judges 11:1-33,* Jephthah fought against the enemy. Jephthah swore to God by saying that he would give a special elevation offering if he was victorious. God heard his prayer, as he had heard that of the Israelites, when they fought against the king of Canaan.

Balak

Chapters: 22:2 - 25:9

Synopsis:

Balak appointed the temporary king of Moab; Balak hired the prophet, Bilam, to curse the Israelites; God warned Bilam twice not to curse the Israelites, but he did so anyway; God's angel stood in the way of Bilam, so his donkey laid down and refused to walk; Bilam hit his donkey three times; the donkey opened her mouth and rebuked Bilam; Bilam saw that the angel of God blocked the way of the she-donkey with a sword; even though Bilam tried to curse the Israelites, against his will his mouth blessed them; Bilam left disgraced after having blessed, rather than cursed, the Israelites three times; Bilam suggested to Balak that the daughters of Moab seduce the Israelites; the Moabite women seduced Israelites and caused them to worship the Moabite idols; a terrible plague struck the Israelites; the zealot, Pinchas, committed an audacious action, thereby stopping the plague.

Question: What is the background to the story in *Parshat Balak*?

Answer: When the Children of Israel first went down to Egypt in the time of Jacob, they were a small group of seventy souls. After more than 212 years of slavery in Egypt, God had Moses lead them out of Egypt and out of slavery. By the time they left Egypt, the seventy had grown to over six hundred thousand despite the hardships of slavery. But slavery had taken its toll: the people were weak, dispirited, tired, and worn out from all the hard years. As slaves they were forced to be obedient to their masters. It was difficult for them to exercise adult judgment and free will. Despite their weakened condition, the Children of Israel managed to defeat the very strong kings of three countries (*Canaan, Emor, and Bashan*).

Question: Who was Balak?

Answer: Balak was king of Moab, the fourth most powerful country in the area. Our sages explained that Balak, who was an ordinary person, incited his people against the Israelites in order to become king. He frightened the people with his demagoguery. Many people followed him, and consequently he was made king of Moab.

Balak saw that the weakened Children of Israel had defeated much stronger adversaries on three different occasions. He carefully analyzed the situation and realized that the Israelites had won these wars not by brute military strength, but by something else. He understood that the "something else" was the power of God. This power was exerted through Moses and accounted for the victories of the Israelites. He learned by careful observation that the big difference was that the Israelites depended on spiritual power rather than the power of the sword. This was evident in Moses' leadership style, in that he spoke to the people, transmitting to them the word of God.

Question: Who was Bilam?

Answer: Bilam was a master magician and sorcerer who practiced black magic. He was also a prophet, because God did speak to him on occasion, but there is a *Talmudic* discussion as to whether or not he was a true prophet (*Babylonian Talmud, Sanhedrin 106b; Bava Batra 15a*). Bilam had no love for the Israelites, and was receptive when Balak offered to pay him handsomely to curse the Israelites, and thereby cause their defeat in battle.

Question: What does the Torah teach us in this *parsha?*

Answer: We learn the importance of the "power of the mouth." Balak saw how the Israelites won their wars, and he tried to mimic it. Since the Israelites were led to victory by a man connected to God, Balak reasoned that if he could get the services of a man connected to God, he would defeat the Israelites. He recruited Bilam, a sorcerer and magician, to curse the Israelites. He hoped to thereby cause the Israelites to lose in battle, as their enemies had lost to them.

God told Bilam not to do the bidding of Balak, no matter how high the price. Bilam could not resist the enticements offered to him, and he went to help Balak. On the way, God gave Bilam one last chance to refrain from this folly. An angel of God appeared in front of Bilam's donkey with a sword, to stop her from moving. Bilam hit the donkey three times. The donkey refused to move. Then the Almighty empowered Bilam's donkey with the power of speech. We see from this incident the enormous impact that speech has on our lives.

Note: This is the second instance in the Torah that an animal is empowered with speech. The first instance is the confrontation of the snake with Eve in the Garden.

Question: Why could Bilam not curse the Israelites?

Answer: The simple answer is that the Almighty refused to allow Bilam to use his powers. His curses came out as blessings. A further understanding is that man cannot force the supernatural to alter the natural order! Consequently Balak failed in his scheme. The parsha teaches us over and over again about the enormity of the power of speech. We must always remember that there is no limit to the amount of damage one can do through thoughtless speech. Words can never be recaptured or undone. The lesson to learn is that one must carefully choose the words one speaks.

Question: What happened to Bilam?

Answer: Bilam returned to Midyan in disgrace over his failure to curse the Israelites. As a last resort to reclaim some pride Bilam suggests to Balak that as the Israelites journey through Moab, he use the women of his nation to seduce the Israelite men to commit forbidden acts and to get them to commit idolatry. This did happen and, as a result, the Almighty sent a plague upon the Israelites causing the death of many thousands. Bilam was killed by the sword as the Israelites conquered Midyan (*Numbers 31:8*).

Question: How is the concept of prophetic dreams explained in the Torah?

Answer: Our sages address prophetic dreams in three contexts: one is random chance or coincidence. These are dreams that can happen to anyone. The person may choose to take it seriously and see it as a prophecy or not. The person who has the dream need not be righteous or wise (*Sefer Hakaida*).

The second idea is that prophetic dreams are sent by the Almighty, and those who receive them deserve them by virtue of living committed spiritual lives. This is exemplified by the lives our ancestors Abraham, Isaac, and Jacob, lived. They ultimately brought the prophecy to the people. On the other hand, secular philosophers, (i.e., Socrates, Aristotle, and Plato) say that people who have this prophetic ability attain this state only through very hard work and self-discipline.

The third idea is put forth by *Rambam*, who says that both concepts are at work simultaneously. The person who has the prophetic dream is one whose life is lived according to the highest possible spiritual level and therefore becomes worthy of being deemed a prophet (*Rambam, Moreh Nevuchim*). *Rambam* differs with the secular philosophers, saying that it is God alone who decides who will receive the gift of prophecy and who will not.

Question: How do we know when to classify a dream as prophetic?

Answer: Let's illustrate our answer through a story. A woman came to a rabbi and told him that her daughter awoke one night sweating and trembling from a dream. She asked for help. She told the rabbi that her daughter had no mental or physical problems. The rabbi told her it was probably nothing but a bad dream. The daughter continued having the same disturbing dreams once or twice a week. The girl was thoroughly checked out by a physician and a psychiatrist and was found to be perfectly normal.

The mother returned to the rabbi, who told her to have her daughter fast for twenty four hours after the next dream. This solved her problem. The sages say in the *Talmud, Gittin: 53b*, that if anyone has a disturbing dream he or she must fast for twenty-four hours immediately following the dream (*ta'anit chalom*). There is a special prayer constructed for concluding such a fast. Our sages further say that if this disturbing dream does not appear three times consecutively (i.e., three days in a row) it can be ignored.

Question: Why is the name of Moses not mentioned until the conclusion of this *parsha?*

Answer: Moses played no active role in any of the events that occur prior to the conclusion of this parsha. The Torah wants to make it clear that those events were directly controlled by God, and were external to Moses and Israel. The *Talmud* states (*Bava Batra 14a*) that Moses wrote the Torah, but intentionally excluded himself from this parsha because he did not want his name to be associated with a person such as Bilam.

Question: God appeared to Bilam and asked, "Who are the people who came to you?" *(Numbers 22:9)*. Did God not know who these people were?

Answer: God asked this question for other reasons than merely to hear an answer. Certainly God knew who these people were and He did not have to ask Bilam to find out. The question was a test for Bilam, to see how he would answer. This is similar to God asking Cain, "Where is your brother, Abel?" Certainly the Almighty knew exactly where Abel was. We can discern from these questions that Almighty was looking for the individual to admit wrongdoing and to repent.

Question: What did we learn from the story of the donkey speaking?

Answer: God gave the donkey the ability to speak in order to humiliate Bilam (*Ohr Hachayim*) and to reveal to the world Bilam's true character (*Rabbeinu Bachayei*).

Only the Creator has the ability to give any creature the capacity to speak. Bilam accused the donkey of mockery, but she did exactly what God had ordered her to do (*Ramban*).

The Almighty gave the donkey the power of speech in this instance for the sake of the Israelites. It also pointed out that Bilam's abilities where granted by God to bring him to the moment in which he would bless Israel and not curse them (*Kli Yakar*).

This was a vision that did not occur in reality; it was only a way to illustrate a vision of prophecies (*Rambam, Moreh Nevuchim*). One should note that many commentators disagree on this point.

The purpose of the donkey speaking was to give Bilam one last chance to repent to the Almighty (*Sforno*).

Question: How many oxen did Bilam offer in sacrifice, and how many times?

Answer: Bilam offered seven oxen in sacrifice, three times. Note that seven is a symbolically important number in the Torah. Bilam was trying to copy the forefathers of the Israelites who sacrificed seven sheep to the Almighty (*Ramav*).

Question: How do we see the concept of freedom of choice in this *parsha?*

Answer: Balak chose to fight the Israelites. He also chose to hire Bilam to curse them.

It would appear from the way the Torah recounts this episode that Bilam was prevented from exercising free will. On the contrary, he made the choice to ignore God's warning and follow his own evil inclination. Bilam's own choices brought God's punishment on him. By changing the curses to blessings in Bilam's mouth the Almighty brought about Bilam's demise.

Rambam explains that God gave mankind freedom of thought and the ability to make decisions. However, the Almighty did not give him total freedom of action. Man does not have the right to indiscriminately use this freedom to hurt others.

Furthermore, the Almighty could not allow Bilam the pleasure of using supernatural means (i.e., having the evil words he spoke be fulfilled) in order to curse the Israelites. God did not want it to seem as though Bilam had the power to entreat Heaven to cause damage to his personal enemies. Bilam was forced to bless the Children of Israel instead of cursing them. He realized from this incident that he was not as powerful as he had imagined himself to be. The powerful faculty of speech is given to man by God. It is to be used carefully and with the utmost discretion (*Ohr Hachayim*).

Question: Bilam delivered the following blessing to the Israelites: "How goodly are your tents, O Jacob, your dwelling places, O Israel" (*Numbers 24:5*). What does this mean, and why is it incorporated into our morning prayers?

Answer: Bilam was referring to the unique way the Israelites erected their tents. The entrances to these tents were positioned in such a way as to obstruct the view into the neighboring tent. This shows the Israelites' desire to be modest. Modesty is seen as a beautiful and elevated trait. According to Jewish law, when one buys a home or builds one, he should make sure that his home exemplifies modesty. We recite this phrase on a daily basis as a constant reminder to ourselves of who we are and how we present ourselves to others (*Rashi; Ramav*).

Question: What advice did Bilam give Balak before he left, and why?

Answer: When Bilam failed to curse the Children of Israel, he advised Balak, "If you really want to make the God of the Israelites angry with them, have the Moabite women seduce the men. Have the women make cohabitation conditional upon the men bowing to the Moabite idols." Unfortunately, Bilam was successful with this advice (*Rashi, Numbers 25:2*).

Question: What was the result of the Israelites bowing to the Moabite idols?

Answer: Bowing to these idols was a great sin. God sent a plague, and 24,000 people died. It might have continued, were it not for the zealous actions of Pinchas.

Pinchas

Chapters: 25:10 - 30:1

Synopsis:

The result of Pinchas' zealous action; the taking of a census of the tribes; the division of the Land by lottery; the story of Zelophehad's daughters; the rules of inheritance; God showed Moses the Land of Israel; God commanded Moses to transfer the leadership to Joshua; the laws regarding the offerings for the Sabbath and festivals.

Question: What were the circumstances that led up to Pinchas reacting in the manner in which he did?

Answer: As we mentioned in the previous parsha, Bilam advised Balak to use the daughters of Moab to seduce the Israelites. The Israelites fell victim to this seduction. They also willingly bowed down to the idols of Moab during this seduction. As a consequence, a plague was sent as punishment to the Israelite nation. God further commanded Moses that the death penalty be meted out to those who had succumbed to this sin. The punishments of the plague and the sentence of death knew neither status nor wealth. Zimri, one of the heads of the tribe of Simeon, took Cosbi, a daughter of the king of Midyan. He made a public demonstration, flaunting his total disregard for the laws of God, by committing a forbidden act with Cosbi. No one in a leadership capacity, including Moses, responded to this flagrant act. Pinchas, who was neither a leader nor a judge, took it upon himself to respond. He stood up and went to Zimri and Cosbi while they were involved in their act together, and with one thrust of a sword Pinchas killed them both instantly. This action by Pinchas was done before the eyes of the entire nation (*Babylonian Talmud, Sanhedrin 106a; Alsheich; Rashi*).

Question: Pinchas took the law into his own hands. Why, instead of punishment, does he receive a reward?

Answer: It seems clear from the story that Pinchas' motivation arises from his deep unselfish devotion to the Almighty and to the rule of law. It appears obvious that he sought neither wealth nor prestige from this act. He was keenly aware of the repercussions of his act: he could have been sought out and killed by members of Zimri's family; he may also have been subject to judgment from the Israelite court system. Pinchas was willing to sacrifice his personal future for the sake of the future of the Children of Israel. Regardless of these consequences he still acted with full conscience. This act avenged the insult to the Name of the Almighty and also put an end to the public ridicule of Moses. Pinchas' zealous action brought about the abrupt end of the plague. As reward for this act the Almighty declared that the future generations of Pinchas would inherit the priesthood (*Babylonian Talmud, Sanhedrin 106a; Alsheich; Rashi*).

It is clear from Jewish law that "a priest who kills unintentionally is forbidden to perform work in the Temple." It was therefore necessary for the Almighty to state from the outset of this parsha that He willed that Pinchas be awarded the role of priest for his zealous actions (*Ibn Ezra; Ohr Hachayim*).

Question: God punished Israel twice for idolatry. The first time was with the creation of the Golden Calf; the second instance occurred with the seduction of the Israelite men by the Moabite women. The nation was punished in both instances but there were marked differences between the two. How so?

Answer: With the incident of the Golden Calf, the Almighty visited upon the Israelites a plague. Moses begged for forgiveness for the nation. God's response to him was, "Now I forgive them, but the time will come when I will take this sin into account" (*Exodus 32:34*). It appears from this verse that the Almighty would continue to impose punishment upon the Israelites for this egregious act for generations to come.

With regard to this parsha and the resulting action of Pinchas, God said that He absolutely forgave the Children of Israel for this incident. For his actions, Pinchas received the "covenant of peace"(*Numbers 25:12*). According to our sages this covenant of peace states that no further punishment will be extracted from the Children of Israel for this particular incident (*Riva; Chizkuni; Zohar*).

Question: A country had attained great honor and status among its neighbors. Suddenly, there rose an evil leader, a man of low morals. He proceeded to destroy the country's prestige. Unfortunately, everyone complained, but no one had the courage to do anything about it. Then one day someone summoned up the courage and took the law into his own hands and killed this leader. After the death of the leader, the country began to reclaim its rightful status. Clearly, the man had committed murder, but justified his actions by saying that it was a zealous action, in order to save the people. In this parsha, it appears that Pinchas acted in a similar way. Was this murder, or someone acting in the Name of God? What is the rabbinical point of view regarding this issue?

Answer: As long as the rabbinical courts are not in power today, we must obey the law of whatever land we are living in. Therefore, any action that is against that law is considered a sin. No one has the right to take matters into his own hands, even if he feels strongly that he is following God's way, as Pinchas felt. The *Talmud* in *Sanhedrin 82b* records a debate on whether Pinchas deserved punishment. Later commentators on the Talmud say that perhaps Pinchas deserved to be isolated from the community. The *Kotz Rebbe* points out that Joshua, not Pinchas, was chosen to lead the Israelites. He suggests that Pinchas' behavior, although praiseworthy, was not leadership quality, therefore he did not deserve a position of leadership. Only because it was clear that Pinchas acted with pure intentions did he get the protection from God, called, "covenant of peace." Even in our time, we must not follow the words or examples of extremists who preach or practice violence, or try to justify their positions by incorrect Torah interpretations.

Question: What do we learn from Pinchas' zeal?

Answer: Pinchas illustrates a principle of Jewish law that "one cannot deduce a tenet of law from a public action." Although the results of the actions by Pinchas had positive effects – the ending of the plague – it is incorrect for us to conclude that one has the right to unilaterally make halachic (Jewish law) decisions. One must consult rabbinical authority. Had Pinchas consulted Moses beforehand regarding Zimri and Cosbi, Moses undoubtedly would have prohibited him from slaying them (*Babylonian Talmud, Sanhedrin 82b; Yavamot 100a; Kiddushin 66b*).

Question: Why is it necessary to mention the lineage of Pinchas: "Pinchas the son of Elazar, the son of Aaron the priest" *(Numbers 25:11)*?

Answer: Our sages say that the people spoke out against Pinchas, saying, "Look at this man, whose grandfather worshipped idols, and he had the nerve to kill one of the leaders of a tribe." It therefore was necessary for the Torah to point out Pinchas' ancestry to show that he had an illustrious background (*Rashi; Babylonian Talmud, Sotah 42b*).

Question: Why does the Bible point out the ancestry of Zimri: "Zimri, the son of Salu, a leader of the tribe of Shimon" *(Numbers 25:14)*?

Answer: The Bible uses this wording to point out that even someone from a prestigious background can easily fall prey to evil if he does not watch his behavior *(Rashi)*.

Question: What was this special prize that God gave Pinchas?

Answer: The Almighty entered into a covenant of peace with Pinchas and granted him and his future generations a priestly role *(Ramban)*.

This covenant of peace protected Pinchas, and his future generations from harm *(Ibn Ezra)*.

God promised Pinchas long life *(Sforno)*. According to the sages the prophet Elijah was the reincarnation of Pinchas years later.

Question: How do we see the Midyanites' hatred for the Israelites?

Answer: The Midyanite king was willing to use even his own daughter as a prostitute to cause the Israelites to sin in front of God *(Numbers 25:18)*.

Question: Why did God tell Moses to count the Israelites (*Numbers 26:2*)?

Answer: Since the Israelites were important to God, He wanted to count them to see how many were left after the plague (*Rashi*).

The Land was to be divided among the tribes, therefore, their numbers had to be determined (*Ibn Ezra*).

The Land needed to be conquered, therefore, the number of eligible men needed to be ascertained (*Abarbanel*).

Question: What qualities does Moses ask God for in Israel's next leader?

Answer: Moses endured much from both the enemies of the Israelites and the Children of Israel themselves. He therefore asked God to install as leader someone who would have the following attributes: the ability to understand the differences in people. Someone tolerant, with the ability to bring divergent groups together as a cohesive unit.

He must be courageous, being in the forefront of his army, placing his own person at risk. He should possess enough righteousness to defend his nation against its enemies.

Above all possess a total faith and trust in the Almighty.

Question: Who followed Moses as leader and why?

Answer: Joshua was chosen by God to succeed Moses because he exemplified the traits Moses believed should be possessed by a leader of Israel. Joshua showed his loyalty and trust by remaining at the side of Moses. To name a few instances: Joshua awaited Moses when he descended from Mount Sinai after receiving the commandments from God; he held up Moses' arm during the war with Amalek; he was one of the twelve spies sent into Canaan by Moses, and one of the two who spoke truthfully upon their return, holding fast to faith and trust in the Almighty.

Matot

Chapters: 30:2 - 32

Synopsis:

The laws regarding vows and oaths; oaths made between men; and between man and God; cancellation of some oaths; God commanded the Israelites to take vengeance upon the Midyanites; Pinchas, the priest, killed the evil magician, Bilam; Moses divided the spoils of war among the Israelites; conflict about land inheritance between Moses and two of the tribes.

Question: What is the difference between an oath and a vow?

Answer: According to our sages there are two types of vows. In one type a person will state that something is forbidden to him. For example if a person had said that apples were forbidden to him, then he would be unable to eat apples. The other type is that which one states obligating himself to do something, for example one states that he will give charity to a particular organization. The emphasis is placed upon the object.

As for an oath, one can do either – prohibit something from himself or require himself to perform a specific act. The emphasis here is on the individual who states the oath.

By declaring a vow, the object's status has changed, as in our example of the apple where it is now in a state of being forbidden to him. By making an oath he has placed himself in a position where he has obligated himself to do or not do something.

Question: What is the general Torah principle regarding oaths and vows?

Answer: God gave man the unique capacity of speech. Man is required, therefore, to guard his speech carefully. Every word that passes out of our mouths is important. The power of speech is seen all too clearly in situations that arise regarding vows and oaths. Once spoken, these verbal commitments are to be followed precisely. One does not have the unilateral right to alter one's statement because it has become inconvenient, troublesome, or burdensome. Rabbinical authorities must be consulted if one has stated or believes he has stated a vow or oath and desires to have it annulled or altered in some fashion.

Question: Why does the Torah discourage people from making vows?

Answer: Torah wisdom suggests it is far better not to swear an oath in the first place.

A story is told of a Jew who immigrated to the U.S. from Russia. He came destitute. He tried to enter a synagogue on the High Holy Days but was denied entry because he was not a member. He got very angry and swore an oath never to enter any synagogue again. A number of years passed and the man was filled with remorse that he had not been to a synagogue for so many years, but he was bound by his oath. He turned to a rabbinical court, describing in detail how he had come to declare this oath, how he had made the oath out of anger and frustration. He convinced the court that he truly had misgivings about making it and that he forgave those who had barred him from the synagogue. After deliberating, the *Beit Din* (religious court) nullified the man's oath. The Torah understands human nature, how someone can be misled into thinking that they can fulfill a vow. It is truly much more difficult than anticipated. One must be careful with spur-of-the-moment speech.

Question: What are the different degrees of oath within Jewish law?

Answer: The most binding form of oath is the one in which the individual pronounces the Name of God before a *Minyan* (group of ten men over the age of thirteen), and in front of a Torah Scroll. A level below is the oath made in the Name of God and in front of a witness. Next comes the oath that mentions the Name of God but with no witness present. The last level is an oath that does not mention the Name of God, has no witnesses present, and yet it is clear to a person that he is either prohibiting something or placing an obligation upon himself.

Question: With the recitation of *Kol Nidrei* on erev *Yom Kippur* are we released from oaths or vows that we made all year?

Answer: Absolutely not. The *Kol Nidrei* prayer is used to free us only from vows that we might have made during the year, but have truly forgotten. We do not want to be prevented from making atonement for promises, that we truly forgot. In no way are we ever absolved by the *Kol Nidrei* from a vow that we knowingly made and still remember.

Question: A man has a nightmare in which he is involved in a serious automobile accident. In his dream, he is very frightened and swears an oath never to talk to the person who caused the accident. He wakes up and remembers the dream. Is he bound by his vow?

Answer: Even though the vow appears to be unintentional due to the fact that it happened in an unconscious state, the person must still be absolved from the formal vow. The *Talmudic* sages suggest that such a man should fast for one day and then he is absolved from his vow. The sages tell us that fasting is a cleansing process; if the person fasts in response to his dream then that cleanses him from his responsibility to adhere to the vow or oath. Or, the person might explain his vow to three Torah knowledgeable persons, who can then absolve him from this vow. Here we see the great importance placed on any vow or promise; even a vow made unintentionally in a dream, seemingly out of the person's control, is not so easily dismissed.

Question: If a man finds that he does not have the physical ability or strength to complete his vow without endangering himself, is he released from his vow?

Answer: There are volumes of controversy surrounding this subject. Generally, it requires a *Beit Din* to meet and decide if the person can be absolved from his oath or vow. Before making a vow it is wise to consult with competent rabbinical authority. It is incumbent upon a person to understand one's own limitations and capabilities.

Question: Is a vow binding, if it goes against Torah law?

Answer: No, one cannot make a vow or oath to something that is in opposition the Torah, i.e., to eat non-kosher food.

Question: Under pressure, a man vows to God to fast for twenty-four hours to try to resolve the problem. The problem is resolved six hours after he starts the fast. Can he stop the fast early?

Answer: No, it remains intact. The man must complete all that he vowed.

Question: The *Nazirite*, who made an oath not to cut his hair for one year, is required to bring a sin offering at the end of that year. Why?

Answer: First, A *Nazirite* is an adult who vows to abstain from cutting his or her hair or drinking wine, and to avoid situations that would bring one to contamination, for a stated period of time.

The Torah does not want us to "take on an extra yoke or burden." God would be pleased if we performed properly those commandments we were obligated to without adding extraneous burdens. Taking on an extra burden, like a vow of *Nazerut,* is a form of sin, and therefore requires a sin offering. It is suggested that this principle of the Torah is an attempt to prevent excesses of religious zeal and fervor.

Question: What was the conflict between Moses and two of the tribes?

Answer: The tribes of Gad and Reuven wanted their land to be east of the Jordan. They saw the land as most suitable for their large herds of livestock. Moses strongly rebuked them for this attitude. He felt they did not have the proper love for the Holy Land, since they were willing to locate themselves outside of its borders. It seemed apparent that they did not have as strong a bond as their brothers, who were preparing for a great battle to conquer the homeland God had promised them. Personal profit was placed over the important principle of being a nation in its own land.

These attitudes of Gad and Reuven made Moses very angry. It seemed that they placed themselves first, rather than looking to the whole nation and its need to enter and conquer the Holy Land (*Akaida; Abarbanel*). Moses also felt that they were somewhat cowardly by attempting to avoid battle, and he was concerned that other tribes might follow their example.

Question: How did Gad and Reuven respond to Moses?

Answer: The answer seems cowardly: they said that they would remain east of the Jordan with their flocks, and that if their brothers had difficulty in battle, they would come to help (*Numbers 32:16-19*).

Question: God commanded Moses to take extreme vengeance on the Midyanites. Why did Moses give this task to Pinchas, instead of doing it himself *(Numbers 31:1-13)*?

Answer: Moses lived for a period of time in Midyan, and did not want to appear ungrateful to the nation by destroying it (*Midrash Rabba*).

There is an adage, "Whoever begins a *mitzvah* should complete it." Moses felt that since Pinchas began dealing with the Midyanites, he should be the one to complete the *mitzvah*.

Question: How did Pinchas happen to kill Bilam?

Answer: Bilam had returned to Midyan to claim payment from Balak for his advice to seduce the Israelites. His counsel led to the deaths of 24,000 Israelites. Unfortunately for Bilam, he happened to be there when Pinchas came to slay the Midyanites (*Yonatan ben Uziel, Numbers 31:8*).

Question: How does this parsha again demonstrate that Moses was an extremely righteous man?

Answer: God said to Moses: "Take vengeance on the Midyanites and after that you will be gathered to your people" (*Numbers 31:2*). Moses is told to carry out this mission and then he would die. We would expect that an ordinary man in this situation would try to delay and stall his death as much as he could. But not so with Moses. He rushed to carry out God's orders with alacrity, even though it brought him closer to his own death (*Meschach Chachmah*).

Masei

Chapters: 33 - 36

Synopsis:

The retelling of the journeys of the Children of Israel; the boundaries of the Land of Israel; the list of leaders of the twelve tribes; the cities of refuge for persons who had unintentionally killed another; the laws of intentional and unintentional murder; the rules of intermarriage among the tribes.

Question: Why is this *parsha* called *Masei?*

Answer: *Masei* is Hebrew for "journey." After forty years wandering the desert, the Israelites came to the border of the land promised to them by God. The Torah lists the places the Israelites encountered during their journey. This rite of passage enabled the Jewish nation to journey from slavery to freedom.

Question: Why does the Torah list the resting places the Israelites stayed during their forty-year journey in the desert?

Answer: Even though the Israelites received God's decree of wandering for forty years in the desert, He gave them many resting places and in each place protected them. When the situation called for it, He performed miracles (*Rashi*). This shows the Almighty's compassion.

It praises the Israelites for following the dictates of God even in the wilderness (*Ramav*).

It shows the tremendous loyalty between the Israelites and God that they went from one unknown place to another over a long period of time (*Sforno*).

In a number of these encampments a different miracle was performed by God. The mention of each place commemorates and publicizes each miracle. The repetition is also seen as an allusion to the future journeys and return to the Promised Land that the Israelites will have to make (*Rabbeinu Bechayei*).

Rambam in his *Moreh Nevuchim (vol. 3, ch. 50)*, said: "...Because it is clear to the Almighty that future generations would doubt all the miracles that happened to the Israelites in the desert, God wanted it written to wipe away all doubt."

Question: What is the chronology of this *parsha?*

Answer: The significant events occur in this order: introduction (verses 1-2); the journey from Ra'amsis to the Sinai desert (verses 3-

15); the journey from the Sinai to Kadesh (verses 16-37); the death of Aaron and the war against the king of Arad (verses 38-40); the journey from Mount Hor to Moab (verses 41-49).

Question: Does the commandment of inheriting the Holy Land exist today?

Answer: This is a controversial issue. The sage *Ramban (Numbers 33:53)* defines the commandment of inheritance and occupation of the Holy Land as a positive commandment that absolutely exists today. Consequently, he considers anyone who lives in the Holy Land to be fulfilling a positive commandment.

However, *Rashi* said that the commandment of inheriting the land is in existence only if one fulfills conditions such as destroying the abomination that exists in the land. Only then is there the chance to fulfill the commandment of inheriting and occupying the Holy Land. Consequently, *Rashi* considers the Holy Land as "temporarily impure land."

Question: Why were the Israelites required to use a lottery system in order to determine each tribe's inheritance (portion of land)?

Answer: In Israel there is a wide range of climate and land quality. By using the lottery system, no one could claim favoritism.

Question: How was the Land divided?

Answer: The Land was divided into territories and distributed among nine and a half tribes. This was done by blind lottery. The reason only nine and a half tribes participated in this lottery was that Reuven, Gad, and half the tribe of Manashah took possession of land east of the Jordan, outside the boundaries of the Holy Land.

There is a difference of opinion among the earlier sages as to how the land was further divided among members of each tribe. One possible way was through the lottery system. Another was through a census of each tribe (*Babylonian Talmud, Bava Batra 117a; Ramban; Grah*).

It is a worldwide custom that when the Torah reader finishes the
last sentence of each one of the five books of Moses, the entire
congregation stands and encourages one another
with the following proclamation:

"CHAZAK CHAZAK V' NITCHAZEK!"

(STRENGTH...STRENGTH...AND BECOME STRONG)

The Book of Deuteronomy

Devarim

Chapters: 1 - 3:22

Synopsis:

Moses repeated the Torah; reprise of Moses' hardships; just before his death, Moses reviewed the history and deeds of the Israelites; Moses rebuked the Israelites for their past sins; Moses instructed the Israelites by repeating some of the commandments; the spies' mission; crossing the border of Moab.

Question: Why is the Book of Deuteronomy referred to as the *Mishnah Torah?*

Answer: Our sages teach that the *Divine Presence* spoke through Moses. Moses did not write even one letter to the Torah without God's instruction (*Ramban; Ibn Ezra; Abarbanel; Ohr Hachayim*).

Mishnah Torah means "second Torah." Deuteronomy is a repetition of parts of the first four books. Therefore, our sages refer to this Book as the *Second Torah.* Deuteronomy emphasizes certain parts of the Torah. There are instances where the event has been recalled but the language used is different. For example, in the *Book of Exodus* the tenth commandment is originally stated as, "Thou shall not covet thy neighbor's house, wife, and possessions." In restating the commandments in Deuteronomy, the order is changed, listing the wife first. This undoubtedly reflects God's experience with the Israelites, causing Him to instruct Moses to make such changes.

Question: What is this *parsha* about?

Answer: It begins with Moses recounting recent history, rebuking the people, and talking to them about their relationship with God. The word *devarim* means "things." The first phrase of the parsha states, "These are the things that you have done wrong to anger God." Moses then lists the names of places that stand for times that the people lost faith in God, from the incident of the golden calf through the rebellion led by Korach, the lack of appreciation for *manna* (the food provided by God from heaven), Miriam's *loshon horah* (gossip) and all the other acts of resistance to God's Will.

Question: For what reasons will God let the people inherit the Land?

Answer: Moses tells the people that God will allow them to inherit the Land not because they are "entitled to it," but rather because God is compassionate and merciful, and because the

Almighty had made a covenant with their forefathers, Abraham, Isaac, and Jacob.

Question: Why is this parsha usually read on the Shabbat before the ninth of the month of Av?

Answer: The Hebrew word *aicha* means to "lament"; it appears four times in the Bible. The first time is in this *parsha*, as Moses laments, "How can I bear all you unruly and difficult people" (*Deuteronomy 1:12*). The second time is in the *haftorah* for this *parsha*, *Isaiah 1*. The prophet Isaiah lamented how Jerusalem "...would become an empty city when all would be killed or sent into exile." The third time is in the *Book of Lamentations*, recited on *Tisha B'Av*, the ninth day of Av. Here, the prophet Jeremiah also laments that the Israelites will suffer a holocaust or be sent into exile (*Babylonian Talmud, Sanhedrin 97b*).

Question: What happened on *Tisha B'Av?*

Answer: In the *Book of Numbers*, the spies were sent into the Holy Land and returned with an evil report. Instead of rejecting the report, the Israelites reacted with much complaining and lack of gratitude. God decreed that because of their complaining, they would wander the desert for forty years, and those living at that time would not live to enter the Holy Land. The people cried and lamented all night. This decree was given on *Tisha B'Av (Talmud Sotah 35b)*.

Jewish history recounts many disasters that happened on this date. For example, during the time when the Temple stood in Jerusalem, we see that the city of Betar was captured and destroyed and hundreds of thousands died.

In 1492, on this date, King Ferdinand and Queen Isabella expelled the Jews from Spain.

World War I began on *Tisha B'Av*. During World War II, the rounding up of Jews from the Warsaw Ghetto to be sent to the Treblinka Concentration Camp began on *Tisha B'Av*.

Yet most important was the desecration of both Temples on the Ninth of Av.

Question: Why was the first Temple destroyed?

Answer: The *Talmud* says that the first Temple was destroyed because the Jews committed the three most serious transgressions: murder, adultery, and idolatry. Israel is supposed to be a holy nation and even though a small segment of the population sinned in those three most egregious ways the entire nation was held accountable. The *Talmud* also suggests that since the gift of prophecy was prevalent at this time there had to be an equal but opposite attraction to evil in order to maintain free will. This explains why some Jews sinned.

Question: Why was the second Temple destroyed?

Answer: The *Talmud* brings the following story: "Because of Kamtza and Bar Kamtza, Jerusalem was destroyed; because of senseless hatred, the Temple was destroyed" (*Babylonian Talmud, Gittin 55b-56a*).

The famous story is about a very important and honored man who made a big party at his palace. He invited all the judges, sages, and notables of the time. He had an enemy named Bar Kamtza, who was himself a highly respected and honorable man. The host sent an invitation intended for his good friend Kamtza, but by mistake the messenger delivered it to his enemy, Bar Kamtza. Bar Kamtza was surprised at receiving the invitation and surmised that the man had sent the invitation as a peace offering. Bar Kamtza thought, "Since he wants to make a reconciliation, I must make every effort to attend the affair."

With mixed feelings, Bar Kamtza went to the affair. He sat and ate the first course, when suddenly, the host discovered his presence. The host approached Bar Kamtza and said loudly in front of all the guests, "What are you doing here at my party?" Bar Kamtza replied, "You invited me and I accepted. Here is the invitation you sent." The host yelled, "Bring the servant who delivered the invitations."

It was soon apparent that the whole matter was an error by the servant. The host said loudly to Bar Kamtza, "You have to leave." Bar Kamtza replied, "Since I am already here, may I please stay? I will pay for what I eat." The host responded, "No, you have to leave right now." Bar Kamtza then said, "Please don't embarrass me. If I can stay, I will pay for my entire table." Again, the host loudly refused. For the third time, Bar Kamtza asked "Please don't embarrass me. If I can stay, I will pay for the entire party." In reply, the host and one of his servants lifted Bar Kamtza and physically removed him from the party. Bar Kamtza was very hurt and embarrassed but thought, "I am much more angry at the important people who sat quietly by and did nothing than I am at the host." All the important people including judges, sages, great rabbis, and scholars, sat silently by because they were intimidated by a man's wealth. Bar Kamtza vowed revenge.

At that time, the Romans ruled the Holy Land. Bar Kamtza had a strong business relationship with the emperor of Rome. Bar Kamtza traveled to Rome and told the emperor that the Jews had betrayed him. The emperor demanded proof that this was true. Bar Kamtza said, "Send them your messanger with an offering to put on the altar, and you will see that they will not accept it." the emperor did so, sending a prize bull to the Temple for sacrifice. On the way, Bar Kamtza had the animal injured in such a way as to make it unfit for sacrifice. When the animal arrived at the Temple there was a debate among the priests of the Temple and the leading sages as to what to do. The sages wanted the *korban* to be accepted, because they needed to adhere to the rule of the government (which was Rome), while the priests looked to the condition of the animal, which had a defect. The defect made it unacceptable for sacrifice on the altar. The animal was rejected. The emperor's messenger returned to Rome, reporting, "It is true, the Jews did not accept the offering." As a result the emperor sent his army to destroy Jerusalem, burn the Temple, and send the Jews into exile. All this happened because of senseless hatred.

It is written in the *Talmud* that the Temple would once again be rebuilt if the people would judge each favorably, with unconditional love, and live as a single unit.

Question: To what other fast day do the sages compare *Tisha B'Av?*

Answer: The fast of *Tisha B'Av* is obligatory like *Yom Kippur.*

Question: "Judge with justice...do not fear any man" *(Deuteronomy 1:17).* What does this mean?

Answer: This admonishment is directed toward judges or any one in a position of authority. Judgments are to be made fairly, independently, and fearlessly. All men should have total faith in God, and should depend upon Him alone. If one truly believes in God, he knows that no man can harm him and, therefore, he has no reason to fear. Leaders and judges should not be intimidated into making a decision.

Question: What connection does the *haftorah* have to this *parsha?*

Answer: The *haftorah* for this *parsha* is referred to as *Chazon Isaiah.* Several generations after Moses, the prophet Isaiah speaks to the Israelites and tells them of his visions of the future and of God's dissatisfaction with their lack of faith. God says that it is not enough to hold public prayer and sacrifice. People must act in private in ways that reflect the principles and ethics that God had taught. Simply put, "practice what you preach."

In our own day, people often feel that it is enough if they follow certain requirements, such as prayer, eating kosher, giving charity, and fasting. These behaviors are certainly commendable. However, a person is not permitted to pick and choose the commandments he or she wishes to follow and ignore the others. The Almighty has set into motion a whole set of commandments (found in the Bible) that one is obligated to follow without exception. The main thrust of Isaiah's warning is to provoke people into behaving in their private lives as they do publicly. By living that way we avoid repeating the mistakes of the past.

"A nation that does not learn from its mistakes is doomed to repeat them" (*Winston Churchill*).

Question: In the *haftorah* why does the prophet Isaiah make a comparison to animals when rebuking the people?

Answer: Isaiah wanted to point out how ungrateful the people were to God. God had done much more for man than man could ever begin to do for animals. Man was empowered with speech, intelligence, and comforts to a degree that animals could never approach. Yet man chose to disobey the laws set down by God. Isaiah stated that the loyalty, obedience, and trust of animals in man exceeded the trust and faith that man had in God. God had saved them so many times and had given them the Land and prosperity, but still their behavior was inferior. Therefore Isaiah rebuked them.

Question: Since all this happened in the past, why are we required to fast on *Tisha B'Av?*

Answer: Our sages say that as long as Jews are capable of senseless hatred, tragedies will continue to strike us. As long as there is strife and unnecessary division among us, we can expect disasters to continue to befall us. Though the fasting that occurs commemorates the tragedies that befell the Jewish people on this date, it is not its main purpose. Of course we are to lament the destruction of the Temples in Jerusalem, but we fast to call to mind the lack of unity among us. The hope is that by fasting each of us will gain a perspective on himself and work to correct inappropriate habits. We can create positive attitudes that can lead to unity. Then, as the prophet says, instead of a day of fasting, *Tisha B'Av* will be a joyous day (*Babylonian Talmud, Sanhedrin 97b*).

Question: What are the laws of *Tisha B'Av?*

Answer: We are prohibited from eating, drinking, bathing, and the wearing of leather, from sunset to sunset. Sexual relations are also prohibited. On the eve of *Tisha B'Av*, we sit on the ground to express our sense of mourning, and chant the *Book of Lamentations* using a sad melody. In the morning prayer service, men do not wear the *tallis* or *tefillin*. In the afternoon prayer service, we wear both. From the first until the *ninth of Av*, parties commemorating joyous occasions are not held. Only non-meat meals are eaten. Men do not shave or cut their hair during this period.

Question: How do we today commemorate the destruction of Jerusalem?

Answer: Traditions include the breaking of a glass by the bridegroom under the *chuppah*, the wedding canopy. There is the tradition, especially in Israel, of leaving a small part of one's house unpainted; it is usually on the wall opposite the front door, so as to remind one of the destruction of the Temples when one enters one's home. This symbolizes our feeling that the world is incomplete with the absence of the Temple. Sometimes we find the verse, "If I forget thee O Jerusalem...," written in this unpainted space.

V'Etchanaan
Chapters: 3:23 - 7:11

Synopsis:

Moses begged God to let him enter the Holy Land; God's final decision let Moses see the Land before he died; Moses instructed the Israelites in detail before he died; the Ten Commandments are repeated; the famous prayer called, "Shema Israel" ("Hear O Israel").

Note: The haftorah for this parsha is called "Consolation" or Nachamu.

This week usually contains the festival of the fifteenth of Av.

Question: Why is the fifteenth of Av a joyous holiday?

Answer: The *Talmud* presents six different reasons; here is one of them: "Rabbi Shimon ben Gamliel said that there is no day happier to Jews than the fifteenth of Av. On this day, all the daughters of Jerusalem went out with borrowed white fancy dresses (in order that no one be embarrassed because one could not afford a dress). They danced through Jerusalem and said, "Men open your eyes and judge by the quality of the person, not by appearance." This holiday became known as *Chag Hashadchanim*, or "The Festival of the Matchmakers" (*Babylonian Talmud, Ta'anit Ch. 4*).

Question: "You shall not add or subtract anything from the commandments" *(Deuteronomy 4:2)*. What does this mean?

Answer: The simple understanding of this verse is that we are to follow God's instructions exactly, without adding anything to or removing anything from them. The Torah comes from the Almighty and no one is allowed to amend it. An example is the Torah commandment calling for the use of four species during the festival of *Sukkot*. We must use exactly the four called for. Using three or five species, or substitution of one, is forbidden (*Rashi, Deuteronomy 4:2*).

Question: Why are the Ten Commandments repeated in this *parsha*?

Answer: Moses wanted to be sure that the people understood their exact meaning. Repetition is a way of emphasizing importance.

Question: What are some of the changes to the Ten Commandments as recorded in the *Book of Exodus* and the *Book of Deuteronomy*?

Answer: In Exodus the commandment is to "Remember the

Sabbath...," a positive commandment. In *Deuteronomy* the commandment is written in the negative "Thou shalt not..." In another example, the commandment written in Exodus states "Thou shalt not covet thy neighbor's property or thy neighbor's wife..." In *Deuteronomy*, stronger language is used, and the order is changed: the wife is listed before property. Since desire for a neighbor's wife could lead to the destruction of the family, the order was changed to the prohibition against coveting another man's wife first. Note: The reader is cautioned not to assume that women are being equated with property in any way. In Jewish law and custom the woman is held in high regard. Her integrity and values are to be guarded with the utmost scrutiny.

Question: The first commandment is, "I am the Lord your God..." What do these words mean?

Answer: The first commandment demands absolute and total faith in God as Master of the Universe. We must acknowledge Him as the true "owner" of everything, and accept the reality that He has created for us. The *Ramav* says that a violation of one of the other commandments is also a violation of the first commandment as well. If someone else has something, it is because God gave it to him. Therefore, if one desires it, one is showing a lack of faith in God, a violation of the first commandment.

Question: How does one fulfill the commandment of honoring one's father and mother *(Deuteronomy 5:16)?*

Answer: Biblical commentators tell us that the obligation to honor one's parents is tantamount to honoring the Almighty Himself. The sages explain, that there really are three partners in the creation of a child – the father, the mother, and the Almighty. In *Talmud Kiddushin 20b-31a,* God says, "I did well not to live among them, for if I had dwelled among them they would have tormented Me, as well." The *Ha'amek Davar* comments that the phrase "your God commanded you" stresses the point that regardless of the natural love one feels for one's parents, one must be aware that this respect is an obligation to God. It is also considered a focal point, the cornerstone of one's faith in the entire Torah. A story helps to illustrate the point:

In 1945, Mrs. Shoshana (Susan) Berkowitz and Mr. Yussel (Joel) Green got married, shortly after having met each other at a liberation camp in Europe. Shoshana was a survivor of Auschwitz, Yussel a survivor of Birkenau. Two months later they emigrated to the United States.

Twenty-one years later, in 1966, in a hospital, there was a terrible commotion in the labor and delivery room. Susan and Joel were finally about to have their first and long-awaited child. Joel was so thankful to the Almighty; he was also busy handing out large chocolate bars to everyone he saw. It was a miraculous day for Susan and Joel Green. Everyone felt a part of their simcha ("happy celebration").

Susan was being monitored very carefully. She was forty-three years old, a holocaust survivor with a history of illnesses and high blood pressure. The pregnancy was a tremendous strain on her body. She was pale and weak during the beginning stages of labor, but she thought that this was normal. Her husband, Joel, was very concerned and called the doctor over to make sure that Susan was okay. The doctor looked at Susan and rushed her immediately into the delivery room. Joel began pacing the halls of the hospital, waiting for more news on his wife's condition. He allowed himself to fantasize about how beautiful his new baby would be, and how beautiful their life would be with this long-awaited baby.

Suddenly, noise of heavy equipment shook Joel out of his thoughts. He stood up and saw nurses with concerned faces rushing into his wife's room. He panicked, but no one would let him see his wife.

Joel waited outside, afraid and confused. Finally, the doctor came out. He was red in the face and sweating. The doctor looked at Joel and said, "Joel, can I speak to you for a moment?" The doctor put his arms around him. He looked at Joel with compassion and said, "Listen to me. I hate to tell you this, but Susan's blood pressure has soared, and it looks like we are losing her. We cannot bring her blood pressure down, and she is not responding to any drugs. Joel, I am really so sorry, but we cannot save them both. Joel, you, and only you, have to make a decision immediately. You must pick either Susan or the baby. We have no time to discuss this further. You must decide right now which life you want us to save, Susan's or your baby's."

Joel cried out, "What are you asking me to do? I cannot make this decision."

The doctor grabbed him by the shoulders and said, "Listen to me. Right now Susan is unconscious and she cannot make any decisions." Again the doctor said, "Listen to me, Joel. I must tell you this. When Susan was alert, she kept on screaming to me, 'Please, doctor, save my baby, save my baby. I cannot live without my baby.'" The doctor continued, "My dear Joel, you have to decide, but I must tell you that these were her last words. Joel, I know that this is the hardest choice, but you have no more time to think. Every minute we waste means that there is less chance that even one life can be saved." Joel cried bitterly, "Save the baby."

Joel sat down in the waiting room and started trembling. He closed his eyes and saw gray all around him. Suddenly, the faces of his past appeared before him. He saw his sister, Basya, and her husband, Reb Yerucham, a *shochet* (Jewish butcher). They had lived together in the same *shtetl* (neighborhood) in Eastern Europe, so many years ago, before the Holocaust.

Suddenly, a vision came to Joel. He remembered the *Yom Kippur* when the Nazis came and kicked everybody out of the synagogue, took the Torah scrolls and threw them on the ground, burned them, then burned the synagogue. He remembered how his sister, Basya, had cried when the Nazis cut off his *peyes* (side hair), and forced him from the train. Joel saw how the Nazis separated his brother-in-law from his sister, and how they forced her to give up her baby. Basya screamed, "No, no. Please take me and leave my baby here, with my parents. Please don't send my baby on the train."

"Joel, Joel, wake up." The nurse's voice woke up Joel. He opened his eyes and saw a nurse holding a cup of water. He tried to stand but felt dizzy. "What has happened with Susan? What has happened to my baby?" Joel asked and passed out.

When he awoke, he found himself in a hospital bed, the doctor standing over him. He told Joel that he had fainted and had been unconscious for several days. The doctor told him, "Joel, I must say, you have a beautiful baby boy."

Joel cried. "Let me see my baby, Susan's baby."

Joel made a funeral for Susan and prepared for his son's bris (circumcision). He named his son Samuel, after his brother, who had perished during the war. He put all his energy into raising Samuel as Susan would have wanted, but Samuel made each day a challenge. When Samuel grew older, Joel decided that the best idea would be to send Samuel away to school, even though it broke his heart to do so. Nothing seemed to change; Samuel remained a difficult boy.

Years passed, and Joel grew older. He became very sick and knew that he didn't have much time left to live. He called for his son to return home. He told his son that he wished to spend his few remaining days with him.

When Samuel arrived, Joel decided that he had to tell his son about his mother. "Can you come with me, please, to your mother's grave?" Joel was surprised when he replied, "Sure, Dad. Let's go together to the cemetery." Joel felt guilty, because he had kept her death a mystery. When they arrived at the cemetery, Joel could not contain his feelings anymore. "Samuel," Joel started to cry, "I have to tell you something very important. I know that I will not live much longer, but I can't go to my death peacefully without knowing that you will take care of your mother's *yahrtzeit* (the Jewish memorial day). I want you, to please say *Yizkor* (memorial prayer) for your mother and pray for her soul. I have done this for years, and now it will be your turn to uphold this important tradition."

As usual, Samuel was rebellious and said, "Dad, I'm sorry, I never even knew my mother. It's you who took care of me. How can I feel something for somebody that I never knew?" Joel fell apart and began to tell to Samuel about his mother's death.

Samuel listened in awe. For the first time in his life, Joel could see that Samuel was deeply touched. Samuel hugged his father and said, "I'm so sorry, dad. After hearing all of that, I feel truly embarrassed and ashamed of myself."

They hugged each other tightly, and then Joel looked into Samuel's eyes and said, "Please, Samuel, please tell me that you will take care of your mother's memory."

He turned to his father and looked into his eyes. "Dad, I can barely face you at this moment. How can I face my mother, who literally gave her life for me? What would Mom think of me now if she saw what I have become? But I promise, Daddy, that I will take care of everything."

Today, we don't recognize Dr. Sam Green as Samuel, the troublemaking son of Shoshana and Yussel Green. He is a committed Jew, a pillar of his religion, and a dedicated son.

Question: Moses received two tablets of stone on which God had inscribed the commandments. What is the significance of this?

Answer: God could have simply put all ten on one tablet, but He chose to divide them for a purpose. The five commandments shown on the right side are commandments between God and man, while the five on the left are the laws between man and his fellowman.

Question: Why is the prayer, "Hear O Israel...," the *Shema*, considered the single most important phrase in the Torah *(Deuteronomy 6:4)*?

Answer: This phrase represents the total and absolute belief in a single God, Who is supreme over all Creation. Our sages tell us that even if a person does not understand any other prayer, he must concentrate totally on this one, the source and foundation of Jewish faith. The need for the utmost focus on this prayer is the reason for the custom of covering our eyes when we recite the opening phrase.

Several years ago we had a Jewish baby-sitter in our home, a girl sixteen years old. She considered herself an atheist. When she heard my wife recite the Shema with my older son as she was putting him to sleep, she asked my wife, "What kind of baloney is this, trying to teach a two-year-old such things?" When I heard this, I told her a story, that occurred several years after the Holocaust.

Rabbi W. in Jerusalem heard many survivors say that many Jewish children were saved by the church during the Holocaust. Rabbi W.

initiated a plan to redeem those lost children. He approached a number of affluent people, and flew with his wife to France. They went to one of the large churches there, known to have a dormitory with over 700 orphans. They met with two priests and thanked them for saving the children's lives and asked if there were any Jewish children living there. "There are no Jewish children here," one of the priests replied. As Rabbi W. and his wife were about to leave, another priest called them over and said, "You have to understand, my dear friends, the children here are between six and eight years old. Some of them came from Eastern Europe, but I bet you that even if there are a few Jewish children here, they have no memories or feelings toward Judaism anymore." Rabbi W.'s wife replied, "Can you please let us meet the children here?" The priest answered, "For what reason? I already told you that there is no purpose in that." Rabbi W. and his wife begged the priest by saying, "Please sir, we ask you just to let us meet them for a few minutes." The priest refused. Rabbi W.'s wife started to cry and said, "Just let me meet them for two minutes, and I will show you who among them are Jews." The priest answered, "You know what, we will make a deal. At 7:00 p.m., the children have dinner. Right after dinner, I will arrange to have all the children in the main auditorium and I will give you two minutes to speak with them. Whoever identifies himself as a Jew, you can take with you." The rabbi and his wife agreed.

After dinner, the children were all seated in the auditorium. It was very dramatic when Rabbi W. and his wife entered the auditorium. The priest made sure the room was quiet; the rabbi went to one side of the room and his wife to the other side, and they started to yell, *Shema Yisrael.* "Hear O Israel, the Lord is our God. The Lord is One." They yelled this once, twice, three times. Suddenly, a number of children stood up and started to scream in Yiddish, "Mamma, Mamma," and went over to the rabbi's wife and clung to her and crying "Mamma, Mamma." Because of the *Shema,* fourteen children returned with Rabbi W. to Israel.

Q **uestion:** What is the principal *mitzvah* of Passover (*Deuteronomy 6:20*)?

Answer: "If your son will ask you tomorrow, 'What is this that God commands...' you shall tell your son the story of Passover." The principal mitzvah of Passover is telling the story of the Exodus from Egypt. We are obligated to tell our immediate family, relatives, and friends about the miracles of the Exodus; how the Israelites were redeemed from Egypt. To appreciate the miracles in all their magnificence, it is important to retell the story.

Ekev

Chapters: 7:12 - 11:25

Synopsis:

Moses promised, on behalf of God, a blessed land; the Jordan is crossed; the wooden Ark and the new Tablets; the glory of the land of Israel; the relevance of the commandments to the Land of Israel.

Question: Why do we have to make a blessing after each meal?

Answer: The Torah requires that one must recite a blessing after a meal; the source for this commandment comes in this parsha. "You shall eat and be sustained and bless God" (*Deuteronomy 8:10*). Our sages teach us that it is a positive commandment to thank God for our sustenance (*Babylonian Talmud, Brachot 21a*). The commentators ask, "Does God really need our blessing?" The answer is that the blessing is actually man's recognition of God's providing food to all His creatures for their survival. It is man's testimony that God watches over all creatures. The Almighty wants man to recognize and appreciate Him, and it is that recognition alone that elevates man above all the other creatures (*Rabbeinu Bechayei*). This in turn leads to a two-way relationship between man and God. The sages say, "Whoever eats without blessing the Almighty, it is as if he were stealing" (*Babylonian Talmud, Brachot*).

Question: Who is the composer of the Blessing after Meals (*Birchat HaMazon*)?

Answer: The Blessing after Meals, *Birchat HaMazon,* is constructed of four blessings. Our sages say in the *Talmud, Brachot 48a* that Moses composed the first blessing when the Israelites received Manna in the desert. This is called the blessing for nourishment. The second blessing, called blessing for the land, was composed by Joshua when the Jews entered the Holy Land. The third blessing, written by King David and his son, King Solomon, when they fought for and built Jerusalem, is called the blessing of the building of Jerusalem. The fourth blessing, composed by Rabban Gamliel, the head of the *Sanhedrin* (supreme rabbinical court), commemorates the miracle at Betar at the time of Bar Kochba. At that time, the Romans conquered the city of Betar and killed more than 100,000 of its inhabitants. The Romans forbade the Jews from burying their dead. What was the miracle? The Almighty prevented the decay that normally occurs in a corpse. Rabban Gamliel named the fourth blessing "the good that does good," to express the gratitude the Jews had to the Almighty (*Talmud, Yerushalmi 7a*).

Question: How does this *parsha* show the Torah's relevance to our daily lives?

Answer: This *parsha* is an excellent example of how relevant the Torah is to important aspects of our daily lives. In it we see God's promise to the Israelites that those who obey the commandments will be rewarded by receiving the Land of Israel in which to live. The bulk of the *parsha* describes the Land and all the benefits that will accrue to the people living there. The blessings and beauty of Israel are mentioned over twenty times as proof of the importance of this concept.

Most Jews in the Diaspora have always felt a strong bond with Israel. In our time, most Jews feel a powerful connection to Israel as part of their daily lives. We react strongly to every event that impacts the welfare of Israel. We feel joy when something good happens, and we feel sorrow for every tragedy.

One of the concepts we take from this *parsha* is that the existence of the world depends on the spiritual essence of the Land of Israel.

Question: Why is the word "remember" repeated so many times in our *parsha*?

Answer: All the biblical commentators agree that the expression of ego and human nature are central in this *parsha*. It is human nature that as long as people need God they beg Him, they cry out, they go to the holy places and pray to the Almighty for salvation, but suddenly, when people get whatever they want, they turn away from God or even betray Him.

In a famous story a man named Yosef (his friends called him Joe) moved to the United States as a young boy. He was very poor. Yosef tried many different kinds of work but unfortunately couldn't make a living. By force of circumstances, he went to the synagogue but when people wanted to give him a donation, he refused. Instead, he offered to work for the synagogue. He became the *Shamesh*, the person who took care of all the little jobs around the synagogue. Yosef came to the synagogue early in the morning to open the doors, prepare the books, and open the ark. He sometimes used to sleep there, because he often closed the synagogue very late at night. Yosef was a very trustworthy man, but he was an ignorant man. He had never learned how to write, or even how to sign his name.

Years passed by. One day, a few days before the festival of Passover, the president of the synagogue sat with Yosef and gave him the names of the big donors to the synagogue. He asked Yosef to prepare a letter for them, asking for donations for poor people before Passover. "Here is the list," the President said, "just prepare a short letter."

"Mr. President," Yosef replied, "don't you know that I don't know how to write anything, or even sign my name?"

The president looked at him and became very upset. "You are going to tell me that you don't even know how to sign your name, and that we have such an ignorant person working in our synagogue. Get out of here. I don't want you here," the president yelled. Yosef left.

Yosef walked on the streets and looked to the Heavens. He raised his hands and said, "God of the Heavens, what can I do now? I have a wife and children to feed, and I have lost my job." Yosef started to cry and said, "Master of the Universe, I know that you and only you are the only one who gives and takes jobs, you give prosperity to all, I beg you, please help me." He walked and walked through the streets, and did not want to go home. His inner voice led him to his best friend's, a man who owned a children's clothing business. Yosef cried out and told him what had happened. His friend wanted to give him some money, but Yosef refused. Instead, he offered his services to his friend's business. His friend said, "You know what? I have here a clothing business. Take whatever you can carry in your hands. I will give you each item for $1.50, and you should go sell it for $2.50 or $3.00, and keep the profit for yourself." He gave this to Yosef on consignment, not taking any money until the items would be sold.

Yosef started knocking on doors, trying to sell the clothing. In those days, people used to open their doors, so very quickly, after only a week, he had sold all the merchandise at a very nice profit. He began doing this on a steady basis. His wife joined him in the endeavor; each took one side of the street to sell their clothing. Shortly thereafter, their elder daughter joined in, and finally, after some time, they were making quite a good profit and doing well.

One day the daughter said to the parents, "Why do you need to do this hard work all day? Why don't we open a bazaar in the house, advertise, and people will come to us to buy." They did as the daughter suggested, and opened the bazaar in their home; they were very successful. A very short time later, they opened up a little store. Within several years, Yosef, who was called Joe, owned a few retail stores and wholesale businesses, and a shopping mall.

One day, Joe (Yosef) sat in his fancy office, leg on leg, smoking a cigar. The president of the bank came to him, to convince him to take a mortgage, at a very low rate, for a new commercial building. Joe agreed with the terms, and a deal was negotiated. The president of the bank handed him all the papers and said, "Just sign here at the bottom, please." Joe looked at the president and said, "Mr. President, don't you know that I don't know how to sign my name?"

The bank's president looked at him and exclaimed, "What? You have over a hundred employees in all of your businesses and you're going to tell me that you don't know how to sign your name?"

Joe stood up and smirked, and very calmly said, "Mr. President, if I knew how to sign my name, I would still be a *shamesh* in a synagogue!"

R'ehe
Chapters: 11:26 - 16:17

Synopsis:

Blessings and curses used by Moses as "stick and carrot"; the prohibition against private altars; the prohibition against the use of blemished animals; tithes to be eaten only in Jerusalem; the prohibition against drinking blood; the prohibition against false prophets, black magic, and sorcery; the prohibition against self-mutilation; forbidden foods; the cancellation of loans in Israel (Shimittah laws); circumstances under which a Jew may be sold into slavery; rules regarding the festivals of Pesach (Passover), Shavuos, and Sukkot.

Question: "See, I present before you today a blessing and a curse" *(Deuteronomy 11:26).* The quote begins in the singular but the rest of the passage is in the plural. Why?

Answer: Our sages teach us that an individual cannot exclude himself from society. We have to be aware that everything that happens in society affects every individual to various degrees, and the individual affects society. We cannot ignore occurrences around us but must think how we can make the world a better place in which to live. This *parsha* begins with the word "see." Our sages tell us that this is a reference to the individual. The next part of the verse, "I present before you today," refers to people as a whole, a group or society. The verse ends with "a blessing and a curse"; this demands freedom of choice, to bring blessings or the opposite (God forbid). One cannot turn a blind eye to the tragedies that befall one's fellowman or the disasters that occur, as a result of the choices we make. Otherwise, we become as Sodom and Gomorrah, described in the *Book of Genesis*, as cities full of individuals totally self-centered and egocentric. Because of this, they incurred God's punishment and were totally annihilated (*Babylonian Talmud, Kiddushin 40a*).

Question: What do we learn from the words "blessing and curse" *(Deuteronomy 14:21)?*

Answer: Our sages teach us that whatever comes out of the mouth becomes either a blessing, or the opposite (God forbid).

Question: "If there should stand up somebody who will proclaim that he is a prophet or dream interpreter and gives you a sign to prove this...and later on he tries to convince you to follow the gods of others in order to worship them ... don't listen to this man, for the Lord your God is testing you to know if you love the Almighty your God with all of your heart and soul" *(Deuteronomy 13:2-5).* If God knows all men's thoughts and actions, what is the purpose of testing people?

Answer: The purpose is for man to discover that he has the ability to stand up for his beliefs and respond with courage to God's adversaries (*Ramban*).

Question: "If a prophet should appear…" *(Deuteronomy 13:2).* Why does the Torah refer to this man as a prophet?

Answer: There is a discussion among biblical commentators as to whether a man who makes claims to be a prophet is a real prophet. The discussion is based on the issue found in the *Babylonian Talmud Sanhedrin 90a:* "Rabbi Yosse Haglili said, 'If there is a man who stands in your midst and declares that he is a prophet of God, even if he stops the sun from moving, don't believe him, because he will require you to worship idols.'" "Rabbi Akiva said, 'It is impossible that the Almighty follows man's orders or that man has the ability to force the supernatural to do something against the nature of the world.'" The fact that the prophet led people to worship idols shows who he really is, and that, although he was a real prophet before, he is not one anymore. *Abarbanel* states that he is a real prophet but that he later became a wicked man. However, *Ramban, Rabbeinu Bechayei,* and *Rav Sa'adya Gaon* suggest that this so-called prophet is a crook and a liar, and the Torah is using the word prophet in connection with his proclamation of prophecy, even though it has nothing to do with reality. The *Ramban* adds that it is true that at times there have been people who were called *kehinah* ("medium") who had the ability to interpret dreams and anticipate the future.

Question: Through time, it has been common for people to seek help in decisionmaking by using supernatural means such as astrology, psychics, fortune-tellers, gypsies, Tarot cards, Ouija boards, and tea leaves, among others. What is the Torah's attitude about the use of these methods?

Answer: The *parsha* clearly states that we must reject all so-called supernatural methods and divinations. If a "prophet" rises up among us and attempts to lead us by signs and miracles, he is to be rejected outright. A true prophet is always motivated by the unselfish desire to do good for people, and to spread God's word. A true prophet never benefits personally. A false prophet can appear to be quite convincing. Sometimes, the false prophet is just a very accomplished trickster. There are times when this false prophet seems to be doing something that defies all known laws of science. What then? Then, the Torah says, God is causing "the wonder" merely as a means of testing us.

The *parsha* says that if a false prophet should rise up among us and try to lead us to worship other spirits or gods, he is an abomination to God; the Torah demands death for such a false prophet. The *Talmud (Sanhedrin 90a)* says that even if the false prophet makes the sun stop in the sky, we are not to heed his sign. The Torah uses the word prophet because the pretender may call himself a prophet, but in fact he is not. If we have full faith in God, we will follow Him obediently and have no need to know what the future has in store for us. God often may tempt us with the potential benefit of knowing the future as a means of testing us and our faithfulness. The test's purpose is to create an ever stronger bond between God and us. The *Ramban* suggests that the very act of resisting the attraction to a false prophet brings about a stronger bond between God and His people.

Incidentally, the phrase "death to false prophets" has been taken out of context by anti-semites who try to use it as some sort of "proof" that the Jews killed their messiah. However, a medium or spiritualist that, for example, helps the police, or in other ways benefits the community, is tolerable (*Rav Sa'adya Gaon*).

Question: How does the Torah teach us to recognize a false prophet?

Answer: The Torah tells us that a false prophet will first perform some unexplainable deed to get attention and to impress people. Then he will lead them on until one day the cat is out of the bag. The false prophet will speak against God and the Torah (*Deuteronomy 13:2-6*). One must carefully investigate such a presumed "leader" to determine exactly what his goals and objectives are. At first it is extremely difficult to recognize the false prophet. One must remain vigilant and true to the Torah. The reader is referred to *Rambam's Book of Science* in which he spends numerous chapters discussing nature and how to determine who is or is not a prophet.

Question: Why is the drinking of blood prohibited by the Torah *(Deuteronomy 12:16)*?

Answer: At the time of Creation, before the great Flood, man had no need to eat meat. God had placed him in the *Garden* and gave him the nourishment of the land. All meat was forbidden. Only after the Flood, when there was a great lack of food, did God allow Noah's sons to eat meat, but without its blood *(Genesis 9:4)*. With the giving of the Torah, God specified the conditions by which animals are to be slaughtered for food. Kindness to animals is an integral part of these laws. Blood is the essence of life. It is for animals as well, so it becomes a matter of cruelty to consume it. All lower animals consume the blood of their prey without giving thought to it. However, man, the highest level of creation, is commanded to control himself from consuming the blood of his food *(Abarbanel; Ha'ikarim Ma'amar 3:16; Ramban)*.

Question: Does the Bible allow us to eat giraffes? *(Deuteronomy 14:6)*

Answer: The sages are divided on this point. The *Talmud Chulin 80a* states zemer, meaning "wild goat." However, the *Raddak* and *Rav Sa'adya Gaon* interpreted zemer to mean the giraffe.

Question: "You shall not cook a kid together in his mother's milk" *(Deuteronomy 14:21)*. What does this mean?

Answer: This is the prohibition against eating milk and meat together. There are different customs regarding when one is permitted to eat something dairy after one has eaten meat. Some communities wait half an hour after drinking milk. Others just brush their teeth. On the other hand, after eating meat, most communities wait six hours, although some wait less time.

Question: "You shall not cook a kid in his mother's milk" (*Deuteronomy 14:21*). Why is this not taken literally?

Answer: This prohibition appears in the Bible three times. The sages state that each one suggests a different facet of the prohibition against mixing milk and meat together. The prohibitions exist against: cooking the two together; eating the two together, or receiving any benefit whatsoever from the two being together in a mixture.

The Written Torah is not to be taken literally,"These are the laws, decrees, and Torahs…" (*Leviticus 26:46*). The plural of Torah is used to signify that Moses was transmitting both the written and the oral law to Joshua. *Rashi* explains that the use of the plural means that both the written Torah as well as the Oral Torah were given together by God to Moses on Mount Sinai.

Only the group *Tzedokim* used to interpret the written Torah literally, in contradiction to the sages, who used Oral Law to explain and interpret the written law. We believe with complete faith in both – Written and Oral Torah – and therefore we interpret the sentence, "You shall not cook a kid in its mother's milk" figuratively, and observe the tradition of our forefathers, that this sentence meant the prohibition of cooking, eating, and obtaining any benefit from mixing meat and milk together.

It is important to understand the concepts of the Written and Oral Torahs.

The Bible relates that Moses wrote the five books of the Torah during his forty days and nights on Mount Sinai. On the forty-first day, he descended from the mountain with the two stone tablets engraved by God and the entire Written Torah. The people miscalculated Moses' return. The agitators, the rabble, who were seeking to take over Moses' leadership, managed to convince their fellow Hebrews that Moses' return was unlikely and that God had abandoned them in the barren wilderness to fend for themselves. The majority of the Hebrews agreed with this despairing attitude. Those wanting to build a Golden Calf to worship – and thereby be relieved of their tenuous situation – overwhelmed even Moses' brother, Aaron. Aaron offered little resistance to this blasphemous undertaking. Most of the male Israelites willingly donated their jewelry for this project. Moses, upon viewing the Golden Calf at the time of his descent from the mountain, became so enraged that he smashed the stone tablets and took the Written Torah back up the mountain. He later returned with a new set of tablets and the Written Torah. In the Torah portion *Bechukotai* it says: "These are the laws, judgments, and Torahs…" The plural of Torah is used to signify that Moses was transmitting both the written and oral law to Joshua. *Rashi* says that the use of the plural means that both the oral and written Torahs came from Sinai.

"Moses received the Torah from Sinai and transmitted it to Joshua. Joshua transmitted the Torah to the Elders. The Elders transmitted the Torah to the Prophets, who then transmitted the Torah to the *Great Assembly*." One of the Thirteen Principles of Faith, by *Rambam*, which we include in daily prayers, is, "I believe with complete faith that the written Torah and the Oral Torah were both received by Moses at Sinai." Another of these principles states, "I believe with complete faith that this is the original Torah, with no changes or additions or subtractions."

One of the basic tenets of Judaism is the belief that Moses received the written and oral Torahs over 3,000 years ago on Mount Sinai, directly from God. During the subsequent transmissions through the time of the *Great Assembly*, other books (such as the *Prophets* and *Megillot*) were added to form the Bible (also known as the *Tanach*).

Much later, we have the early sages (*Tanna'im*). This group, which persisted for many generations, studied in a place called the *beit hamidrash* (house of study) and expanded the rules of the Oral Torah. Then the head of the *Sanhedrin* in that time, Rabbi Yehudah Hanassi (*nassi*, president of the Court), not only wrote additional rules, but edited the entire work of all the early sages into six volumes, known as the *Six Orders of Mishnah*.

Much later, in the Diaspora, there were great centers of study and learning in two Babylonian cities. Many thousands of scholars developed and refined the principles of both the Oral and Written Torahs. At the end of that time, the main leaders, Rabbina and Rav Ashi, organized, compiled, and edited all of the writings and discussions into twenty volumes, known as the *Babylonian Talmud*. At about the same time, a large group of scholars in Jerusalem completed a similar work in six volumes, structured on the *Mishnah*. This *Talmud* is known as the *Yerushalmi*.

The scholars and rabbis who worked on these *Talmuds* are known as the later sages (*Amora'im*).

The purpose of the *Talmud* is to provide us with a guide on how to live our lives. The Written Torah itself (*Five Books of Moses*) does not always have sufficient detail and interpretation to enable us to resolve the many complex practical problems of life. The *Talmud* and Oral Torah show us how to analyze and solve questions that arise in life. It is an essential part of the Jewish legal system containing case law, as well as procedures, that even describe how to investigate a particular matter for adjudication. Certainly, the written Torah is important and the Oral Torah is equally important. Just as we cannot survive missing any one of our vital organs (e.g., heart, brain, lungs, and so forth), we cannot authenticate our religious dogma if even a minute part of the *Talmud* is altered or lost.

In real life situations, the *Talmud* must be heavily relied upon in order to make appropriate decisions. A recent example that comes to mind involves *Agunot* (abandoned wives). When a submarine of the Israeli Navy, the *Dakar*, sank in very deep water, with all aboard presumed dead, the question arose as to the status of the wives they had left behind. The Torah clearly states that when a woman's husband dies, she is a widow, and allowed to remarry. But what of this case, when we cannot be as certain that each man died as we would be if his body were accessible? As it happens, the author's father-in-law was chief rabbi of the Israeli Navy at the time, and so he knew firsthand the tremendous amount of investigation and research that had to be performed in preparation for getting a decision by the religious court. The court's investigation and decision was largely based on detailed principles that are stated in parts of the *Talmud*, rather than the Written Torah.

As difficult as the case of the *Dakar* submarine was, much more complicated and painful cases are encountered. For example, there was a couple (civil marriage only) that lived together for four months, during which time they alternated between a loving, harmonious relationship and a bitter, antagonistic one. Nevertheless, the woman got pregnant during this time. She went away for a week to visit her mother, and when she returned, the man was gone. He left a letter saying that he went on a business trip to South America and signed the letter, "I love you."

From that day on, she never heard from the man again. She had the baby and about a year later she fell in love with another man and became pregnant by him. The couple applied to the religious court to clarify their status. They asked for permission to marry by religious law. The civil court would not sanction a civil marriage because there was no evidence that the first marriage had ended by death or divorce. To further complicate the matter, the woman was found to be pregnant with twins, and the father of the twins threatened to leave her and the children if the court did not find her free to marry. The civil authorities agreed to change her civil status, according to what the religious court decided. This posed a terribly sad and painful problem for the court. The religious court had to decide whether the first husband was still alive and if so, whether or not the first marriage was valid and binding. The court also had to think of the status of the unborn children and had to decide quickly, as the pregnancy progressed. The court turned to the FBI, which responded that the man had gone to South America but that all traces of him had been lost.

Before a decision could be made, the father of the twins was badly injured in an automobile accident, remained in a coma for a long time, and died. The religious court is now faced with deciding the status of the child of the first husband, the twins yet to be born, and the woman herself.

There are many questions. If the first marriage was valid, then the twins to be born are *mamserim*, children from an adulterous relationship, and the woman's status must be determined. If the first marriage is not valid, then all the children are legitimate and the woman is free to marry. In this quandary, the judges are able to search the entire *Talmud* for cases with similarities, and thereby find methods to analyze and decide even so complicated a problem. The *Talmud* contains many instances of similar cases, upon which the court can base a decision consistent with Jewish law and human needs. It is almost impossible to resolve such difficult and complicated matters without relying on the *Talmud.*

In order to understand the system of the *Talmud,* we must first understand how and why the *Talmud* was created. Here is what the main authority in that era stated: "Rav Zayra said, 'If the first generations were angels, then we are human beings; but if the first generations were human beings, then we are donkeys.'" "Rav Yochanan says that the heart of the earliest generations was like an enormous hall, the heart of later generations was like a regular hall, but the heart of our generation is like the eye of a needle." These examples illustrate one of the fundamental principles of Judaism – that there has been a spiritual decline throughout the generations. At the time of the wandering in the wilderness and giving of the Torah, everyone was on a very high spiritual level. All could hear God's voice and all understood what was required of the people by God. As the generations passed, the spiritual level of the people declined, and the ability to understand the meaning of the Torah and God's requirements continually lessened. During this decline, at first the elders survived, then there was a generation with fewer prophets. Subsequently, it came down to a *Great Assembly* of 120, with a few elders and sages of that era.

According to the *Rambam's Introduction to the Mishnah,* there are exactly forty generations from Moses to Rav Ashi. Each era made significant contributions to the *halachah* (Jewish law). Each era is known by the name of its most outstanding leader.

Each one listed in the following table is considered a great Torah scholar of his time, and contributed greatly to Jewish thought and practice, including prayers, laws, and sometimes even amendments or repairs to existing laws. The creations of these leaders have survived for many hundreds of years to the present, and are part of our regular religious practice today. They have stood the test of time. The names of these forty are listed in chronological order.

1. MOSES
2. YEHOSHUA (Joshua)
3. PINCHAS
4. AYLEE
5. SAMUEL
6. DAVID
7. ACHIA
8. ELIAHU
9. ELLISHA
10. YEHOYADA

11. ZECHARIA
12. HOSEA
13. AMOS
14. ISAIAH
15. MICHA
16. JOEL
17. NACHUM
18. CHAVAKOOK
19. TZFANIA
20. YIRMIYAHU (Jeremiah)

21. BARUCH

22. EZRA

23. SIMON the RIGHTEOUS

24. ANTIGONOUS

25. YOSSI ben YOEZER
    and JOSEF ben YOCHANAN
26. YEHOSHUA ben PERACHIA
    and NITAI Ha'ARBELEE
27. YEHUDAH ben TABBAI
    and SHIMON ben SHETACH
28. SHEMAYA and AVTALLYONE
29. HILLEL and SHAMMAI
30. RABBI SHIMON son of Hillel)

31. RABBAN GAMLIEL HaZAKEN
    (son of Shimon)
32. RABBAN SHIMON
    (son of Rabbi Gamliel)
33. RABBAN GAMLIEL
    (son of Shimon)
34. RABBAN SHIMON
    (son of Rabbi Gamliel)
35. REB YEHUDA HaNASSI
    (President)
36. RABBI YOCHANNAN
    RAV and SHMUEL
37. RAV HUNAH

38. RABBAH
39. ROVEH
40. RAV ASHI and RAVINA

Joshua circled the walls of Jericho seven times before he conquered the Holy Land. He then composed the prayer *Aleinu L'shabeach*, which we recite three times daily.

The *Great Assembly*, composed of Elders, prophets, and scholars of those days, wrote the *Amidah* prayer (referred to as the *Shmoneh Esrei*, which means eighteen blessings). The prayer was divided into three parts and confirmed by the prophets in order to ensure that there would be no change, and that the prayer would be eternal. The

Amidah has remained unchanged, even to this day, as the *Great Assembly* wrote it.

Shimon ben Shetach and Yehudah ben Tabai originated the rule that all children have to go to school to be educated. Prior to this rule, education was quite prevalent, but on a haphazard basis. This rule resulted in an organized system of schools and compulsory education that is still followed today.

Hillel authored the *Pruzbol*, which was an amplification of the Written Torah, with all the force of law. In the Written Torah, there is a commandment that designates every seventh year as a *shmittah* year. In a year of *shmittah*, crops are not planted, slaves are freed, and all debts are canceled. Therefore, some people would take advantage and borrow just before a *shmittah* year. As a result, people refused to lend money even to the needy, thereby going against the commandment to lend to those in need. To remedy this situation, Hillel composed the *Pruzbol* which allows a borrower to waive the possibility of cancellation of the debt by *shmittah*. This solution to the problem has also endured to modern times. Hillel was only able to create the *Pruzbol* (in apparent contradiction to the Written Torah) because of two conditions that had changed since the time of Moses. First, the majority of Jews were not living in the Holy Land; and second, the Temple in Jerusalem was no longer in existence.

The next period, which lasted 400 years, began with the conquest of the Holy Land by the *Sloki'im* (from their centers in Syria and Greece). This period started with a single leader called Simon the Righteous. After him came another single leader, Antiginous–Man of Socho, and then began the Era of the Pairs (e.g., Shimon ben Shetach and Yehudah ben Tabai, Hillel and Shamai, etc). The end of this 400-year period was the end of the era of the *Mishnah*.

When we speak about the *Era of the Pairs* (the era of the matched sages), we begin with Shimon ben Shetach and Yehudah ben Tabai. Although the *Mishnah* speaks only of them as a pair, there was really a third partner, King Yannai, who was not accepted by them and did not himself accept Shimon ben Shetach and Yehudah ben Tabai. The *Mishnah* does not mention Yannai because he belonged to the *Tzedokim* movement, which believed only in the Written Torah, not the Oral Torah. The *Tzedokim* refused to accept any interpretation of the written Torah and were, in effect, opposed to the *Mishnah* itself. The *Tzedokim* were a small group of wealthy, powerful people who sometimes succeeded in controlling the *Sanhedrin.* They put on airs, as though they were royalty. Control of the *Sanhedrin* at that time was tantamount to control of the nation.

Despite these struggles and conflicts, the Oral Law continued to be transmitted only by word of mouth, from generation to generation, until the time of Hillel and Shamai, the last of the pairs. Hillel had a generally more permissive and less literal attitude toward the Law than did Shamai. Their conflict was not based on any competition between the two, but rather on a sincere desire to find the way for us to follow the laws given by God. This kind of dispute is called "controversy for the sake of Heaven," meaning that each had a different viewpoint, with no animosity toward the other.

After the passage of many hundreds of years, we find that modern *halachah* (Jewish law) follows the way of Hillel in all but eighteen of the laws, which are observed in accordance with the views of Shamai. Hillel was a greater and more influential leader than Shamai, no doubt because his interpretations were more flexible than those of Shamai. A leader who allows his followers to do things takes the risk that he might be proven wrong in his decision (*Pirkei Avot 1:11*), whereas a leader who always forbids his followers to do things never takes the risk and rarely finds out if his decision was wrong. Furthermore, the *Talmud* describes Hillel as a very gentle and forthright man. As the *Talmud* states, "There should always be men who are patient and humble, like Hillel, and not strict and exacting, like Shamai."

In one example of the difference between the philosophies of Hillel and Shamai, consider the case of a person who forgets to recite the blessing after eating a meal, and travels to a distant place before remembering. Shamai would say that he must return to the place where he ate and then recite the blessing while Hillel would say that he should recite the blessing in the place where he was when he remembered. Both sides agree that one must recite a blessing after eating, but that there is a time limit. Both are considered correct, but as a practical matter, it is considered too burdensome for the people to follow Shamai's way. However, we, as students of the *Talmudic* system, must learn and understand both ways. It is not just enough to follow the law blindly, without understanding all that the law is based on. We are to follow the laws with knowledge and intention. Therefore, we must have knowledge of all the procedures that led to each of the laws that the Oral Torah teaches, so that when we fulfill any duty, we do so with full understanding, which is one of the purposes of the *Talmudic* system.

The *Talmud* says that the phrase in the Bible, "an eye for an eye... a tooth for a tooth...." is an example of a statement that needs explanation. This is not to be taken literally. For example, if a man takes out another man's eye, what good does it do for the man who lost an eye to take out the eye of the one who hurt him? After taking out the eye, he would be no better off. Obviously, this is not the intention of the Torah, but it is there to emphasize that in rectifying the damage, there must be total equality. To do justice in a case like this, one must consider whether the injury was accidental or deliberate, whether the injured party contributed to causing the injury, and many other factors. The *Talmud*, like the Torah, is written in a very concise form, while many things are not spelled out in great detail. At a first superficial glance, much of the meaning of the Torah is not apparent. Therefore, much explanation and amplification is required, to achieve the full understanding of both Torah and *Talmud*.

The Torah was passed orally from era to era. As *Rambam* said, "From the time of Moses to Rebbe Yehuda HaNassi (referred to as *"Rebbe"*), thirty-five generations, nobody wrote down any copy of the Oral Torah." In every generation, the prophet or the Head of the Court wrote for himself what he heard from his rabbis, but taught it publicly by memorization, and it was this way for all generations until Rebbe Yehuda HaNassi.

The leader of that time, *Rebbe*, saw that as the Romans were defeating and dispersing the Jews throughout the world there were fewer and fewer Torah scholars. Jews were being exiled, leading Rebbe Yehuda Hanassi to fear for the future survival of the Torah and causing him to take the great responsibility of writing the Oral Torah. This was done in order to preserve God's laws for future generations, which may otherwise not have had the opportunity of hearing the Oral Law. Also, *Rebbe* and all his court sat and publicly taught the *Mishnah*.

Some groups in history believed only in a literal reading of the Law. Members of such groups felt that if a person injured another, either intentionally or unintentionally, then that person must be injured to the same extent. Only a *Beit Din* (Jewish Court of Law) would decide that the law could be interpreted to mean that monetary damages should be used to compensate a person for loss, rather than have the injured one merely injure the other. The *Beit Din* does not limit itself only to a literal reading of the Law, but also considers the many factors used to determine the amount of damages. If we were to limit ourselves to strict reading of the words, without explanation, we would have to call our forefather, Moses, a murderer, because he technically took a life. This example from the Torah shows us that we must incorporate the Torah with the *Talmud.* There are more intricate issues with many more factors that occur in life. These issues must be judged deeply.

The commentators record many cases that have been judged in the past, and describe all the factors that were the basis of judgment. The explanations also include descriptions of the processes used to analyze and investigate cases. This can serve not only as a useful guide to a judge trying to analyze a new case, but it is often the very source of the decision itself. A major purpose of the *Talmud* is to explain and fill in ideas that are not explicitly stated in the original Torah. The *Talmud* is a large series of explanations of laws, and a guide that helps us navigate our way through the complexity of life.

Question: What is the *Sanhedrin?*

Answer: The *Sanhedrin* was the highest court in Israel during the times of the first and second Temples. God commanded Moses to establish the first *Sanhedrin.* The structure of this court consisted of seventy-one learned Torah scholars. To qualify, each member had to know a number of the languages spoken in the world at that time. They had to be extremely intelligent, upright community members, and spiritually minded. Each member had only one vote; all votes were of equal weight. The body functioned as both judge and jury. They had their own specific seat with the *sanhedrin* from where they handed down their decisions. The court, when it met, could not hand down a decision unless they were in a specific location.

Not all cases were handled by this judging body. Cases that dealt with certain types of crime, such as those resulting in punishment by death and other complex cases, were handled here.

Question: What was the Great Assembly?

Answer: We learn in the *Book of Exodus*, in *Parshat Yitro* that Moses' father-in-law Yitro, advised him to bring together a group of leaders from among the tribes whose goal was to disseminate the Torah to the entire nation. It was their goal to act as instructors, teachers, and interpreters to ensure that even the most minuscule of ideas contained within the Torah was passed on to future generations. During the second Temple, the *Great Assembly* took on a special significance. It had 120 members consisting of the rabbinical scholars of the nation, the judges, and the last of the prophets. This institution formulated the prayers and the liturgy that we use today. The *Great Assembly* differed from the *Sanhedrin*, which dealt only with legal matters.

Question: "You shall tithe everything in your possession..." (*Deuteronomy 14:22*). How much should one *tithe*?

Answer: There are differences of opinion as to the amount to be tithed. Our sages teach us that one should not give less than 10 percent of one's income, nor more than 20 percent. This was a decision made by the *Sanhedrin*. Sephardic communities, which follow opinions handed down by *Rambam* and the *Yerushalmi Talmud*, hold that there is no limit to the amount one may tithe. Our sages teach us that, rather than becoming poor from giving charity, one's fortunes increase greatly from this act.

The *Talmud* states that anyone who observes the law of giving away one-tenth of his produce will get riches *asher bishvil shetitasher*. The *Talmud* is filled with stories relating to the giving of charity and the rewards one receives for performing this commandment. Here is one of them:

There was an Israeli farmer whose land produced a thousand bushels of wheat year after year. A pious man, his first act at harvest time was to set apart a full tenth of the produce as a tithe – that meant 100 bushels of wheat, quite a substantial amount. The farmer cheerfully gave it away, and the remaining 900 bushels were more than enough to take care of all of his needs, with a tidy sum of money in savings. Consequently, the man was getting more prosperous every year. Before he died, he called his son to his bedside. "My dear son," the dying man said, "the Lord is calling me to the next world, and I am happy to go, for I have lived such a good life, in accordance with God's way. Now, all my possessions belong to you, to do with as you please. But, only one thing do I advise you. As you know, our property produces a thousand bushels of wheat a year. Never fail to tithe, and believe me, it will not fail you."

After the man died, his son, now owner of the land, gave the 10 percent tithe, as his father had done before him. A year passed, and again it was the time to tithe. Unfortunately, in that year, the possession of wealth had had a bad influence on the young man. He thought it foolhardy to give away such a fortune, and he decided to give only 9 percent, instead of the full 10. The following year, the yield of the land decreased, and the young farmer reduced the tithe further by giving only 8 percent, to make up some of the loss. He waited for the next year's harvest quite impatiently. To his consternation, the land produced even less.

Do you think that the young man realized that he was playing a dangerous game? Indeed no. He became stubborn, and kept on reducing the quantity of his tithe year after year. At last, a point was reached when his land produced only 100 bushels, the same as the original tithe his father gave. Instead of regret, the foolish young man was filled with anger.

A few friends came to comfort him in his misfortune. Instead of sharing his sadness, they started singing and dancing, as if at a happy celebration. The young man lost his temper and said, "Did you come here to insult me and mock me in my misfortune?" "No," the guests replied cheerfully, "we have come to celebrate with you the transfer of your land from your hand into the hands of God. Until now, you had been the owner of the fields, and you had given less then you were obligated to God's charges. Now, God owns the land and you are His charge, receiving a tenth part of what the land can produce. You have, thus, joined the ranks of the Levites, and we have come to congratulate you." Eventually, the young man learned the lesson his friends had taught him. He gave up his wicked ways and learned the lesson of the sages, *Asher bishvil shetitasher.* The *Talmud* concludes that the young man was once again blessed with plenty.

Question: According to *Rambam,* how many levels of charity are there?

Answer: According to *Rambam* there are eight. The Hebrew term for charity, *tzedaka,* is the sharing of one's possessions with others. Not only is it money, but it is also knowledge, wisdom, food, clothing, and anything else that may be of help to another. According to *Rambam* the levels of charity are: giving someone the means by which to support himself, either by hiring the person or by finding a position by which he can support himself; the giving of charity without either the giver or the receiver knowing the other; giving anonymously, in which the giver knows to whom he is giving but the recipient does not know from whom it came; the giving in which the recipient knows who the giver is but the giver has no knowledge to whom it is given; the giving of charity without being asked; the giving of charity after being asked; the giving of charity with a smile; the giving of charity without a smile.

Our sages teach us that *tzedaka* will save one's life. I would like to share with you a story that took place a few years ago in Israel. Reb Shlomo and Chaya G., a religious couple, lived with their eleven children. It was an hour before *Rosh Hashanah* and they had just finished preparing the house and setting the table. Reb Shlomo was a scribe, and his wife, Chaya, a teacher. The week before *Rosh Hashanah,* Chaya still had not received her paycheck. The school did not have any money, and they told the teachers to wait until they could raise some money to pay the salaries. To compound the situation Reb Shlomo had, unfortunately, been ill, and unable to work. Two days before Rosh Hashanna, they had no choice but to borrow money for food. This was the very first time that they had to borrow money for food, and it was done with great reluctance.

Just as they had finished their preparations, there was a sudden knock at the door. One of their children opened the door, and there stood an elderly stranger.

"Please come in," Reb Shlomo said to the woman.

"I need help," she said. "All the stores are closed now and I need a chicken for the holiday. Can you please help me out?"

Chaya glanced at her husband and said, "I'm sorry, but we only have three chickens, and we have eleven children to feed, and there are two days of *Rosh Hashanah.* Can we give you something else instead?"

"No," the woman replied, "I need meat for the holiday. I must have a chicken."

Chaya and Reb Shlomo looked at each other and Chaya said, "I am sorry, but we cannot help."

"I beg you, please give me a chicken," she continued.

Reb Shlomo said, "I will give you the chicken." He turned to Chaya and said, "Please, Chaya, go and give her a chicken."

Chaya had no choice. With a heavy heart, she went to the kitchen, opened the freezer door and started screaming hysterically. Reb Shlomo ran to the kitchen and found Yehuda, one of his little children who was two years old, inside the freezer, almost frozen to death. The children had been playing hide and seek, and Yehuda had hidden in the freezer.

In the meantime the elderly woman disappeared.

The doctor told Reb Shlomo that it was an absolute miracle from God that the child had survived. "If you had waited another few minutes, the child surely would have died," the doctor said.

This is a strong example of what our sages teach us: *Tzedaka* will save your life.

Shofetim
Chapters: 16:18 - 21:9

Synopsis:

Commandment to appoint judges and peace officers; prohibition against planting a tree of the type worshipped by pagans; prohibition against statues and idols; prohibition against offerings with defects; the Jewish court system; the requirement for at least two qualified witnesses in order to convict someone of a crime; the requirements for a witness in court; petitioners must accept a judge's ruling in its entirety; Moses' instructions for future kings of Israel, regarding their rights and limitations; prohibition against black magic and all attempts to communicate with the dead; the commandment to build three cities of sanctuary for innocent people fleeing prosecution; prohibition against infringing on another's territory; rules of conscription of men for war; prohibition against cutting trees and roots; the case where a dead body is found in the country outside of any city.

Question: What factors must be considered in the appointment of judges?

Answer: A judge must be wise, intelligent, and God-fearing. He is not to take bribes or accept favors of any kind. He must pursue justice. He may not judge any case of which he has prior knowledge or connection to anyone involved.

Question: What is the system under which the *beit din* operates?

Answer: A minimum of three judges is required, one of whom is the head judge. A *beit din* is a Jewish court of law. Each litigant chooses one judge and the two judges then pick the third. There is no jury. The judges ask the questions and examine the witnesses. The decision is made by the three judges in consultation, and announced by the head judge. This system is still used in Israel today, where it is part of the general legal system, as well as elsewhere in the world where it only has religious significance.

Question: What is the purpose of the three cities of sanctuary?

Answer: In a case where a person unintentionally causes the death of another and is found not guilty by a *beit din*, there is a fear that the victim's family might still seek revenge for the death. The Torah obligated the establishment of three cities to harbor individuals found in this circumstance. To enter one of these cities of sanctuary, the refugee needed an order from the court proving that he or she indeed was found innocent of the alleged crime. If evidence was produced that proved the person is truly guilty, then the *beit din* had to remove its order of protection and bring him to trial.

Question: The Bible holds witnesses as an integral part of the legal process. In other words, the court cannot decide on a death penalty without two acceptable witnesses. What makes witnesses acceptable?

Answer: Many requirements need to be met for one to be considered acceptable to give testimony. Some of these are: the person must be at least 13 years of age, he must not be a simpleton or retarded, and he must not be a gambler or a usurer.

Question: Why is a gambler disqualified as a witness?

Answer: The Oral Torah (*Mishnah*) states (*Rosh Hashanah, Chapter 1:8*), a gambler is disqualified as a witness for reasons of sinfulness. A professional gambler, because he does not have a profession that benefits society in any way, lacks credibility. He already is an outcast in society; consequently, he could be tempted to accept a bribe to testify falsely (*Talmud Sanhedrin 24b*). Another sage explains that the gambler is considered ineligible because the money that he makes is an *asmachta*, which comes from the Hebrew root, *samach*, meaning, "to depend on something." In this instance, a gambler depends on other people losing money in order for him to win.

The sages explain that the Torah allows business transactions only if both parties agree on a trade of a product, service, or property for a product, service, property, or money. The transfer is a legal transaction because both sides enter into it and agree to it with a full heart. In the case of gambling, one anticipates winning, or at least not losing the money he has put down. It is clear that if the gambler knew in advance that he would surely lose his money, he would not put any money down. Therefore, the winner did not receive it in exchange for anything, which by definition means that the loser did not give the money with a full heart. Consequently, the sages consider this money as stolen. The gambler is not considered a thief, yet his testimony is not acceptable in a *beit din* (Babylonian Talmud, Sanhedrin 25a).

Question: "If a matter of judgment is hidden from you…you will go to the judge who will be in that day…you shall do exactly according to the word that the Authority tells you,…you shall not deviate from the words that they tell you, right or left" (*Deuteronomy 17:8-11*). What do the sages teach us through this?

Answer: The sages teach us (*Babylonian Talmud, Rosh Hashanah 25b, Sanhedrin 52b, 87a, Sifri 154; Rambam*) that if you make a decision to go to a rabbinic authority with a question, you must adhere to the reply, and not deviate whatsoever from their counsel. If you do not follow their counsel, it is considered a transgression. The sages explain, "Do not deviate right or left," to mean that you cannot go against what a rabbinic authority tells you, even if you have an opposing viewpoint.

There is a famous story about Rabbi Israel Cohen, the *Chofetz Chaim*, a rabbinic judge of Radin. Two people once came to him for a *Din Torah* (a dispute brought before a rabbinic authority). The *Chofetz Chaim* required that each party sign an agreement compelling the parties to accept absolutely the rabbi's decision, with no right to appeal.

Each side told his story, then the *Chofetz Chaim* weighed the testimony and made his decision. The decision was absolutely without prejudice to either side. Unfortunately, the party that lost left and tried to defame the *Chofetz Chaim's* character by saying that he had judged unjustly and he refused to follow the decision handed down as he had previously agreed to do.

In Israel the *beit din* is an accepted form of judgment by the constitution of the state. Therefore, any decision handed down by it has the full weight of the government behind it to enforce the decision.

Question: In the middle of the *parsha*, there are several verses that seem out of place (*Deuteronomy 18:9-15*). Right before discussing the role of the prophets, there is a long and apparently unrelated warning to Israel about dealing with soothsayers, wizards, and all forms of sorcery. The Torah states that this is an abomination before God. This commandment is first mentioned in *Parshat Kedoshim* in *Leviticus 19:31*. Why is it repeated here?

Answer: We know that God has a specific purpose for the placement of each letter or verse in the Torah. Joining together these two very different laws (prophets and soothsayers) teaches us an important lesson. God sees that in forming a government and developing a structure for our lives, the desire to know the future is all too tempting, and to see if our plans will be successful. The Israelites lived among nations who turned to sorcerers to ensure their own success. It only seems natural then that the Israelites would look to imitate their neighbors to find comfort and hope in the words and magic of enchanters and their witchcraft.

But the Torah tells us that this "seeking to know" is an abomination before God, because it would show the Israelite as placing his faith in man rather than in God. An Israelite strong in his belief knows that God tells him to do right, and he has faith in his future. The conviction that God always protects us and knows what is best for us is what religion and faith are all about. This is what we must remember as we set up new living situations. We must forge ahead and become involved with God's wishes and commandments, with ultimate faith that good will prevail.

In return for doing this, God promises us in the next verse *Deuteronomy 18:13*, "You shall be complete with the Lord your God." By climbing the heights of faith in God and His Torah, one achieves the highest form of spirituality, a oneness with God. From this flow the many blessings one prays for each day (*Rashi*).

Question: In this *parsha*, what is the meaning of the sentence, "You shall not move (encroach upon) the boundary of your fellow's property" (*Deuteronomy 19:14*)?

Answer: Moses, in advance, divided the Holy Land among the tribes. He commanded that each tribe recognize and respect the others' ownership. The commandment is in the negative form, in order to emphasize that anyone who trespassed clearly would be in violation of the rules of ownership.

Question: How do the sages interpret this boundary issue, *Hasagat G'vul?*

Answer: The concept does not only apply in Israel, but everywhere. It applies to transactions as well. For example, a person is forbidden to sell at a loss, attempting to deliberately put his competition out of business. In this way, the *Talmud* was many years ahead of the antitrust laws that became necessary in the U.S. and elsewhere. A man may not offer a product or service cheaper than another, solely for the purpose of destroying the other man. If the lower price is his normal price, that is not considered encroachment, and is permitted. Only offers that have the intent to damage a competitor are forbidden. There also exist many subtle situations that may only be settled by consulting rabbinic authority.

The Written Torah prohibits a man from moving his fence past the boundary of his land, especially if his neighbor is unaware. This is particularly true if the man moving his fence is aware of what he is doing. To illustrate our point is the instance of a *mohel* who earned his livelihood by doing circumcisions in a small hospital. A new *mohel* moved in and began offering to do the circumcisions at a lower price. Since this would take away the first *mohel's* livelihood, the second *mohel* is totally prohibited from working in that territory.

However, in the case of teaching, a second teacher, who increases the wisdom being taught without affecting the first teacher's livelihood, is not infringing on another's territory. Furthermore, in a big city, for example, where many restaurants can be supported, adding additional restaurants will not take away or destroy anyone's livelihood, and so that is not infringement of territory (*Talmud Bava Batra 21b, 22a; Aruch Hashulchan Choshen Mishpat 156; Rambam Hilchot Talmud Torah 2*).

Question: How does this *parsha* demonstrate that we must hold fast to both the Oral and Written Torah?

Answer: *Parshat Shoftim*, which means "judges," deals with the status of judges, kings, priests, and prophets, all of whom are considered officers of the Israelite nation. Many verses in the Torah are concerned with the issues of organizing a civil government, where justice is free, easy to obtain, and absolutely impartial.

This *parsha* also contains many negative commandments that at first glance seem very harsh. This is precisely why it has become axiomatic that the Written Torah must always be interpreted by means of the Oral Torah. Where the Written Torah says "an eye for an eye" or "blood for blood," the Oral Torah teaches us that compensation is something other than blood, for example money. A story in the *parsha* tells of a body found between two cities; without the Oral Torah we would not know the requirements necessary to bury the deceased person (*Deuteronomy 21*). The interplay between the Written and Oral Torah can best be exemplified by this *parsha*.

KiTetzei
Chapters: 21:10 - 25

Synopsis:

Passion of soldiers in battle; a firstborn son's right not to be deprived of his father's inheritance; death of wayward and rebellious son; hanging of a person executed by stoning for blasphemy; protection of prosperity; avoidance of excessive mingling between men and women; forbidden relations in a marriage; sexual promiscuity; vows to God; divorce; remarriage; death penalty for kidnapping; slander; debtors; payment of workers, orphans, widows, and the poor; embarrassment; honesty in monetary issues; Amalek.

Question: What does this *parsha* deal with?

Answer: This *parsha* deals with many details of the institution of marriage. We know that in the past, marriage took place only between people of the same ethnic background. Sephardim married Sephardim, Litvaks married Litvaks, Chassidim married Chassidim, and so on. After the Holocaust, Jews from all over went to Israel and America, among other places. The result of this is a wonderful, paradoxical phenomenon.

On the one hand, we feel like this fulfills the prophecy of different types of Jews living together as one. This diversity strengthens the quality of the nation. Life is made more interesting through exposure to different cultures. Some families might have four sons-in-law, one from Yemen, one from Germany, one from Mexico, and one from Egypt. Imagine how interesting family gatherings must be for them.

On the other hand, this also can lead to conflicts within a marriage and families. For example, a newlywed Sephardic bride and her Litvak husband sit down to their first Seder. She brings him a beautiful dish of rice that she has worked extremely hard to prepare, in hopes that he will enjoy it. He looks at her in amazement and asks her if she has forgotten that it is *Pesach* and that rice is *chometz*. This is one difference of custom between Ashkenazic and Sephardic Jews.

The beauty and wisdom of the Oral and Written Torah is that both enable us to differentiate between *minhag* and *din*. *Minhag* is a custom associated with a specific place or group. As King Solomon wrote, "Don't abandon the customs of your mother." *Din* is biblical law.

America's foremost Torah scholar, Rabbi Moshe Feinstein, may he rest in peace, ruled in one of his famous books (*Shut Egrot Moshe, Even Haezer, Ch. 59*) that as long as the conflict is not clearly a matter of written law, but is a personal *humra* (personal stringency), neither the husband nor the wife has the right to force the other to follow his or her customs.

Rabbi Feinstein also answered another question on the merging of communities, where the merging of divergent customs is the issue. This problem exists in countries like America, a nation of immigrants, where there are no clear customs established. Rabbi Feinstein answered that an individual must be willing to compromise in the area of *minhagim* (custom) for the stability of the community.

Question: What is the commandment of *shiluach hakain,* the chasing away of a mother bird from her nest before taking her eggs *(Deuteronomy 22:6)?*

Answer: The Torah states that if you pass by a bird's nest with a mother bird sitting on her eggs or caring for her chicks the Torah requires that you chase the mother away before you can take the eggs or baby birds.

Question: What is the reason for this commandment?

Answer: There are many answers to this question:
This a law of God that has to be accepted *(Rashi)*.
God is teaching us the essence of compassion *(Talmud Chulin 80a)*. If you took the mother instead of the chicks, all her future off-spring would be lost. If you take the chicks, the mother can still reproduce. If you take mother and chicks together, that could destroy the species *(Ramban)*.
When you approach the nest, the mother tries to protect her chicks and she will not flee. One must continually attempt to send the mother away before taking her young *(Ha'amek Davar; Rambam, Hilchot Schittah 7)*.

Question: What is the underlying principle of this commandment?

Answer: In the *Garden of Eden* God created a world in which no creature had to be harmed for the sake of another. Each creature was able to sustain its life on plants alone, without any need for meat.

Man did not have to harm any animal in order to survive. Because of man's evil deeds, God created the great Flood. After the Flood, there was no longer enough vegetation to sustain all animals. Therefore, God allowed man to eat meat. He did so under very carefully controlled conditions (*kashrut*). These conditions forbid us from taking the parent and its offspring on the same day, and require us to kill animals painlessly.

Question: What reward does the Torah promise for the *mitzvah* of sending away the mother bird?

Answer: The Torah promises a good and long life (*Deuteronomy 22:7*).

Question: Why does the Torah promise a long life?

Answer: This is an example of the Torah's process of "measure for measure." In the same way that you extend the existence of a species, your existence is extended (*Chatam Sofer*). The same idea is demonstrated by allowing us to cut the fruit from the tree, but prohibiting us to cut the root of the tree (*Abarbanel*). This idea appears to contradict the suggestion of compassion, since one might propose that it would be more compassionate to kill the parent together with its offspring, rather than have them suffer the separation.

Question: Why does the Torah require us to have a fence around our roof (*Deuteronomy 22:8*)?

Answer: The Torah requires an owner to be responsible and to make sure that harm does not come to his fellowman while on the homeowner's property.

KiTavo

Chapters: 26 - 29:8

Synopsis:

Moses instructed the Israelites on how to build the Altar; commandment to write a Sefer Torah; the blessing and cursing.

Question: What is the main idea of this *parsha?*

Answer: Right before they entered the Holy Land, Moses told the Israelites how their behavior would cause God either to reward or punish them. If we read Jewish history, we see that all the tragedies that Moses described in his prophecy came to pass. We learn a very crucial lesson from this. As Winston Churchill said, "Nations that do not learn from their own mistakes will surely repeat them."

Question: "...Because you have not worshipped your God with gladness and good-heartedness..." *(Deuteronomy 28:47).* What does this mean?

Answer: The Ba'al Shem Tov, the founder of the Chassidic movement some 230 years ago, teaches that we must be happy and light-hearted in our approach to the service of God. From the beginning, Chassidism has been based on worshipping God with joy and happiness, deriving enjoyment from the worship itself. Moreover, the basic principle of Chassidism is that any worship or service to God without feelings of joy is of no value.

Rabbi Zalman, the Lubavitcher Rebbe, went further. He says in the *Tanya, chapter 6,* that not only are joyous feelings necessary for service, but bad feelings and sadness will prevent us from appropriate service to God. Feelings of sadness lead to depression and a reluctance to perform good deeds. Rabbi Eliyahu (*The Grah*) from Vilna agrees with this point.

The *Chyda,* Rabbi Chaim Dovid Azulie, leader of the Sephardic community in the Middle East about 120 years ago, suggests that one must pray with a melody that exudes joy and happiness in the praising of the Almighty. When praying in a Sephardic minyan one can feel the great joy and happiness alluded to by the *Chyda* and other sages.

Nitzavim

Chapters: 29:9 - 30

Synopsis:

Last day of Moses' life; warnings against idolatry; repentance and redemption; accessibility of Torah; concept of freedom of choice.

Question: How old was Moses when he passed away?

Answer: He was 120 years old (*Deuteronomy 31:2*).

Question: What else do we learn from this *parsha?*

Answer: The verse says, "I am 120 years old today." Since Moses died the very same day this was said, we know that he died on his birthday (*Babylonian Talmud, Sotah 13:2*). This was the seventh day of Adar.

Question: Before Moses died he gathered the entire nation before him. He restated the covenant that the Almighty had made with him, and warned of the severe consequences that would befall the nation if this covenant was breached. The covenant was made with the expressed intent that future generations would also be obligated to uphold it. "Not only standing with us today…, but also with those who are not with us today" *(Deuteronomy 29:14)*. How was Moses able to obligate future generations to this covenant?

Answer: The Children of Israel cried out to the Almighty for freedom during their period of slavery in Egypt. The Almighty heard their pleas and took them out. They came to the mountain of Sinai and the Almighty offered freedom, but with the condition that they accept the yoke of the Torah, and perpetuate it. Even before hearing of the conditions, the Israelites accepted the Torah by saying, "We will do, and we will listen" (*Exodus 19:8*). This obligated the present generation.

Rabbeinu Bachayei points out that the statement, "and whoever is not here," refers to future generations because parents and children are likened to a tree with branches; and the children become bound by obligations made by their parents. Futhermore, it is a widely accepted concept that all souls were present at the disclosure of this covenant at Sinai (*Zohar; Tanya*), where they obligated themselves to its adherence.

Abarbanel refers us to *Ezekiel 20,* where he tells that the prophet is referring to this convenant and that the behavior exhibited by the Israelites leads to exile. The nation acted like the other nations, attempting to disassociate itself from the Almighty. The Almighty told the nation, "This is My Land," and any behavior done which was outside the bounds of the covenant would lead to further exiles. And so it was. Other commentaries, from a legalistic point of view, state that an inferior or lesser court cannot overrule a judgment made by a greater court. Moses and his generation were of a superior status, therefore decisions reached by them cannot be overruled by any later generation (*Ramav*).

Vayeylech
Chapter: 31

Synopsis:

End of Moses' leadership; Joshua assumed leadership;
the commandment of the unity of Israel.

Question: What is the last commandment mentioned in the Torah, and how may one perform it?

Answer: "Now you have to write this song [Torah] and teach it to the future generations of the Children of Israel, so it will be for an everlasting testimony" (*Deuteronomy 31:19*).

The obligation of this commandment is that each person is to write a *Sefer Torah* for himself. Our sages tell us there are various ways by which one can fulfill this obligation. The highest level is to write the Torah oneself. Those who do not know how to write a *Sefer Torah* may hire an expert scribe to do so their behalf. The third level is to join others and share in the cost of having a scribe write one. The fourth level, for those who cannot afford to share in the cost of a complete Torah, is to write or pay for one column or a few sentences (*Ramban; Rosh; Chinuch 613*). Other commentators say one can buy holy books for the sake of studying and learning the Torah, if one does not have the financial wherewithal to purchase a share in the writing of a Torah Scroll. This was commanded so that every holy place will have enough *Sifrei Kodesh* (sacred books). (*See the Babylonian Talmud, Nadarim 38a, Chagigah 12a; Rambam, Hilchot Sefer Torah 7; Tur, Yorah Deah 270 Prisha; Chatam Sofer, Orh Chaim 52, Yorah Deah 252*).

Question: The Torah gives us 613 commandments. How many are positive? How many are negative?

Answer: The Torah lists 248 positive commandments and 365 negative.

Question: How many of the 613 commandments are meant for all people, regardless of their religion?

Answer: The Torah tells us that all people are obligated to act morally. The Torah gives us that prescription to follow. For the Children of Israel there are 613 commandments. For the non-Jew there is the code of seven referred to as the *Noachite Laws*.

Question: Is it possible to perform all 613 commandments in our day?

Answer: No. Some commandments are required to be fulfilled only under certain conditions, or in specific places. There are commandments that pertain specifically to the Holy Land, or commandments that have to be fulfilled in the Holy Land only if the Temple is in existence and then only by certain people. Some commandments have the condition that the majority of the Jews must be living in the Holy Land, otherwise they cannot be fulfilled. For example, first fruits, jubilee, *shmittah,* and *tithe* of the harvest.

Ha'azinu

Chapter: 32

Synopsis:

Moses' poetic final oratory

Question: At the beginning of the *Book of Exodus* it tells how Moses was unable to talk to Pharaoh. How does it happen that Moses is now able to deliver one of the most magnificent, poetic speeches in the entire Bible?

Answer: The beginning of the *Book of Exodus* tells of Moses' inexperience and seeming lack of self-confidence. He felt himself unworthy of being God's agent in leading the Children of Israel out of Egypt. After forty years of wandering in the desert and being the leader of a nation that was extremely unruly and difficult to manage, Moses was able to look back on many difficult times and crises that he had been able to overcome. As is the way with most human beings, the experience of overcoming hardships and successfully conquering difficulties builds up a person's confidence.

The *Ramav* suggests that Moses was inspired by God to deliver this magnificent oration, causing him to speak so eloquently and prophetically of the future.

Question: What was one of the prophecies of Moses?

Answer: Moses foretold of the times to come when the Jewish nation would be almost wiped out! That is, a great number of the Jews would be killed but enough would survive to ensure that the nation would continue into the future (*Ramban*). This prophecy has been fulfilled many times by such events as the Spanish Inquisition, the pogroms in Eastern Europe, and the Holocaust of the Second World War.

Question: How was this *parsha* read in the time of the Temple?

Answer: This *parsha* was considered so important and so much the essence of the whole Torah that it was read differently from all the other *parshiot*. It was divided up into small parts and each part was given to the *Leviem* to read each week for the entire year. In this way the message was kept alive all throughout the year and its poetry was honored (*Babylonian Talmud Rosh Hashanah 31a*).

Vazot Haberachah
Chapters: 33 - 34

Synopsis:

Noses blessed all the Israelites; God buried Moses in an unknown place.

Question: Why is the burial site of Moses unknown (*Deuteronomy 34:6*)?

Answer: Moses wanted to avoid having anyone worship him as an idol, especially since many people worship deceased religious leaders as idols (*Ralbag; Ba'al Hakaida*).

The Egyptians used to mummify their leaders, and many Egyptians recognized Moses as one of the great leaders, so he was fearful that they might do this to his body (*Abarbanel; Radak*).

As it is written in the beginning of *Parshat Bereishit 2:7*, "God blew into man the soul of life." The sages explain that just as a balloon needs to be inflated to make it move and fly in the air, so too, man required God's action to change this lifeless, immovable object into a human being. Through the very act of blowing His breath, God created the combination of body and soul. The origin of the soul is absolutely spiritual, and the soul cannot be physically touched; the source of the body is made entirely from the earth. God created this perfect combination, forming man's body from dust and energizing his soul with the breath of life. After death, the soul is returned to the heavens and the body reverts back to dust.

We can appreciate that the main source of conflict within ourselves often lies between our soul, which is completely pure and spiritual, and our body, which is geared to the materialistic world. God entrusted us with the freedom of choice to conduct our own lives and to strike a balance between body and soul (*Rambam; Tanya, Chapter 2*). Moses was the only prophet who saw God face to face (*Deuteronomy 34:10*); therefore, when he died his body totally disintegrated (*Zohar; Shla'a*).

God did not want anyone else to be buried near Moses (*Chizkuni*).

Moses was different from others all of his life, and God wanted him to be different also in death (*Ralbag*).

This is one of the many mysteries of the Bible for which we have no explanation (*Ramav*).

Question: How could Moses write, at the end of the Bible *(Deuteronomy 34:5-12)*, about his own death, and the fact that there would be no other prophet as great as he?

Answer: Some sages teach us that Joshua was ordered by God to write these last seven sentences of the Bible, describing Moses' death and burial *(Ibn Ezra; Rabbeinu Miyuchas)*. Other opinions say that God ordered Moses to write this, and he did so with tears *(Babylonian Talmud, Bava Batra 15b)*. *(See Rambam, Hilchot Tefillah, chapter 13:6; Ra'avad; Talmud Menachot 30a; Shulchan Aruch, Orach Chayim 428:7; Abarbanel; Ohr Hachayim)*.

It is a worldwide custom that when the Torah reader finishes the last sentence of each one of the five books of Moses, the entire congregation stands and encourages one another with the following proclamation:

"CHAZAK CHAZAK V' NITCHAZEK!"

(STRENGTH...STRENGTH...AND BECOME STRONG)

Index

Abraham (*continued*)
compensation for belief in God, 23
daughter of, 41
decision not to bless Isaac, 45–46
differences with Moses, 138
Eliezer's mission to find Isaac a wife, 41–42, 45
establishment of morning prayers and, 45
faith of, 22, 105
God's appearance before, 32
God's blessings of, 23–24, 40–41
God's changing the name of, 27
God's testing of, 22–23
Holy Land given to, 27, 40
honor given to MalkiTzedek, 26
humility of, 33, 179
king of Sodom's property and, 26
kings' war and, 25
love for the Land of Israel, 44–45
marriage to Hagar, 45
minyan and, 33
miracles at midnight, 156
power of blessing given to, 24
prophecy of the Exodus and, 153
purchase of *Mearat Hamachpelah*, 39–40

relationship with God after Lot's departure, 25
sacrifice of Isaac, 36, 247
souls converted by, 24
special sign given to, 27
Tower of Babel as a revolt against, 19
transmission of spiritual power to Isaac, 44
Acacia wood, 239
Acharei Mot (parsha), 271–273
Achashvarosh, 157, 215, 216
Achav, 235
Achiman, 39
Ada, 75
Adam
burial place of, 39
commandments given to, 8
creation of woman and, 7
meaning of the name, 249
number of generations between Adam and Noah, 4
offerings of, 249
punishment of, 8–10, 12
sin of Cain and, 10–11
sin of eating from the Tree of Knowledge, 8, 9, 11, 12
Adar, 215
Adoption, 281
Adultery, 192–193
Afternoon prayers, 45
Agog, 75
Agricultural tools, 13
Agunot, 392–394
Akaidah, 22
Akdamot, 295

Breastplate, 221–222
Brit milah. See Circumcision
Burial
  halakhah on, 40
  of Jacob in Canaan, 118, 119
  of Joseph, 167
Burial places
  Cave of Machpelah, 115, 120
  Kiryat Arba, 39
  of Rachel, 61
Burning bush, 131, 132
Business
  prohibitions against unfair competition, 408–409
  proper behavior in, 286
  theft of money in, 286–287

Cain, 4
  God's mark on, 11
  loss of God's likeness, 18
  punishment of, 11
  sin of murder, 10, 11, 12
Caleb, 315
Canaan, 22, 25
  burial of Jacob in, 118, 119
  the twelve spies and, 315
  war with the Israelites, 334
Candelabra. *See* Menorah
Candles. *See also* Chanukah; Sahmesh candle; Havdalah candle
  lighting on *Shavuot,* 293
  lighting on the Sabbath, 283
  significance of, 309, 310
  symbolism of, 212–213

Cantillation, 34
Cattle disease, plague of, 146
Cave of Machpelah, 115, 120
Censuses, 300
  amount of money given by each individual, 225–226
  by David, 227
  procedure for, 225
  prohibition against counting the Israelites directly, 226, 227
  reasons for, 350
Chag Habikurim, 294
Chag Hakatzir, 294
Chag Hashadchanim, 372
Chaim ben Attar, R. (Ohr Hachayim), 53, 150, 177
Challah, 44, 181
Chamushim, 167
Chananel, Rabbeinu, 329
Chanukah
  Al haNissim prayer and, 85, 90–91
  customs of, 85
  differences with Purim, 92
  displaying the menorah, 87
  dreidel game and, 85, 89
  eating dairy foods, 88
  eating food cooked in oil, 88
  events celebrated by, 85–86
  first day of, 86
  gifts of money to children, 90
  gifts to charity, 91
  how to light the candles, 87–88

lighting candles at the
synagogue and at
home, 87
lighting Sabbath candles
on, 86
lighting the *Havdalah*
candle, 87
oil and, 86, 90
reasons to celebrate, 92
reciting blessings on, 88
sahmesh candle, 86, 87–88
significance of the first
night, 88
Chanukah *gelt*, 90, 91
Charan, 56, 57
Charity
to alleviate poverty,
287–288
Chanukah and, 85, 91
levels of, 402–403
Chassidism, 416
Chatam Sofer, 133
Chayei Sarah (parsha), 38–46
"Chazak chazak v' nitchazek,"
243
Chazon Isaiah, 368, 369
Chesed shel Emet, 280
Chever, 186
Chevrah Kedishah, 282
Chidekel river, 7, 41
Chidushei Harim, 330
Chilazon, 317
Children
Chanukah and, 90, 91
commandment to be fruit-
ful and multiply, 41
commandment to educate
during Passover, 160,
161

parents are not responsible
for the sins of, 317
in the Passover story, 159
Pharaoh's intent to kill
newborn males, 125,
126, 127
Children of Israel. *See*
Israelites
Chinuch, 89
Chizkuni, 67
Chodesh, 154
Chofetz Chaim. See Cohen,
R. Israel
Chometz, 159
Choshon, 221–222
Chukat (parsha), 326–336
Chyda, The. See Azulie,
R. Chaim Dovid
Circumcision
of Abraham and Ishmael,
22, 30
Chanukah and, 90
commandment of, 29
determining the day of, 29
of the Hittites, 72
of Moses' son, 136, 137
significance of viewing
three stars and, 29–30
Cities of sanctuary, 405
Civil law. *See also* Halakhah
on the accidental death of a
pregnant woman, 199
on animal damage cases,
196
on animals injured by falling into pits, 199–120
on assaulting another, 198
on assaulting one's parents,
198

Priests (*continued*)
  Pinchas and, 347
  priestly garments and,
    219–220, 221–222
  purpose of, 303
  raising of arms, 304–305
  recitation of blessings, 303
  refusal to perform priestly
    duties and, 304
Princes of Israel, construction
  of the Tabernacle and,
  237–238
Prohibited behaviors,
  272–273
Property
  respecting, 41
  responsibility for safety on,
    414
Prophecy
  humility and, 130
  by Jacob, 112–113, 115, 117
  in Joseph's story, 77
  Moses and, 130, 173–174
Prophetic dreams, 312
  Joseph and, 117
  nature of, 340–341
Prophets
  Bilam, 339
  recognizing false prophets,
    386–388
  in the world today, 312–313
Prostitution
  by a priest's daughter, 80
  Tamar and, 80
Pruzbol, 396
Pshat, 150
Puah, 126–127

Punishment
  true causes of, 287
  warning before, 34, 145
Purification
  ceremony of the Red
    Heifer and, 327, 328
  laws of, 265
  through *mikvah,* 268–269,
    270
  of vessels for food, 208
Purim
  customs of, 216–217
  differences with Chanukah,
    92
  Hallel service and, 85
  Magillah Esther and,
    216–217
  message of, 217
  reading from *Zachor* on, 213
  reasons to celebrate, 92
  story of, 215, 217
  Yom Hakipurim and, 217
Putiel, 187

Rabbina, 392
Rabbinical courts. *See* Beit din;
    Jewish courts; Sanhedrin
Rachav, 318
Rachel
  death of, 99
  Jacob's agreement with
    Laban over, 59
  Jacob's curse and, 62
  Joseph's protection of, 117
  naming of Joseph, 61
  reward for her righteous-
    ness, 61

Rashi (R. Shlomo Yitzchaki)
  on Abraham's angel
    visitors, 32
  on Abraham's transmission
    to Isaac, 44
  on the angel attempting to
    kill Moses, 136
  on the angel wrestling with
    Jacob, 69
  on Bezalel, 229
  on Bilam, 183
  on the contributions of
    princes, 238
  on Creation, 5
  on the differences between
    Moses and Abraham,
    138
  on Enoch, 12
  on Esau, 46
  on Eve, 10
  on Hagar, 28
  on the Hebrew elders, 137
  honesty and humility of, 53
  "I do not know what it
    means," 53
  on the increase of the
    Israelites, 124
  on Jacob, 57, 95
  on Joseph, 100, 103, 119
  on MalkiTzedek, 26
  method of Torah explica-
    tion, 150
  on Moses and Aaron being
    denied entrance to
    the Holy Land, 329
  on Moses' birth, 128
  on Moses' choice of officers,
    187

  on Moses' mother and
    father, 127
  on offering bread and wine,
    26
  on Pharaoh's prediction for
    the Israelites, 152
  on the plague of frogs, 148
  on priestly garments, 250
  on Rachel, 61
  on the reception of the
    Torahs by Moses, 390,
    391
  on the route of the exodus,
    166
  on Serach, 104
  on the Tree of Knowledge,
    87
  on Yocheved, 128
Ravshaka, 156
Real estate brokers, 286
Rebecca
  burial place of, 39
  consent to marriage, 44
  considerate personality of,
    42, 43
  giving birth to two nations,
    49
  Jacob and Esau fighting in
    the womb of, 48–49
  righteousness of, 48
  switching the blessings of
    Jacob and Esau, 52–53
  the three blessings of Sarah
    and, 44
Receiving the Torah, Festival
  of. See Shavuot
Red calf. See Red Heifer
Redemption, faith and, 137

Vows (*continued*)
recitation of *Kol Nidrei* and,
353–354
against Torah law, 354–355
Torah principle regarding,
352
types of, 352
unintentionally made, 354

Wages, paying promptly, 276
Waldenberg, R. Tzvi, 281
Warsaw Ghetto, 365
Water, 5
Moses and, 125
purifying. *See* Mikvah
turning into blood, 133,
134
"Waters in the desert," 328
Wealth, collected from the
Egyptians, 153, 154
Weeks, Festival of. *See*
Shavuot
Well of testimony, 63
Wicked son, 160
Widows, 204
yibum and, 79–80, 298
Wild beasts, plague of, 146
Wilderness
census of the Israelites in,
300
complaints by the Israelites,
176
how the Israelites survived,
167–168
Israelites speak out against
the leadership of
Moses, 334–335

miracle of manna in, 176–
179, 180
miracle of "waters in the
desert," 328
modern remembrances of,
180–181
organization of the
Israelites in, 300
the Pillar of Clouds and
the Pillar of Fire, 168,
242
the place of bitter water
(*Marah*), 174–175
reasons for forty years
wandering, 308–309
rebellion of Datan and
Aviram, 179–180
rebellion of Korach, 180
resting places in, 359
war with Amalek, 182–183,
213
Wild goats, 389
Wine
and bread, 26
five cups at Passover, 140
Wine steward, in Egypt, 82–
83, 94–95
Witnesses, requirements for,
405–406
Wives, abandoned, 392–394
Wizards. *See also* Magicians;
Sorcerers
Bilam, 183
Pharaoh and, 142
Wolf, 118
Women
consenting to marriage,
43–44

in the construction of the
Tabernacle, 237
creation of Eve, 7
in the creation of the
Golden Calf, 237
Workers, paying wages to
promptly, 276
World War I, 365
Worship, by Abraham and
Isaac, 105
Written Torah
formation of the Talmud
and, 392
Hillel's *Pruzbol* and, 396
interplay with Oral Torah,
409–410
received by Moses, 390–391
transmission through time,
391–392
Tzedokim movement and,
396–397

Yaakov. See Jacob
Yael, 294
Yagar Sahadusa, 63
Yannai, 396
Year
first month of, 282
as the time of remem-
brance, 95
Yehoshua, R., 178
Yehuda, R., 267
Yehudah ben Tabai, 396
Yehudit, 75
Yerushalmi, 392
Yeter, 186
Yibum, 79–80, 298

Yigach, 7
Yitro, 131
advice given to Moses, 187
befriending of Moses and
the Israelites, 185–186
formation of the Great
Assembly, 400
as Moses' father-in-law, 185
political position in
Midyan, 185
seven names of, 186–187
time of his story, 185
Yitro (parsha), 184–193
Yitro's daughters, 129–130,
131
Yitzchak. *See* Isaac
Yitzchaki, R. Shlomo. *See*
Rashi
Yochanan, R., 394
Yochanan ben Zachai, R., 201
Yocheved, 126, 127, 128
Yom Hakipurim, 217
Yom Kippur
fast of *Tisha B'Av* and, 367
Purim and, 217
second reception of the
Tablets on, 235, 237
and the story of Elijah and
Jezebel, 235
vestments worn by priests,
221
Yonatan ben Uziel, 12

Zachariah, 156
Zachor, 213
Zalman, R. (Lubavitcher
Rebbe), 416

About the Author

Rabbi Moshe Pinchas Weisblum is a fourteenth generation rabbi. He is the great-grandson of Rabbi Elimelech of Lijensk and grandson of the famous kabbalists Rabbi Yehuda Leib Ashlag and Rabbi Yehuda Tzvi Brandwein. Rabbi Weisblum has written several books, including the award-winning *Beiury Haklomar Berashi.* He has authored many articles and has appeared on media programs discussing a wide variety of Jewish topics. He has also composed many musical pieces with accompanying lyrics. He completed his Iraeli army service as a commissioned officer with the rank of Major.